Not God's People

Religion in the Modern World

Series Advisors
Kwok Pui Lan, Episcopal Divinity School
Joerg Rieger, Southern Methodist University

This series explores how various religious traditions wrestle with the dynamic and changing role of religion in the modern world and examines how past changes reflect on today's critical issues. Accessibly and engagingly written, books in this series will look at secularization, global society, gender, race, class, sexuality and their relation to religious life and religious movements.

Titles in Series:

Not God's People: Insiders and Outsiders in the Biblical World by Lawrence M. Wills

Not God's People

Insiders and Outsiders
in the Biblical World

Lawrence M. Wills

ROWMAN & LITTLEFIELD PUBLISHERS, INC.
Lanham • Boulder • New York • Toronto • Plymouth, UK

ROWMAN & LITTLEFIELD PUBLISHERS, INC.

Published in the United States of America
by Rowman & Littlefield Publishers, Inc.
A wholly owned subsidiary of The Rowman & Littlefield Publishing Group, Inc.
4501 Forbes Boulevard, Suite 200, Lanham, Maryland 20706
www.rowmanlittlefield.com

Estover Road
Plymouth PL6 7PY
United Kingdom

British Library Cataloguing in Publication Information Available

Library of Congress Cataloging-in-Publication Data

Wills, Lawrence M. (Lawrence Mitchell), 1954-
  Not God's people : insiders and outsiders in the biblical world /
Lawrence M. Wills.
      p. cm.— (Religion in the modern world)
  Includes bibliographical references and index.
  ISBN-13: 978-0-7425-6249-3 (cloth : alk. paper)
  ISBN-10: 0-7425-6249-2 (cloth : alk. paper)
  ISBN-13: 978-0-7425-6250-9 (pbk. : alk. paper)
  ISBN-10: 0-7425-6250-6 (pbk. : alk. paper)
 1. Identification (Religion) 2. Identification (Religion)—Biblical teaching.
3. Christians. 4. Jews. I. Title.

BV4509.5.W55 2008
  220.8'305—dc22   2008004738

Printed in the United States of America

∞™ The paper used in this publication meets the minimum requirements of
American National Standard for Information Sciences—Permanence of Paper
for Printed Library Materials, ANSI/NISO Z39.48-1992.

Contents

Preface

Today's headlines constantly update the accounts of new religious and ethnic violence, hardened boundaries, and definitions of outsiders that allow no ambiguity. The divisions of the world seem to be written in stone—why else would people exhibit such certainty that the Other is dangerous? And yet, just a few decades ago, the categories of "Us" and "Them" were quite different. Religious and ethnic violence also dominated the headlines, but the blanks were filled with a different set of clearly drawn opposites. To oppose the eternal foe of communism, represented most prominently by the Soviet Union, Americans were willing to die to establish control over the tiny nation of Vietnam. The United States was loathed and daily attacked in many Latin American countries, but the Muslim world was more favorably disposed to the United States than to the Soviet Union. Internally as well, J. Edgar Hoover was mounting a full-scale investigation of Martin Luther King's communist ties while insisting that the mafia did not exist. At the time, who could imagine that lines would be drawn differently just thirty or forty years later? One of the ironies of modern nationalism—almost inexplicable, it has seemed to scholars—is that even though new national identities arise so quickly, people are willing to kill and die for them. Surely, one would insist, only an ancient loyalty could instill that kind of intensity of feeling. And yet identities do change, and change quickly, even though—and this is the startling part—*the participants assume they are unchanging, even primordial.* Before the actual violence between ethnic or religious groups occurs, there is a prior step of definition which attributes a deeper meaning to the conflict.

The Bible functions today to define many of the groups who people our headlines, and these groups assume that their text is a single, ancient oracle which reveals God's notion of community, good, evil, and most clearly, who "they" are, the Other who is not only opposed to us, but opposed to God as well. The Bible is considered clear and unchanging, and totally without ambivalence. And while it is true that the different books of the Bible, both the Hebrew Bible or Old Testament and the New Testament, often define the Other who is arrayed against the community, they do not define the Other in the same way, and there are many parts which also express a great deal of ambivalence. People who want to *use* the Bible as a clear delineation of us and them will have to continue doing what they have always done, and that is avoiding actually *reading* it, because it will not support them. It will support a wide variety of delineations of We and Other, and it will at other points support an attitude of ambiguity and ambivalence and a reconciliation of We and Other, but it will not support any of the "clear" programs of name-calling that it is used for.

Here I propose returning to the text and reading a number of books from the Hebrew Bible, the Catholic and Orthodox Old Testament, and the New Testament and asking the same questions in each case: How is the outsider defined? Is the insider defined as the opposite of the outsider? How does this define God and community in each case? Does this also define some people *within the community* who are likened to the outside enemy? This book does not simply argue *that* the biblical texts construct the Other, but tries to delineate *how* they accomplish this. These reflections also suggest other questions: How were these definitions of We and Other in the ancient communities used by later Jews and Christians to define enemies in *their* day? Are these processes similar in Muslim communities, Hindu communities, and secular states? Are the coordinated processes of community formation and enemy formation that are found in the Bible exhibited in other cultures as well? That is, are they simply part of human nature? And finally, do the processes found in the Bible illuminate our headlines?

Our reading of the Bible, in short, will indicate that the definitions of insider and outsider change dramatically from text to text, even though the definitions are considered eternally true. The dividing lines of us and them shift and change, but the *processes* endure. They have been essentially the same for millennia and are very "modern" in the sense that they crop up again each day in new headlines about Christian, Muslim, or Jewish repudiations of the Other, Russian or Hindu nationalism, or suggestions for the re-partitioning of yet another region. We suppose that our myths of difference define how *different* we are from other cultures, but they actually reveal how we are *similar*. Reading the Bible with this in mind, then, not only illuminates the social divisions in the ancient texts, it allows us to extrapolate the typical and enduring human processes that are at work here and allows us to chart a historical progression from ancient creeds to modern divisions, a genealogy of the Other.

Acknowledgments

This book has been a labor of love and obsession for a number of years. A large number of people have helped me tremendously in the gestation of this text. Every member of the Episcopal Divinity School community has made it an environment in which very serious issues can be explored in a positive spirit of mutual affirmation; I will never forget many of the conversations that I have had there on this topic. Sarah Stanton, Melissa McNitt, Brian Romer, Amanda Gibson, and the staff of Rowman & Littlefield have brought this process to completion in exemplary fashion. Kwok Pui Lan, who is both a colleague at Episcopal Divinity School and a consultant to Rowman & Littlefield, played a crucial role in bringing us together. In 2006–2007 I had the pleasure of teaching courses on the subject of this study at Wesleyan University, and I am grateful to the faculty and staff of the religion department and the students whom I came to know while there. A number of other individuals have led me to clearer insights on this topic: Ellen Birnbaum, Joan Branham, Bernadette Brooten, Denise Kimber Buell, Shaye J. D. Cohen, David Frankfurter, Caroline Johnson Hodge, Shelly Matthews, Richard Horsley, Andrew McGowan, Gregory Mobley, Laura Nasrallah, Saul Olyan, Jack Sanders, and Christine Thomas. In addition, three anonymous outside readers provided valuable suggestions for the final editing. *Journal of Biblical Literature* also kindly allowed me to revise and expand my article, "The Depiction of the Jews in Acts" (*Journal of Biblical Literature* 110 [1991]: 631–54). Last, I want to thank my family, Shelley, Jessica, and Daniel, for providing more than just love and support (as if that weren't enough!); they were my first, last, and best discussion partners on this study.

1

Introduction

Who is an insider and who is an outsider in the Bible, and why? Does this change over the various books? How does the definition of ancient enemies in the Bible affect modern Jews and Christians? The Bible, in its various Jewish and Christian canons, has been and remains constitutional for western society. As part of this constitutional function it defines "us" and "them." It creates an image of the ideal community of God, the identity of the We, and an image of the Other. This has traditionally been understood in this way: In the Hebrew Bible the Israelites conceived of the nations who lived upon the land before them—Canaanites and so on—as Other, and in the New Testament the Christians, in a revolution of the gentiles, inverted this by conceiving of the Jews as Other. But this traditional understanding is very misleading. The construction of the Other in the Bible is much more complicated than that, and it is in the complications that the real story lies. These complications reveal ambiguities of identity and vast differences among biblical texts that are often assumed to speak with one voice. The Israelites, for instance, expressed complex beliefs about other nations, and the early followers of Jesus, most of them Jews, expressed a whole range of quite contradictory notions about Judaism. Further, the depictions of the Other in biblical texts, far from being unique, can be compared with the processes of constructing the Other found in surrounding cultures of the era or in other times and places. And whether we are Jewish, Christian, Muslim, Buddhist, or not religious at all, the Bible continues to influence modern constructions of the Other as well. It has shaped the western world, and through the migratory paths of Jews and the missionary paths of Christianity and Islam, much of the

1

eastern world also. The Bible, directly or indirectly, defines identity for most of the people in the world.

Ambiguities concerning the nature of the Other can be found even in texts that would seem on the surface to be brutally clear. For instance, a number of passages in the Hebrew Bible detail the process that the Israelites are commanded to follow when they take the land that God has promised them. In Deuteronomy 7:1–3 Israel is told:

> When the Lord your God brings you into the land that you are about to enter and occupy, and he clears away many nations before you—the Hittites, the Girgashites, the Amorites, the Canaanites, the Perizzites, the Hivites, and the Jebusites—and when the Lord your God gives them over to you and you defeat them, then you must utterly destroy them. Make no covenant with them and show them no mercy.

And yet when this text was written, some of these nations were hopelessly obscure, or perhaps even invented. The list of peoples is a fantasy concerning the *former* condition of the land. The list contributes to a construction of a mythical past with mythical Others. Even more astonishing, the peoples who are descended from one of these nations, the Canaanites, are in other texts treated quite civilly. The craftsmen of Tyre—the very people whom the Canaanites had become—contributed to Solomon's construction of the temple (1 Kings 5) and, *because of their ancestry*, are enlisted again as welcome guest workers under Ezra (Ezra 3:7). Further, at the same time that the foreign nations in lists such as this were marked for destruction, we also encounter people after people who, according to the narrative, *should* have been on the list of destruction but were adopted as a minority within Israel or as a servant class (Gibeonites, Jerahmeelites, Kenizzites, and others).

In the New Testament as well, the moment one begins to examine closely the depiction of opponents, ambiguities arise concerning the construction of the Other. Although the Gospel of Matthew has some of the sharpest polemical condemnations of individual Jewish groups in the New Testament ("scribes and Pharisees, hypocrites!"), it is also in many ways the most Jewish of the gospels and does not see the followers of Jesus as lying *outside* of Judaism. Matthew probably speaks for a sect within Judaism that claims the title of true Israel. The polemical language, therefore, is that of a segment within the Jewish world that, on the one hand, marks clearly the boundaries with broader Judaism, but on the other, never leaves the fold to start a new religion in the manner of the emerging church of the second century and afterward. The Gospel of John, on the other hand, has shifted the polemical language from that of Matthew's sect within Judaism to that of a new group in some sense separated from Judaism, not as "Christians" but as a self-isolated movement. In John the opponents are rarely Pharisees as in Matthew, but are now simply "the Jews," even though Jesus, John the Baptist, the disciples, and almost all of the crowds are Jews. Matthew and John clearly do not erect the concentric circles of "friend" and "opponent" in the same way, and neither do the other gospels, Paul, or other early Christian texts. Yet out of the variation in the Hebrew Bible and the New Testament there has emerged a series of consensus views that ignore these differences and create a view of unanimity. Each group that claims a descent from these texts can perceive itself as the people of God with a clear Other on the horizon, an Other that is perceived "clearly" in this constitutional document of culture. The construction of the Other in biblical texts is more diverse and interesting than most readers realize, and certainly more diverse and interesting than is admitted by established religious bodies.

Here I have chosen to analyze a number of texts that illuminate biblical constructions of the Other: Genesis, Deuteronomy, the conquest narratives in the history books of the Hebrew Bible, the restoration of Jerusalem in Ezra and Nehemiah, the relation between Judaism and Hellenism in 1 and 2 Maccabees, the condemnation of "scribes and Pharisees, hypocrites" in Matthew 23, the condemnation of "the Jews" in the book of John, Jews and gentiles as Other in the letters of Paul, and the summary descriptions of the relation of Jews and followers of Jesus presented in the Acts of the Apostles. These texts distinguish sharply between "us" and "them": one group is acceptable before God and another is rejected. But the rhetoric of the texts does not simply *describe* the groups that are arrayed against the community, it *constructs* an identity for them as a well-defined opposite.

Although I examine a large number of texts, my treatments are not meant to be exhaustive, but rather illustrative of the process of "constructing the Other." Scholars in many fields have explored this process, and they speak of a web of interlocking conceptions of the Other based on foreignness, race, class, gender, sexual practices, ability, and so on. The various aspects of the Other are interrelated, and the process by which the Other and the We are constituted in societies is a nearly universal aspect of community and identity formation. The "science of the Other," as Jonathan Z. Smith calls it,[1] reminds us that the Other, like gender or race, is *constructed*. It is based less on historical or scientific fact and more on a cultural consensus that is nevertheless transmitted as a fact. It also reminds us that scriptural texts, which for centuries have been constitutional for our society, were also once constructed. They did not appear fully formed, and central to their formation and evolution is a constantly changing construction of the We and Other. The Bible, indeed, and the identity that stems from it, could only be created through a process of closely defining We and Other.

In each chapter I have chosen a text or a set of texts that reveals a particular approach to the construction of the Other. Chapter two, for example, will address selected sections of the so-called Primary History, the historical narrative that runs from Genesis through Second Kings (the Torah or Pentateuch and the historical books of the Hebrew Bible). The passages chosen concern, first, the origins of difference in the naming and spread of the peoples of the earth, and second, the conquest of Canaan. When Israel is commanded not only to conquer and take the land God has promised it, but also to annihilate every person of the nations who occupy the land (the Deuteronomy passage quoted above), this establishes a binary opposition between the "We" of Israel and the "Other," or the nations who reside there. By looking more closely at these passages, we also see how the external Other—the foreign nations—are configured side by side with internal Others, such as slaves, women, those who engage in aberrant cultic practices, men who engage in same-sex love, lepers, resident aliens, and illegitimate children.

While chapter two addresses texts dating from before the Babylonian exile, in chapter three I proceed to Ezra and Nehemiah, which cover the period of the restoration after the Babylonian exile. Although Israel and Judah (the province where Jerusalem was located) had been broken up and defeated, the descendants of the people of these regions still existed in various categories and in various places—Judah, Babylon, and Egypt. Yet Ezra and Nehemiah struggled to reform political and religious life in Jerusalem by redefining the remnants of Israel and Judah. In their view, only those Judeans who had returned from exile in Babylon were worthy to be called "Israel." This group was involved in a power struggle to rule Jerusalem's civil and religious institutions. The parties who opposed them were defined as Other, and presumed to have more in common with foreign nations than with Israel. Marriages to women who were not considered Judean—what in fact they were is not clear—were dissolved, and the women and the children born to them sent away. Ambiguous people within Jerusalem were either defined as foreign or adopted as returning Judeans. A new order was created in Judah by the clarifying of boundaries, the expulsion of certain residents, and a reconstruction of ethnic identity that eliminated ambiguous categories. The middle was cleared out and a new Law of the Excluded Middle was imposed.

In chapter four I turn to 1 and 2 Maccabees, which in historical development stand between the Hebrew Bible on the one hand and the New Testament and rabbinic Judaism on the other. They are important for a discussion of the Other because it is generally assumed that they draw a neat distinction between Judaism and the new Other on the horizon, Hellenism, and that they create a definition of Jewish identity that applies to the situation under Greek control. However, these assumptions may be too simplistic. First and Second Maccabees make varied judgments about the outside nations, and do not even agree with each other. The later memorializing of the actions of the Maccabees has influenced modern readings of these texts.

From here I turn to texts of the New Testament. Those who assume that it is the Hebrew Bible which draws sharp distinctions between We and Other and not the New Testament will be disappointed. The process of constructing the Other remains the same, even if it is often projected onto an apocalyptic scenario. But at the same time, the New Testament texts do not simply substitute Jews as Other for Canaanites. Each of the New Testament authors depicts a different relation to Judaism, an entity which itself would be difficult to define in the first century. After discussing complexities of Jewish and Christian identity in regard to Matthew and John, I consider Paul in chapter seven and argue that his construction of the Other was also more complex than is usually perceived. He does not, as often assumed, oppose Christianity and faith to Judaism and law. Like Matthew, he saw the body of believers in Jesus as part of Judaism, now with gentiles adopted as children of Abraham under a special dispensation from God. Finally, I turn to a very different retelling of Paul's mission, that found in the Acts of the Apostles. Probably the latest of the New Testament texts to be considered here, Acts presents a harmonized narrative after the fact of how the nascent Christian movement had separated from its parent-body, Judaism, and how God's mandate had passed from one body to another. In each text chosen, then, there is a drama of definition. These are among the most influential writings of the Bible in terms of the construction of identity and the Other.

APPROACHES TO IDENTITY AND THE OTHER

The late twentieth century witnessed an explosion of investigations of identity and the Other which we may touch on briefly. If we consider identity first, we note that it is a broad term, an ambiguous term, and a problematic term. Recent discussions of identity have been influenced by new voices demanding to be heard on the public stage. In a series of waves, the elite western man was confronted by the reality of the perspectives of others—women, people of color, workers, people of other religions or sexual orientations, colonized peoples, different cultures on the horizon—the list could go on. This "identity politics" carried with it challenges to "essentialized identity," or the notion that identity has a real essence that is at the core of a certain people's sense of sameness and belonging, that it exists independently of the identity of other groups, and that it preexisted our present situation and is stable over time. Questions began to be raised about all of these assumptions. Does identity exist as an essence, or is it constructed? Following Fredrik Barth's reflections on ethnic identity, many have argued that identity as a whole, not just ethnic identity, arises not only by belonging with those who are in the same group, but also by differing from others, not just by an objective essence but by an invention of identity.[2] Those who challenge essentialized identity argue that individual identity is constructed by social forces, that identity shifts constantly and is not stable, and that it does not radiate from the core *out* but from the boundary *in*.

Here I will not engage all of the problems that have been associated with identity, but I do want to focus on the interrelation of identity and constructions of the Other. Although I do not argue that identity arises *solely* from a construction of the Other, I am most interested in that aspect of identity that is shaped by opposition, the image of the ideal human that is propped up and inflated by the denigration, even demonization of the Other. I recognize that although discussion of identity is often connected with this process of contrast-building, the two are not exact equivalents. I also recognize that identity is both individual and social, yet I focus on the social; identity is found both at the core and at the boundaries, yet I focus on the boundaries; there may be essentialist aspects, yet I focus on the constructivist.

The texts studied here are self-consciously *historical* texts of authors, sometimes anonymous, who retell their own past. Attempting to illuminate this historical process of identity-making are scholars who analyze "social memory" or "cultural memory." It is often assumed that memory is a strictly individual process, a recall of what one has learned. But a dictum of social memory theorists is that groups choose what to remember and what to forget. History has a social utility that determines what people affirm as their collective story. Maurice Halbwachs systematized this: groups possess a shared cultural memory, whether the group is as large as a nation or as small as a local sewing circle. Social memory serves to retain and transmit group history, but also to shape it, articulate it, or even invent it. As Halbwachs says, social memory "retains only those events that are of a pedagogic character."[3] Alan Kirk further summarizes the function of social memory:

> Through narration of its master narrative a group continually reconstitutes itself as a coherent community, and as it moves forward through its history it aligns its fresh experiences with this master narrative, as well as vice versa.[4]

Others note that the expression of the past and the experience of the present cannot even be separated from each other. According to Paul Ricoeur, religious texts like the Hebrew Bible are not important because of their structure, as theorists such as Levi-Strauss would assert, but because of their depiction of constitutive narrative events like Exodus.[5] It is a narrative rather than a structural truth that the Bible communicates (although I would argue that it is both), and in modern society it is interpreted by different groups as constructing *"our* past." The memories of past Others are used to construct the present Others, just as past history is understood as relevant to the present.

Identity, when studied on a social as opposed to individual level, is often explored in terms of ethnicity, gender, race, religion, and so on. Like many of the other terms used in this study, ethnicity is a relatively recent term in the social sciences. It arose among liberal social scientists in the twentieth century when the biological basis of race came to be questioned. Race itself was a relatively young term; it appeared at the time of European colonization to explain the supposed inferiority of dark-skinned peoples. The cultural construction of "ethnic groups" was preferred as a more accurate description of human differences than the idea of permanent and immutable racial characteristics, and this term does seem to correspond more closely to the way ancient peoples talked about cultural differences. Scholars also raised questions about the definability of ethnicity. Is ethnic identity objective or subjective? Is it more fixed or more fluctuating? Is it understood as deriving from an ancient and primordial essence of a group or does it result from an evolutionary process? Is it more basic than religion for defining human identity or less? Do ethnic traits arise from within the group or are they generated more at the boundaries, in opposition to other groups?

Gerd Baumann and many other scholars now view ethnic identity as processual and developmental, which is the view that will be taken here.[6] Ethnicity may be less stable as a marker than is commonly assumed. Barth also proposes that ethnic identity is not based on differences that an outsider might observe but on a small group of characteristics that are subjectively highlighted by insiders. Ethnic groups do not coalesce based on a common culture, but significant markers of culture are constructed to express an ethnic identity. In addition, as noted above, Barth concludes that ethnic groups are defined by their *boundaries*, not their *cores*; that is, identity arises from defining how one is different. Shaye J. D. Cohen would amend this, however, to assert that ethnic identity is a combination of what we might call a sense of the core—how we are the same—combined with boundary definition—how we are different.[7] There is likely an important relationship between the boundary and the core in terms of ethnic definition, yet that relationship may vacillate at times. Identity formation may shift from the center to the boundary under times of stress. Customs of decorum which originally arose more from the core may in another setting and under stress become fervently protected markers of the outer boundaries with others, as one may see in the case of yarmulkes for Jewish men and hijabs (head coverings) for Muslim women. They were at one point in their respective cultures internal markers between men and women, but in a new cultural situation they also became external markers of ethnic and religious boundaries. Interestingly, both have been restricted at times by enlightened western democracies.

Much of what is said of ethnic groups in terms of constructed identities may also be said of nations, and this will inform how identity is constructed in biblical texts. A number of scholars have recently traced a people's belief in the inherent reality of ethnic identity and nation to a shared set of myths of origin. Benedict R. Anderson asserts that ethnic groups and nations alike are "imagined communities," created in a people's consciousness, brought into being as an ideal that perpetuates itself over time. Anderson argues that a nation comes into being out of selective memory of the past and selective amnesia as well.[8] Nations and ethnic groups, then, are products of social memory. They construct their histories out of bits and pieces of information about the past, some true and some false. Anthony D. Smith isolated certain common beliefs that are shared by both ethnic groups and nations: (1) an account of origins in time and space (that is, both the when and where of origins); (2) the group's ancestry and descent; (3) the migration of the group; (4) the liberation of the group; (5) common beliefs about the golden age of the group; (6) the decline of the group at some point in the past; and (7) the rebirth of the group.[9] Even modern nations, artificial communities in an artificially defined territory, and often having come into existence only recently, instill a sense of identity in the newly defined "citizens." There is often a myth of the spirit of the peasantry, a *Volk* who are the embodiment of the very spirit of the nation. The "authentic" roots of the peasantry are considered sacred, unmixed, and primordial.

Scholars of nationalism were once firmly convinced that "nation" as a secular definition of a "people" in a certain territory with recognized borders is a purely modern concept, arising in Europe during the Enlightenment, but this theory on the origins and nature of nationalism has been challenged on two fronts. First, in the ancient world, and certainly in Israel, there was something very like a "nation," and second, the development of nations in the modern period may be religious and not secular. Elie Kedourie had argued the earlier position, but altered this dramatically in 1971, when he wrote that nationalism does not arise out of the secular notions of the Enlightenment and the Romantics who followed, but out of the millennial quest of figures like Joachim of Fiore in the twelfth century and the Anabaptists in the sixteenth.[10] Not only did ancient kingdoms begin to look more like nations, but modern nations began to look more like ancient theocratic kingdoms. As Anthony Smith says,

I began to see that the passion evoked by nationalism, the powerful commitments felt by so many people to their own national identities, could not be explained in conventional economic and political terms. Only religion, with its powerful symbolism and collective ritual, could inspire such fervor.[11]

Thus the evolutionary and constructed nature of both ethnic groups and nations will be important for the present study because their very definitions require a construction of the mirror of identity, the Other.

It is clear that many of these notions of identity are formulated as a contrast with the outsider or Other. An obsession with the Other has dominated the social sciences for the last half century. There is a large body of anthropological literature on Otherness which addresses worldview formation, the concentric circles of the known and unknown that all human beings must be taught. Robert Redfield suggested in 1953 that all cultures see the world in terms of human/not-human and We/They; the We is correlated with the human, the They with the not-human.[12] Jonathan Z. Smith argues that understanding this relationship is a central goal of modern anthropology. As noted above, it is a "science of the 'other'"; its goal is to "decode the other."[13] He makes an important point about this sort of study: it is a process of defamiliarization, "making the familiar"—here the Bible—"seem strange *in order to enhance our perception of the familiar.*"[14] Smith very helpfully describes both sides of this process, that is, making the unfamiliar familiar and the familiar unfamiliar. There is a

dialectic of the "near" and the "far" that is central to the practice of the human sciences. If one aspect of the work of the scholar is to reduce surprise in that which first appears "strange" by enterprises of familiarization (ranging from analogy and translation to explanation), the opposite and equally important impulse must be to introduce surprise into that to which one is accustomed by means of enterprises of defamiliarization.[15]

Sociologists have also turned their attention to processes of the Other, often focusing on sects and "deviants," groups which may be marginalized by the larger society as Other, but which may also choose to differentiate; that is, they may, like the Cynics, define themselves in opposition to society. We will have occasion to speak of sectarian divisions, social deviance, and revitalization movements in more detail in regard to several of the texts in this study. Since the construction of the Other is often expressed in terms of conflict, we may note also those scholars who have developed "conflict theory." Georg Simmel, Lewis Coser, and Lewis Kriesberg outlined a series of descriptive laws which apply to conflict in society, among them: (1) conflict with an external opponent serves to reinforce group boundaries; (2) conflict with an opponent tends to reinforce structures within the group; (3) the closer the opponent is in reality, the more intense the conflict; (4) conflict tends to bind opponents together; and (5) conflict gives rise to a unitary view of the opponent.[16] Despite the chasm of distance between the biblical texts and us, we will find that these processes derived from modern social analysis can be discerned there as well.

Following the groundbreaking work of Gordon W. Allport, *The Nature of Prejudice*,[17] a number of social psychologists have also focused on the social dynamics of prejudice. Allport's research indicated that there are identifiable psychological aspects of the prejudiced person, but he conceived these on an individual psychological model only. Others, especially Henri Tajfel, turned in their research to group identity (social identity theory), and argued that in-groups form with startling ease and generate prejudices against out-groups just as readily.[18] The two main emphases of social identity theorists—a group mentality and an almost instantaneous distinction of in-group and out-group, even when the distinctions are trivial, have been applied to modern ethnic conflict by Donald Horowitz.[19] This would seem to provide the script for our analysis of constructions of We and Other in ancient texts as well.

Running parallel to this list of various approaches from the social sciences is a second list of reflections on identity and the Other from literary and critical theory. The twentieth century was seen as both the period of the triumph of western capitalism and individualism, and also the period of a growing awareness that the triumphant western male was not the center of the universe.[20] The assumption of a universal knowledge was challenged and even ruptured by any recognition of the validity of the Other's experience. One may even say that the "crisis of modernity" *was caused by* the discovery of the Other. It resonated as a negative presence, focalizing the anxiety of individualism in the mid-twentieth century, but the Other also often appears in a much more positive way in the works of the later deconstructionist philosophers Jacques Derrida and Emmanuel Lévinas. Deconstruction destabilizes the supposed relation of thought and reality; recognizing the Other will by necessity push the Self out of the center of its own universe, decentering the Self and initiating a Copernican revolution in everyday life.[21] The relation of the recognition of the Other and the decentering of the Self could hardly be stated more idealistically than by Tzvetan Todorov:

> The first phase of understanding consists of assimilating the other to oneself. . . . There is only one identity: my own. The second phase of understanding consists of effacing the self for the other's benefit. . . . Here again, there is only one identity; but it is the other's. In the third phase of understanding, I resume my own identity, but after having done everything possible to know the other. During the fourth phase of knowledge, I "leave" myself once

again, but in an entirely different way. I no longer desire, nor am I able, to identify with the other; nor can I, however, identify with myself. . . . My identity is maintained, but it is as if it is neutralized; I read myself in quotation marks. . . . By interacting with the other, my categories have become transformed in such a way that they speak for both of us and—why not?—for third parties also. Universality, which I thought I had lost, is rediscovered elsewhere: not in the object, but in the project.[22]

His optimism concerning universality may not be shared with all post-colonial or postmodern critics, but the emphasis on the process would be.

This awareness gives rise to an entirely new "way in" to historical and cultural discussions. In postmodernist thought knowledge in general is often understood to arise from perception of oppositions: God/world, death/life, Other/Self. Entities cannot be known *in themselves,* but can be perceived *in opposition* to each other, like atomic particles whose existence can only be detected when they collide. The *tension* between A and B in an ancient text may be comparable—not identical, but comparable—to the *tension* between entities A' and B' in another culture, or in the modern world. It is for this reason that it may not matter whether, say, "homosexuality"—a purely modern term—was understood in the same way in ancient cultures as in the contemporary West. The tension between the We of the text and those who engage in same-sex love may be comparable—not identical, but comparable—in two different cultures even if they have defined the "essences" differently.[23]

Much of the affirmation of the Other in the late twentieth century was promulgated by theorists who *were* the Other. In addition to the large number of Jewish thinkers who have addressed this issue, we may note briefly three other critical approaches: feminism, race theory, and postcolonial theory. Feminism attempted to reveal the male construction of the woman as Other, which is quite analogous to the construction of the ethnic outsider as Other. Race theory in the United States focused on prejudice, class, and slavery, issues noted above and treated in the chapters which follow. Literary scholars, philosophers, political economists, and social scientists who were born outside of European culture also converged to describe the peculiar ambiguity of the colonized person—interesting here because all of the texts of the Bible were written or edited by colonized scribes. Armed with the literary and intellectual techniques of the colonial powers, the colonized intellectual saw the artificiality of the colonizer's idealized Self and identified instead with those who were relegated to "native" status, the colonial Other. Feminism, race theory, and postcolonial theory all found a congenial ally in deconstruction to critique the idea that the categories of western culture possessed an inherent truth-value and universality.[24]

What all of these varied approaches would seem to require at this point is a comprehensive theory that might integrate multiple approaches into one, and this was attempted by Baumann.[25] He proposes that three widely known theories of identity and Otherness can be used to cover all manifestations. First, Edward Said's *Orientalism* provides a model for the colonial Other at the border who is constructed as the ethnic opposite of the We. Louis Dumont's *Homo Hierarchicus*, a structural study of the caste system in India, provides the model for the member of one's own society who is consigned to a relatively low rung on the social hierarchy. The third theorist, E. E. Evans-Pritchard, analyzed segmentation among the Nuer in Africa. What I will propose is that the first theory, that of Said, corresponds to my analysis of the construction of the external Other; the second, that of Dumont, to my analysis of the internal Other. The third model, that of Evans-Pritchard, has little application in the present study—segmentary organization implies an essential equality of segments—but Baumann's work as a whole demonstrates that various manifestations of constructions of the Other can be considered in a single, dynamic matrix. His overarching categories, however, though helpful, still remain too much of an abstraction. That is, we may need more than three hermeneutical lenses to view manifestations of identity and the Other in the biblical texts.

THEOREMS FOR THE ANALYSIS OF THE OTHER

The goal of this study is not to argue *that* biblical texts construct a vision of the Other—that is generally assumed now by biblical scholars—but to elucidate *how* they do it and *why*. These theoretical approaches provide photographs of our subject matter taken from different angles, and there will be opportunities to bring many of them to bear on one or more of the texts at hand. We must develop a method of integrating the theoretical advances outlined above and analysis of particular texts and particular cases. Therefore, I postulate here nine theorems about the construction of the Other, theorems which apply not only in the biblical texts but in other contexts as well. They may act as a matrix between the various methods discussed above and the texts under study. (They are listed as well in the appendix for easy reference, and at the end the reader can also find an index of references to each theorem where it is treated in the text.)

Theorem 1: From Other to We. The construction of the Other serves to construct the We. Not all outsiders are constructed as Other; the distant stranger is not necessarily Other. The Other must be defined and mythologized as an opposite and be the object of an obsession, but the stranger is simply distant and different.

Theorem 2: From We to Other. Just as the construction of the Other serves to construct the We, so also the construction of the We serves to construct the Other. The social practices that hold society together are affirmed by the We, while their opposites, which threaten to destroy social bonds, are projected onto the Other.

Theorem 3: Other similar to We. The Other is often in reality very similar to the We. Viewed by an outside third party, the Other is often almost indistinguishable from the We, but certain traits are magnified by the We in order to impose a gulf between them, just as ethnicity is often expressed by a selection of traits. This is what Freud referred to as the "narcissism of small differences."[26] Jonathan Z. Smith also emphasizes that the anxiety over the Other is more often not in regard to the distant Other but the "proximate Other"; not the one who is different from us, but the one who is too much like us, who must be meticulously redefined as Other.[27] And surprisingly, studies of ethnic conflict indicate that it occurs just as often and is just as intense even when the groups are of the same race, language, or religion. Differences can always be "discovered."

Theorem 4: Seductive power of Other. The Other has the ability to corrupt or infect the We, and the We is vulnerable. A strong argument for imposing strict boundaries around the We is that the Other always threatens to invade or undermine the We. Despite the grotesque inhumanity of the Other, the We is felt to be in constant danger of being seduced by the Other. There are great ambivalences of fear and desire. Closely related to the emotional reaction of abjection or horror of the Other, says Julia Kristeva, is the desire for the Other, and anxiety over this desire.[28]

Theorem 5: Other distorted. The depiction of the Other is often unreal, distorted, monstrous, mythical, and taboo. As Robert L. Cohn says, "Groups project onto the Other what they fear most in themselves."[29] Further, the construction of the Other often occurs in the absence of any meaningful contact or information. Cross-culturally, the same stereotyped list of traits is projected onto the Other: cannibalism; incest and other sexual perversions; murder and human sacrifice; inverted religious practices; savage customs that strike at the very notion of civilization. Conversely, multiple aspects of the Other may be reduced to one identity, one type. While in reality human beings exhibit multiple and nested identities, constructing someone as Other erases all those identities and replaces them with one inaccurate identity.

Theorem 6: Internal Others. There are internal as well as external Others, and they are often seen as linked. The external Other is that antagonist on the horizon who is perceived as the opposite of everything we are, who is inhuman while we are human, and who is always threatening to attack us at the borders. The internal Other, on the other hand, lives among us, often as the instrumental Other or the invisible Other. Even intimates can be

Other, such as people of the Other gender, of the Other sexual orientation, of the Other class, or of the Other race. It is ironic that Others often have the most intimate contact with the bodies of the defining group: servants, barbers and hairdressers, tailors and shoemakers, prostitutes and wives, child-care providers. The internal Other is held in check by a domesticated social order, but if that order fails for one second, there is a danger that the internal Other will become the external Other, because they are linked. As a result, condemnation of the external Other is a way of controlling the internal Other, and vice versa. In reading ancient texts, *it is often difficult to discern whether the motivating fear is of an external or internal Other, regardless of which is being discussed; either can be a cipher for the other.*

Theorem 7: Ambiguous groups reassigned. Ambiguous groups are often reassigned either as an Other or as a special case of an adopted We or internal Other. This is an application of the Law of the Excluded Middle: everything found between the two extremes must be cleared out and redefined as one or the other extreme. It is very difficult to predict in which way a group will be redefined, Other or adoptee, but a reassignment in both directions often occurs to different ambiguous groups simultaneously. Some cases defy belief. In the segregated American South, an American with "one drop of Negro blood" was excluded from white hotels and restaurants, while Africans were occasionally served as visitors. In Nazi Germany, some German officers with Jewish ancestry were declared to be non-Jewish, even by Hitler himself, and "adopted" as Aryan.[30] Homi Bhabha investigates well this in-between category in regard to colonized persons: from the perspective of the colonized person, the marginal ambiguity remains; it cannot be reassigned. "Mimicry" is one way of negotiating this ambiguity, which is invisible from the point of view of the colonizer. We will see that some small nations that would normally be associated with the Canaanites were appropriated as subservient groups within Israel while originally Israelite practices were rejected as Canaanite.

Theorem 8: Origins of practices reassigned. Ancient, native, or traditional practices may be redefined as new or foreign and associated with the Other, while an originally foreign practice may be redefined as ancient, native, and traditional, now associated with the We.

Theorem 9: Eternal Other. The Other is viewed as having existed from time immemorial and continues to exist, and cannot be permanently extirpated. The threat of the Other lies partly in its antiquity. The Other has threatened in the past and will continue to threaten again in the future. Heresies in Christianity, for example, have traditionally been traced back to the original arch-heretic, Simon Magus; in the modern world a major Nazi propaganda film was entitled "The Eternal Jew." There is thus a continuing tension concerning the eternal Other: there is a command to destroy it finally, yet it will always endure to threaten again.

NOTES

1. Jonathan Z. Smith, "What a Difference a Difference Makes," in *"To See Ourselves as Others See Us": Christians, Jews, "Others" in Late Antiquity,* ed. Jacob Neusner and Ernst S. Frerichs (Chico, CA: Scholars Press, 1985), 15–16. A few texts that have synthesized some of the results include Howard Eilberg-Schwartz, *The Savage in Judaism: An Anthropology of Israelite Religion and Ancient Judaism* (Bloomington: Indiana University Press, 1990); Regina Schwartz, *The Curse of Cain: The Violent Legacy of Monotheism* (Chicago: University of Chicago Press, 1997); Saul Olyan, *Rites and Rank: Hierarchy in Biblical Representations of Cult* (Princeton, NJ: Princeton University Press, 2000); Robert L. Cohn and Laurence J. Silberstein, eds., *The Other in Jewish Thought and History: Constructions of Jewish Culture and Identity* (New York/London: New York University Press, 1994); Steven L. McKenzie, *All God's Children: A Biblical Critique of Racism* (Louisville, KY: Westminster/John Knox, 1997); and E. Leigh Gibson and Shelly Matthews, *Violence in the New Testament* (Edinburgh, UK: T & T Clark, 2005). A number of other scholars have addressed the issue of the Other in particular biblical texts, to which reference can be found in the chapters that follow.

2. Fredrik Barth, "Introduction," in *Ethnic Groups and Boundaries: The Social Organization of Cultural Differences,* ed. Fredrik Barth (Boston: Little, Brown, 1969), 1–26; Andre Gingrich, "Conceptualizing Identities: Anthropological Alternatives to Essentializing Difference and Moralizing Othering," in *Grammars of Identity/Alterity: A Structural Approach,* ed. Gerd Baumann and Andre Gingrich (New York and Oxford: Berghahn, 2004), 5–6; Gerd Baumann, *Contesting Culture: Discourses of Identity in Multi-Ethnic London* (Cambridge, UK, and New York: Cambridge University Press, 1996). Critics of an overly broad or tendentious use of identity include Rogers Brubaker and Frederick Cooper, "Beyond 'Identity,'" *Theory and Society* 29 (2000): 1–47, and John Rex, "The Fundamentals of the Theory of Identity," in *Making Sense of Collectivity,* ed. Siniša Malešević and Mark Haugaard (London and Sterling, VA: Pluto, 2002), 88–105.

3. Maurice Halbwachs, *On Collective Memory* (Chicago: University of Chicago Press, 1992), 223. See Elizabeth A. Castelli, *Martyrdom and Memory: Early Christian Culture Making* (New York: Columbia University Press, 2004), 10–24; Doron Mendels, *Memory in Jewish, Pagan and Christian Societies of the Graeco-Roman World* (London and New York: T & T Clark International, 2004); Yosef Yerushalmi, *Zakhor: Jewish History and Jewish Memory* (Seattle: University of Washington Press, 1996).

4. Alan Kirk, "Social and Cultural Memory," in *Memory, Tradition, and Text: Uses of the Past in Early Christianity,* ed. Alan Kirk and Tom Thatcher (Atlanta, GA: Society of Biblical Literature, 2005), 5, referring to the work of Yael Zerubavel, *Recovered Roots: Collective Memory and the Making of Israeli National Tradition* (Chicago: University of Chicago Press, 1995), 7.

5. Paul Ricoeur, "Structure and Hermeneutics," in *The Conflict of Interpretations: Essays in Hermeneutics,* ed. Don Ihde (Evanston: Northwestern University Press, 1969), 27–61. An entire parallel study could be carried out on the construction of We and Other in terms of archaeological remains and the categorization of space; see Joan Branham, "Hedging the Holy at Qumran: Walls as Symbolic Devices," in

Qumran, the Site of the Dead Sea Scrolls: Archaeological Interpretations and Debates, ed. Katharina Galor, Jean-Baptiste Humbert, and Jürgen Zangenberg (Leiden, Netherlands: Brill, 2006), 117–31; and David Frankfurter, "Spaces of Crisis, Locations of Destruction: Violent Christianization in Late Antique Egypt," forthcoming.

6. Gerd Baumann, *The Multicultural Riddle: Rethinking National, Ethnic, and Religious Identities* (New York: Routledge, 1999), esp. 90, 95. See also Jonathan M. Hall, *Ethnic Identity in Greek Antiquity* (Cambridge, UK: Cambridge University Press, 1997); Mark G. Brett, ed., *Ethnicity and the Bible* (Leiden, Netherlands: Brill, 1996); and Kenton L. Sparks, *Ethnicity and Identity in Ancient Israel* (Winona Lake, IN: Eisenbrauns, 1998).

7. Shaye J. D. Cohen, *The Beginnings of Jewishness: Boundaries, Varieties, Uncertainties* (Berkeley: University of California Press, 1999), 5–6.

8. Benedict R. Anderson, *Imagined Communities: Reflections on the Origin and Spread of Nationalism*, 2nd ed. (London and New York: Verso, 1991), 6. Homi Bhabha, *The Location of Culture* (London and New York: Routledge, 1994), 139–70, contrasts Anderson's assumption of a stable core of a nation with a consideration of the nation's colonial margin.

9. Anthony D. Smith, *The Ethnic Origins of Nations* (Oxford: Blackwell, 1986), 192. On the belief in the primordial roots of the peasantry, see Anthony Smith, *Chosen Peoples* (Oxford and New York: Oxford University Press, 2003), 36–38.

10. Earlier view: Elie Kedourie, *Nationalism* (London: Hutchinson, 1960); later view: Elie Kedourie, *Nationalism in Asia and Africa* (London: Weidenfeld & Nicolson, 1971), 92–103. See also Ilana Pardes, *The Biography of Ancient Israel* (Berkeley: University of California Press, 2000), 1–2, 16; Doron Mendels, *The Rise and Fall of Jewish Nationalism: Jewish and Christian Ethnicity in Ancient Palestine* (Grand Rapids, MI: Eerdmans, 1992); David M. Goodblatt, *Elements of Ancient Jewish Nationalism* (New York: Cambridge University Press, 2006); John Armstrong, *Nations before Nationalism* (Chapel Hill: University of North Carolina Press, 1982); John Armstrong, "Religious Nationalism and Collective Violence," *Nations and Nationalism* 3 (1997): 597–606; Donald Akenson, *God's Peoples: Covenant and Land in South Africa, Israel and Ulster* (Ithaca, NY: Cornell University Press, 1992); and Walker Connor, *Ethno-Nationalism: The Quest for Understanding* (Princeton, NJ: Princeton University Press, 1994).

11. Smith, *Chosen Peoples*, vii.

12. Robert Redfield, *The Primitive World and Its Transformations* (Ithaca, NY: Cornell University Press, 1953), 92; Edmund Leach, "Anthropological Aspects of Language: Animal Categories and Verbal Abuse," in *Reader in Comparative Religion: An Anthropological Approach*, ed. William Lessa and Evon Vogt (New York: Harper & Row, 1979), 153–65.

13. Smith, "What a Difference," 15–19.

14. Jonathan Z. Smith, *Imagining Religion: From Babylon to Jonestown* (Chicago: University of Chicago Press, 1982), xiii.

15. Jonathan Z. Smith, "Dayyeinu," in *Redescribing Christian Origins*, ed. Ron Cameron and Merrill P. Miller (Atlanta, GA: SBL, 2004), 483; Jonathan Z. Smith, "Differential Equations: On Constructing the Other," in *Relating Religion: Essays in the Study of Religion* (Chicago: University of Chicago Press, 2004), 231–37. See also Cheyney Ryan, "The Two Faces of Postmodernism, or the Difference between Dif-

ference and Otherness," in *Who, Exactly, Is the Other? Western and Transcultural Perspectives*, ed. Steven Shankman and Massimo Lollini (Eugene: University of Oregon Books, 2002), 15–21. Smith's startling ability to perceive and describe cross-cultural constructions of worldview has allowed him to compose an oeuvre that is one of the richest contributions in recent discussions of religion, but he does not turn to the power relations inherent in the construction of the Other. The construction of the Other is described by Smith almost neutrally, as a compelling instance of intellection—the Other is good to think with—but in the analysis here it will be the power relationships that will be highlighted.

16. Georg Simmel, *Conflict* (Glencoe, IL: Free Press, 1955); Lewis Coser, *The Functions of Social Conflict* (Glencoe, IL: Free Press, 1956), esp. 67, 72; Lewis Kriesberg, *The Sociology of Social Conflicts* (Englewood Cliffs, NJ: Prentice-Hall, 1973). Applied to biblical studies, see Jack T. Sanders, *Schismatics, Sectarians, Dissidents, Deviants: The First One Hundred Years of Jewish-Christian Relations* (Valley Forge, PA: Trinity Press International, 1993), 125–29; and John G. Gager, *Kingdom and Community: The Social World of Early Christianity* (Englewood Cliffs, NJ: Prentice-Hall, 1975), 79–87.

17. Gordon W. Allport, *The Nature of Prejudice* (Cambridge, MA: Addison-Wesley, 1954); John F. Dovidio, Peter Glick, and Laurie A. Rudman, eds., *On the Nature of Prejudice: Fifty Years after Allport* (Oxford: Blackwell, 2005). A cognitive-linguistic approach to the categories by which people conceive social relations is presented by George Lakoff, *Women, Fire, and Dangerous Things: What Categories Reveal about the Mind* (Chicago: University of Chicago Press, 1987).

18. Henri Tajfel and John C. Turner, "The Social Identity Theory of Intergroup Behavior," in *Psychology of Intergroup Relations,* ed. W. G. Austin and S. Worchel (Chicago: Nelson Hall, 1986), 7–24; and Henri Tajfel et al., "Social Categorization and Intergroup Behaviour," *European Journal of Social Psychology* 1 (1971): 149–78. Elisabeth Young-Bruehl, *The Anatomy of Prejudices* (Cambridge, MA: Harvard University Press, 1996), esp. 27–30, 69, 184–99, following in the tradition of Allport, distinguishes sharply between ethnocentrism—what I will call construction of the external Other—and charged prejudices against certain groups in modern society, the internal Other. Rather than drawing a link, however, between the construction of external Other and internal Other (as I do), she emphasizes the difference. For instance, the obsessive nature of modern prejudices in her view is generated by repressed desire for the Other, which is not the case with ethnocentrism. The biblical evidence would suggest that it is true in both cases; see the postcolonial critiques of ideologies of desire in western views of colonial peoples in Robert J. C. Young, *Colonial Desire: Hybridity in Theory, Culture and Race* (London and New York: Routledge, 1995).

19. Donald Horowitz, *Ethnic Groups in Conflict* (Berkeley: University of California Press, 1985), 141–84.

20. Michel de Certeau, *Heterologies: Discourse on the Other* (Minneapolis and London: University of Minnesota Press, 1986), 181; Silberstein, "Others Within and Others Without: Rethinking Jewish Identity and Culture," in Silberstein and Cohn, *Other in Jewish Thought,* 5.

21. Jacques Derrida, "Deconstruction and the Other" in *Dialogues with Contemporary Thinkers,* ed. Richard Kearney (Manchester, UK: Manchester University

Press, 1984), 107–26. Emmanuel Lévinas became the quintessential philosopher of the Other; see *Ethics and Infinity: Conversations with Philippe Nemo* (Pittsburgh, PA: Duquesne University Press, 1985), 77; Emmanuel Lévinas, *Time and the Other [and Additional Essays]* (Pittsburgh, PA: Duquesne University Press, 1987). Compare also Certeau, *Heterologies,* xv–xvi; John T. Lysaker, "Who, Exactly, Is the Other? Western Philosophical Perspectives," in Shankman and Lollini, eds., *Who, Exactly,* 5.

22. Tzvetan Todorov, "Postscript: Knowledge of Others," in *The Morals of History* (Minneapolis/London: University of Minnesota Press, 1995), 14.

23. This approach, very common in much of cultural studies, also allows for the possibility that there was a repressed meaning in the ancient tension between A and B that may have been unrecognized by the first audience and by every audience thereafter until today. Cf. the differing views in Clifford Geertz, *The Interpretation of Cultures* (New York: Basic, 1973), 25–26; Clifford Geertz, "Distinguished Lecture: Anti Anti-Relativism," *American Anthropologist* 66 (1984): 263–78; Silberstein, "Others Within," 12; Massimo Fusillo, "Modern Critical Theories and the Ancient Novel," in *The Novel in the Ancient World*, ed. Gareth Schmeling (Leiden, Netherlands, and New York: Brill, 1996), 300–301.

24. Silberstein, "Others Within," 5, 11. A good introduction to issues of colonialism and the Other is that of Zhang Longxi, *Mighty Opposites: From Dichotomies to Differences in the Comparative Study of China* (Palo Alto, CA: Stanford University Press, 1998), 1–54; see also Edward Said, *Orientalism* (London: Routlege & Kegan Paul, 1978); Bhabha, *Location of Culture,* esp. 85–92; R. G. Sugirtharajah, ed., *Postcolonial Bible* (Sheffield, UK: Sheffield Academic Press, 1998); Michel de Certeau, *The Practice of Everyday Life* (Berkeley: University of California Press, 1984), 35–39; Young, *Colonial Desire.*

25. Gerd Baumann, "Grammars of Identity/Alterity: A Structural Approach," in Gerd Baumann and Andre Gingrich, eds., *Grammars of Identity/Alterity*, 18–50; Louis Dumont, *Homo Hierarchicus: An Essay on the Caste System* (Chicago: University of Chicago Press, 1970), and E. E. Evans-Pritchard, *The Nuer: A Description of the Modes of Livelihood and Political Institutions of a Nilotic People* (New York: Oxford University Press, 1969). Partial attempts at integration of different Others can be found in Young-Bruehl, *Anatomy of Prejudices*; Young, *Colonial Desire*; and R. I. Moore, *The Formation of a Persecuting Society*, 2nd ed. (Oxford: Blackwell, 2007), 144: ". . . persecutions of heretics, Jews, lepers, sodomites and others in twelfth- and thirteenth-century Europe cannot be considered or explained independently of one another, as they almost always had been hitherto."

26. Sigmund Freud, "Taboo of Virginity," in *The Complete Psychological Works of Sigmund Freud*, 24 vols. (London: Hogarth, 1957–1974), 11:193–207.

27. Smith, "What a Difference," 46–47; "Differential Equations," 245. The point is pressed by other scholars as well: Simmel, *Conflict*, 48; Julia Kristeva, *Powers of Horror: An Essay in Abjection* (New York: Columbia University Press, 1982), 9; Robert L. Cohn "Negotiating (with) the Nations: Ancestors and Identity in Genesis," *Harvard Theological Review* 96 (2003): 149; Toril Moi, *Sexual/Textual Politics: Feminist Literary Theory* (London: Methuen, 1985), 150; Esther Benbassa and Jean-Christophe Attias, *The Jew and the Other* (Ithaca, NY, and London: Cornell University Press, 2004), ix–18, esp. 3–4; and Horowitz, *Ethnic Groups*, 15–16.

28. Julia Kristeva, *Powers of Horror; Strangers to Ourselves* (New York: Columbia University Press, 1991), 191; Derrida, "Deconstruction," 116; Young, *Colonial Desire*; and Young-Bruehl, *Anatomy of Prejudices* (but see the caveat in n. 18).

29. Cohn, "Negotiating (with) the Nations," 149; "The Second Coming of Moses: Deuteronomy and the Construction of Israelite Identity," in *Proceedings of the Twelfth World Congress of Jewish Studies* (Division A: The Bible and Its World), ed. Shmuel Ahituv et al. (Jerusalem: World Union of Jewish Studies, 1999), 66; David Frankfurter, *Evil Incarnate: Rumors of Demonic Conspiracy and Ritual Abuse in History* (Princeton, NJ: Princeton University Press, 2006); and Amartya Sen, *Identity and Violence: The Illusion of Destiny* (New York: Norton, 2006).

30. Bhabha, *Location of Culture*, 5, 9; Bryan Mark Rigg, *Hitler's Jewish Soldiers: The Untold Story of Nazi Racial Laws and Men of Jewish Descent in the German Military* (Lawrence: University of Kansas Press, 2002).

2

⟨✍⟩

The Beginning of Difference and the Origin of Others in the Hebrew Bible

In the beginning, there was no Other. Something did exist, for creation in Genesis is not *creatio ex nihilo*, but there were no differences that would allow one to distinguish one thing from another. Rather, there was only a formless void, a primeval plasma, undifferentiated both in terms of form and in terms of time; it is formless and timeless. How, then, will Genesis show the process of differentiation? Although God speaks and light is created, this is not considered sufficient, for the text then says that "God separated the light from the darkness," and "called the light Day, and the darkness Night." Time begins when light and dark are *separated* and this separation differentiates one time segment from the next. On each day God separated one thing from another, or gathered one thing together, or made various distinctive kinds, each in its own place. Even the human being is created "male and female." The verb "to separate" is thus used more often than the word "create," as we move from an undifferentiated mass, through new entities and distinctions, to culminate with human beings. Where there had been only undifferentiated plasma, there is now day and night, land and waters held back, plant life and animal life, and human beings, male and female. But the Eden that is created is still a relatively undifferentiated place; parts come to take shape or are divided off, but remain in a primitive state of pastoral innocence: there are few people, few living things, no difference in roles, no conflict, no shame, no striving or competition.

One biblical scholar, Susan Niditch, compares myths of creation from a number of cultures and perceives certain important similarities.[1] She notes that although creation myths may differ in terms of whether at the

21

beginning there is nothing (Scandinavian) or formless matter (Chinese, Apache, Greek), they are alike in positing creation as the process of differentiation. The process of differentiation that is found in creation also characterizes the subsequent history of the world. When Adam and Eve eat from the tree of knowledge of good and evil, this does not introduce the knowledge of sexual sin as Christian tradition would have it, but knowledge of the *separated* orders of good and evil, a divine prerogative; the first humans have crossed a boundary into divine knowledge. Their subsequent expulsion is presented as negative, but it also gives rise to an important development. The negative aspects of expulsion contain within them the various new differentiated dimensions of life for human beings. After the fall, there are other family members now present, work, and the pain of childbirth, in addition to the knowledge of good and evil. The birth of Cain and Abel—one who plants fields and one who shepherds livestock—represents a differentiation of roles that are necessary for providing sustenance. Losing the peace and innocence of the undifferentiated Eden brings with it new aspects that make us human: other family members and "cities" are now mentioned, the challenge of childbirth and work is described, and even death plays a role in allowing humans to go beyond the timelessness of Eden. Death, we find, is necessary for history; fall and differentiation are necessary for growth.

The first part of Genesis is composed of a series of falls. There will be a repeated cycle of violation of God's boundary, God's curse and punishment, a re-creation of a new order with further differentiations and new, more specific laws. In Genesis 6 the mysterious "sons of God" violate the boundary between earth and heaven and mate with human women. In Genesis 11 humans try to cross a boundary by building a tower to heaven. They are punished and there is a further separation of peoples, now differentiated by language, with both a tragic and a typically human result: the human race is differentiated into language groups and people have difficulty communicating with each other. People are scattered and unable to communicate, resulting in a spread of human culture and difference over the face of the earth. Difference, but no Other. Differentiation becomes alienation from God and each other, but the result is the story of humanity, and the repetition of the cycle of differentiation, fall, and re-creation is in each case expanded until the differentiation becomes increasingly like the picture of society in the author's own day. Without sin, there is no history. This sounds so "biblical" to our ears, but as Niditch also points out, this pattern of fall and differentiation is found in other cultures as well. The explanation of how human categories came into being is in many cultures a story of a tragic fall or a series of falls from a state of undifferentiated innocence. Ironically, we suppose that our myths of difference define how *different* we are from other cultures, but they actually reveal how we are *similar*. Here we first encounter a manifestation of one of the theorems from the introduction, the Other is similar to the We (Theorem 3).

At the same time that human groups are being differentiated, the origin of categories that we would call ethnic groups begins to emerge. At Genesis 9:18 human difference is described in terms of genealogy, the scientific anthropology of the ancient world. As we learned in the introduction, ethnic identity is generally seen cross-culturally as a primordial essence that is transmitted through kinship. All of human ethnic diversity is seen in Genesis as deriving from a particular ancestor:

> The sons of Noah who went out of the ark were Shem, Ham, and Japheth. Ham was the father of Canaan. These three were the sons of Noah, and from these the whole earth was peopled.

After the flood Noah's three sons become the patriarchal heads of the families of the earth. Shem is the ancestor of Abraham, Ham is the progenitor of the peoples to the south—Egypt, Cush (Nubia or Ethiopia), Put (Libya), and Canaan; and Japheth is the progenitor of the peoples of Asia Minor and the Aegean region. Shem is the origin of the word Semitic, but in Genesis the Canaanites, in reality a Semitic people closely related to the Israelites, are reckoned as distant; they are the offspring of Ham and associated with Egypt. This illustrates Theorem 8: Origins of practices reassigned: the recent separation of Israel and Canaan is redefined as something old.

Immediately after the introduction of the three families of human beings there is another sign of growth and differentiation followed by another sin. Noah learns to plant a vineyard, a new human occupation, but becomes drunk on the wine, and while lying in his tent is seen naked by Ham. Sexual relations between Ham and Noah may also be implied in the story. Ham's sin incurs the curse of his father, Noah, but his curse falls not on Ham but upon his son, Canaan. This unexpected turn of events—that Canaan and not Ham is cursed—is best explained as an attempt to focus the curse on Israel's perpetual enemy. Canaan is said to move from the area of Ham and occupy the region of Shem (Gen 10:15–20), violating the primeval boundaries laid down in this story. And yet it is ironic and quite significant that the movements of Canaan parallel the movements of Israel, from Egypt to Palestine, the region that Israel will come to occupy. Other than the Canaanites, none of the other families mentioned so far has been marked as positive or negative. But this first differentiation in the narrative into specific, named peoples is also accompanied by the first clear characterization of a people as Other. Although in the beginning there was no Other, now there is. The origin of the antagonism that the framers of the biblical narrative felt toward Canaanites is *read back into primeval history* as a way of explaining their *present* enemies.

OTHERNESS AND COVENANT

Humankind has differentiated into human families, one of which is now cursed—the one that has moved outside its original boundaries and circled around to occupy the land that will become Israel. Abraham is also called forth to become the patriarch of a new kinship group. He is promised a progeny as plentiful as the stars of heaven who will enter the land which the Canaanites now occupy, a land flowing with milk and honey. The religion of Israel, and the history of Jews as well, is understood as the history of the family line of Abraham.[2] The fact that the first Other is introduced very near the first announcement of the promise to Abraham is not coincidental. In Abraham and Canaan we see a single patriarch of the We and a single patriarch of the Other. Later it will become more complex, with a number of patriarchs and a number of Others, but no matter how the description of the We or the Other may change or become more complex, they are always easily perceptible as mirror images of each other, each deriving from its respective ancestor. We already see evidence here for several of the theorems stated in the introduction: the Other defines the We, the Other and the We are similar, the Other is mythologized and distorted, the Other is reduced to one essence, and the Other is eternal.

A subsequent story in Genesis, that of Lot's daughters (Gen 19), also describes the genealogy of the Other. The daughters, living alone with Lot and realizing that they will not marry and have children, conspire to get their father drunk, lie with him, and become pregnant. Just as Ham fathers a cursed progeny (Canaan), so also the daughters of Lot give birth to Moab and Ammon, the progenitors of the Moabites and the Ammonites, two perennial enemies of Israel. In two stories, then, incestuous sexual relations—the violation of strict boundaries—give rise to the birth of enemies of Israel (Theorem 5: Other distorted, with a list of stereotyped traits, including incest). The stories of Canaan's and Lot's daughters demonstrate that sexual relations with those who are too close are dangerous, while later (Gen 26:34–35) it will be said that Ishmael's foreign wives created enmity. As Regina Schwartz says, union-too-close and union-too-distant both produce perennial enemies of Israel.[3]

In Genesis, the special nature of the patriarchs is not based on their *religious* observances as it will be in later texts; it is based on lineage and territory, acted out in struggles over women and land. The *moral* acts of the patriarchs are not crucial for the future history of Israel; for the most part the patriarchs do not act more nobly than the other figures. However, what they do that *is* correct is marry women from the right families. At the early stages of the narrative, the underlying moral value of the Israelites that is threatened at every turn is not exclusive worship of Yahweh, but endogamy (marrying within a particular group). It is crucial in the flow chart of the narrative that the patriarchs choose a descent line that is endogamous and which will eventually become the Israel of the biblical author's day. Various explanations for this emphasis on endogamy have been suggested. Albrecht Alt argued that the religion of the patriarchs was tribal and nomadic, so that geographical and territorial differences *were considered* religious differences. Yehezkel Kaufmann thought that Israelite religion before Sinai was not truly monotheistic, and more recently Rainer Albertz has argued that early worship of Yahweh was not exclusive and did not require rejection of other gods. Robert L. Cohn suggests, however, and I would agree, that endogamy predominates over the worship of God *because of the genre*.[4] The patriarchs are depicted in epic-time, a prehistoric period in which things were simply different. Cohn refers to this as a distinction between family myth and political myth. (The distinction in ancient Scandinavian saga between the oldest layers—family saga—and the later layers—royal saga—is very similar.) Things could be depicted in a different way in a primordial, preinstitutionalized period in which single patriarchs stood for later peoples. The presentation of a preinstitutional world of Genesis might be compared to American westerns which looked backward to create origin-myths of a time before white people had established a European order. As Wild Bill Hickok says in Cecil B. DeMille's *The Plainsman*, "There is no Sunday west of Junction City, no law west of Hays City, and no God west of Carson City." "Our" ancestors, primal people, struggled to establish farmsteads without the safeguards of civilization, before there was a God in Nevada.

Although the narratives of the early patriarchs and matriarchs treated above may have arisen in older mythic and epic sources, the structure of the larger narrative of Genesis through Kings makes up one continuous story of the founding of Israel, often referred to as the Primary History.[5] There are close parallels in the other literatures of the ancient near east for many of the genres found in the Hebrew Bible, from psalms and proverbs to the creation myths and patriarchal sagas of Genesis 1–11 analyzed above, but Moshe Weinfeld argues that the great ancient near eastern empires do not have accounts of the founding of their nations; they "were not cognizant of a beginning of their national existence."[6] Greece, he argues, does provide such parallels in its stories of the founding of new colonies, as does Rome in the epic accounts of the founding of the city, but Israel's neighbors did not emphasize historical narratives of their own founding.

The revelation of God in the Hebrew Bible takes place in the context of God calling upon Israel to make a contract or covenant:

> If you obey my voice and keep my covenant, you shall be my treasured possession out of all the peoples. Indeed, the whole earth is mine, but you shall be a kingdom of priests for me and a holy nation. (Exod 19:5–6)

The parts of the covenant are found in slightly different forms in the earliest sources of the five books of Moses, presented as part of a dramatic narrative of promise, sin and a threat to that promise, and renewal. It was left to the Priestly Source (P), the last of the Pentateuch sources (sixth century BCE), to put all the pieces of the covenant history into one sequence of increasingly specific covenants:

(1) creation: blessing
(2) Noah: rainbow covenant
(3) Abraham: covenant of circumcision
(4) Moses: covenant of law

Other references to covenant in the Hebrew Bible are divided and categorized in various ways by scholars: Abrahamic versus Mosaic versus Davidic, early versus late, unconditional or promissory (without stipulations) versus conditional (with stipulations), ritual versus theological, modeled on ancient near eastern treaties versus not modeled on treaties, and so on. We need not rehearse the history of covenant theology in order to conclude that Israel perceived in the covenant with God the essence of its identity, the construction of the We *par excellence*. As noted in the introduction, a scholar of modern nationalism, Anthony D. Smith, perceives strong parallels between the Israelite covenant and the religious basis of modern nations.[7] The concept of covenant creates a drama of a people; there is a theme of the necessity of decision and signing on. The conscious choice by God and then by the people is the essence of Israelite tradition. The experience at Sinai, then, could be taken as the charter or constitutional moment of Israelite identity and religion. In the P arrangement of covenants, it is only here that Israel is told the true name of God. The Israelites, centuries after the Exodus supposedly occurred, expressed in these chapters their understanding of an *identity-less* people who moved toward identity. Michel de Certeau refers to "Exodus as a voyage through the other," and Ilana Pardes says that "the journey through the land of the other [was] indispensable to the emergence of Israel as a character."[8]

CONQUEST AND NATIONS

An important stage in the clarification of Israel's relation to surrounding peoples is found in the "promise" passages. Genesis 1–11 has presented the recurring phenomenon of fall and differentiation; Genesis 12 begins the positive arc of the narrative. God has stated that he will never again punish humanity with complete destruction, and has visited Abraham to bestow a promise upon him: "I will make of you a great nation, and I will bless you and make your name great, so that you will be a blessing. . . . In you all the families of the earth shall be blessed." But what is not mentioned is what will happen to the peoples who live where that great nation will be; in other words, the necessity of a *conquest* of the land is not mentioned at this point. A similar phenomenon can be observed at Deuteronomy 26:5–9, a beautiful statement of Israel's understanding of its origins as a people, its identity:

> An Aramean on the verge of perishing was my ancestor; he went down into Egypt and lived there as an alien, few in number, and there became a great nation, mighty and populous. When the Egyptians treated us harshly and afflicted us by imposing hard labor on us, we cried to the Lord, the God of our ancestors; the Lord heard our voice and our affliction, our toil, and our oppression. The Lord brought us out of Egypt with a mighty hand and outstretched arm, with a terrifying display of power, and with signs and wonders; and he brought us into this place and gave us this land, a land flowing with milk and honey.

But alongside such positive, bloodless depictions of the conquest are descriptions that outline *how* the displacement will occur. First, Exodus 23:23–28 (relevant verbs italicized):

> When my angel goes in front of you, and brings you to the Amorites, the Hittites, the Perizzites, the Canaanites, the Hivites, and the Jebusites, and I *blot them out*, you shall not bow down to their gods, or worship them, or follow their practices, but you shall *utterly demolish* their gods and break their pillars in pieces. . . . I will *send my terror* in front of you, and will *throw into confusion* all the people against whom you shall come, and *I will make* all your enemies *turn their backs* to you. And I will *send hornets* [or pestilence?] in front of you, which shall *drive out* [*garash*] the Hivites, the Canaanites, and the Hittites from before you.[9]

It is God, the angel, and the hornets who drive out the nations, not the Israelites, although the latter are to take up a crucial parallel mission in destroying the gods and their cult objects. This parallel administration of the conquest is not accidental. Unlike Genesis, where the difference between

Israel and other peoples is marked by genealogical or ethnic aspects alone, here the difference is based on *cultic observances* as well. The Other is marked by religious worship, not by a lack of a kinship connection. When this passage was composed and read, God's role would have been in the ancient past, but it would have been understood that the duty of the Israelites contemporary to the author was to cleanse the land of foreign cults.

In Deuteronomy 7:1–4, however, the bluntest of the passages, the necessity of violence is taken to its extreme conclusion and a stronger verb, *heherim*, is utilized:

> When the Lord your God brings you into the land that you are about to enter and occupy, and *he clears away* many nations before you—the Hittites, the Girgashites, the Amorites, the Canaanites, the Perizzites, the Hivites, and the Jebusites, seven nations mightier and more numerous than you—and when the Lord your God *gives them over to you* and *you defeat them*, then *you must utterly destroy* [*heherim*] them. *Make no covenant* with them and *show them no mercy. Do not intermarry* with them, giving your daughters to their sons or taking their daughters for your sons, for that would turn away your children from following me, to serve other gods.

We will return to the surprising command at the end that Israelites should not marry those whom they have supposedly killed, but first take up the command of total extermination. This injunction is one of the most difficult in the Hebrew Bible for modern readers, for it involves a commandment of God to *exterminate* opponents. As Weinfeld notes, this text avoids the use of "drive out" (*garash*) because expelling would fall short of extermination.[10] The verb *heherim* is related to the noun *herem* or "total ban," a holy war doctrine found in Israel and elsewhere in the ancient near east: what God commands to be destroyed must be totally devoted to God, like the whole burnt sacrifice in the temple; that is, there can be no booty in human captives as slaves, children, or wives, no taking of livestock, and no material booty. The reason that there must be a total ban is that these peoples are guilty of a fundamental wickedness; they worship in ways that are abhorrent to God. The nations are called an abomination (*to'evah*; Deut 20:18, 12:30–31), which is a term associated elsewhere with impurity on a national scale.[11] The land must be cleansed before Israelites can occupy it.

The continuation of Deuteronomy 7 broadens the commandment:

> This is how you must deal with the peoples of the land: break down their altars, smash their pillars, hew down their sacred poles, and burn their idols with fire. For you are a people holy to the Lord your God; the Lord your God has chosen you out of all the peoples on earth to be his people, his treasured possession.

The division of labor found in the earlier passage of Exodus 23—God will drive out the people and Israel will destroy the cult objects—is merged into one job description for the Israelites: they will kill the people and dismantle their shrines. The extermination of the inhabitants is treated on the analogy of a sacrifice to God that will purify the land. The conquest theme is pervasive in the Hebrew Bible, appearing in multiple sources. E. Theodore Mullen goes so far as to say that "the theme of the possession of the land is so widespread that it might have a legitimate claim to being even more central to the Hebrew Bible than the concept of covenant."[12] However, they are not competing themes in any sense, but mutually related. The conquest and the covenant go hand in hand, as the construction of the Other and the construction of the We (Theorems 1, 2: From Other to We, From We to Other). Conquest presumes the Other, covenant presumes the We, and the presence of either of these themes presupposes the other.

It is possible that Deuteronomy 7 is a sharper and more violent image of the conquest because it was composed at a particular time in Israelite history. According to 2 Kings 22, King Josiah was in the midst of his centralizing reform of the cult and the destruction of outlying cults when a "book of the law" was discovered in the temple in 621 BCE. This book was probably an early version of Deuteronomy, and Josiah was the king in Judah who most closely conformed to the royal and religious ideal in Deuteronomy. Although this book was successfully promulgated as an additional book of Moses, it was more likely composed at least in part during the reign of Josiah.[13] With the new book of the law in hand, he renewed the covenant with God, and set about purging Israel of cult objects and practices identified with the pre-Israelite peoples, first in the vicinity of Jerusalem and then at the cult sites to the north. In one of the most chilling scenes in this narrative Josiah completes the destruction of proscribed cults in northern Israel: "He slaughtered on the altars all the priests of the high places who were there, and burned human bones on the altars as well" (in order to defile them; 2 Kings 23:19–20). If this program was in fact carried out much as it is described, would this have been seen as the realization of the divine command in Deuteronomy 7? Or was the command to annihilate in Deuteronomy in fact written to provide a sanction for Josiah's reform?

Two other observations about this passage are relevant here. First, much of the condemnation of *external* groups like Canaanites and Amorites in the Deuteronomistic History (the historical books Joshua through Kings) may really have been aimed at suppressing *internal* groups, that is, those within the broader cult of Yahweh who opposed Josiah's reforms (Theorem 6: External and internal Other linked). This parallelism between external abominations and internal practitioners is most dramatically presented in Deuteronomy 13, where it is said that Israelites who follow practices of the nations are to be committed to the *herem* and blotted out just as are the peoples on the land.[14] Second, the command in Deuteronomy 7 to annihilate these nations is linked to a positive motive-clause: "You are a people holy to God." As Theorem 1 would indicate, a strong definition of Otherness is juxtaposed with a strong definition of We; the Other creates identity. In the midst of the program of purging the land of (supposedly) foreign practices, Josiah oversees a renewal of the covenant and the celebration of the Passover, which were said not to have been celebrated properly since Israel had entered Canaan (2 Kings 23:1–3, 21–23). His actions reassert a clarity of We versus Other that had supposedly been lacking.

The perceived need for Josiah's reform also raises a question about the earlier narrative of the conquest: if the Israelites had indeed swept the foreign nations out as God had commanded, why were their descendants still present? The conquest narrative contains differing assessments of how successfully God's command to annihilate the people had been carried out. In some passages it is said that Joshua had been successful in destroying all of the cities of the pre-Israelite peoples (Josh 11:16–23), and yet the absolute destruction is contradicted by other texts that recognize the continued existence of these peoples in the land (1 Kings 9:20–21). Thus a great irony hangs over the commandment to destroy the Other in Deuteronomy 7:1–4. Not only does it contain an absurd contradiction—Israel should *utterly destroy* all the peoples *and also* should not have relations with them—but from the vantage point of the author's own day, there is also the realization that although God commanded the extermination of these peoples, it did not occur, and the unsettling political influences and religious observances of these peoples remain a threat (Theorem 4: Seductive power of the Other). The Deuteronomistic Historian seems to say, "God told us to get rid of these people. We failed to do that. Now look at the trouble they're causing" (compare Judg 2:1–4).

Yet despite the danger associated with the cults of the nations, not much detail is given for their practices. The practices include: worshipping other gods or idols, engaging cult prostitutes, offering unclean food sacrifices, practicing divination, cross-dressing, using prostitutes' wages for a religious vow, using false measures, and eating carrion.[15] The list of abominations seems varied and minor in some cases, but they are violations of basic social norms, a list very similar to the stereotyped list of evils that is associated with the Other in all cultures (Theorem 5). Furthermore, they are invested with "Canaanitism," and are thus associated with an irredeemable wickedness. But in addition, two other specific sins are returned to again and again: cult prostitution and the child sacrifice associated with the god Molech. Both male and female cult prostitutes are associated in the biblical texts and in some Greek historians with temples to the goddess Asherah. Male adherents of Asherah would presumably come to the temple to engage official prostitutes and the moneys would be placed in the temple treasury. This is treated in the Bible as a degraded practice that should be wiped out in the land of Israel (Deut 23:17, 1 Kings 14:24, 15:12), but most scholars question whether cult prostitutes really existed at these temples, or were instead a polemical invention of their opponents.[16] Such charges are often made for the purposes of identity and *self*-definition, that is, the affirmation of the humanity of one's own group by projecting that which is deemed savage or inhuman onto others (Theorem 2: From We to Other). Child sacrifice, however, is a different matter. It was once argued that this practice was also a charge invented by Israel's reformers, but archaeological discoveries in Carthage indicate that child sacrifice was carried out in Phoenician sites (Phoenician is a later name for Canaanite). This gives credence to the notion that child sacrifice existed as a real practice even in Israel.

The extreme view of the Other found in Deuteronomy 7, however, is not a peculiarly Israelite belief, but is also found in the inscriptions of the great empires of the ancient near east, inscriptions that are earlier and may indicate that there were outside influences on the Israelite authors. The various theorems of the Other apply here as well. Enemies of these empires were described in stereotyped manner as an evil Other, and rebels within the Assyrian kingdom were called "sinners against Assur and the great gods" and were cruelly exterminated. Assyria, in turn, had been an Other to the Sumerians.[17] Surprisingly, also similar is the motif of oppression by foreign Others as the justification for extermination. As is the case in the Deuteronomistic History, the terror inflicted on the enemy is seen as a compensation for former oppression. The Hittites had claimed to suffer from their neighbors, as had Egypt from the Hyksos. The just revenge that they exacted upon their enemies gave rise to expansion, just as it had in Israel. Even the motif of God judging the nations is paralleled in the inscriptions of the ancient near eastern empires.

Another question that should be examined more closely at this point is, in the Hebrew Bible, who precisely were the people who would be destroyed? Most of the conquest passages contain a stereotyped list of the nations to be conquered. In the two most violent passages above, Exodus 23 and Deuteronomy 7, the nations listed are almost identical:

Exod 23: Hittites, Amorites, Canaanites, Perizzites, Hivites, Jebusites
Deut 7: Hittites, Amorites, Canaanites, Perizzites, Hivites, Jebusites, Girgashites

At the time the texts were composed, the nations listed were either long gone or hopelessly obscure. Were they perceived to be unreal, or understood as former nations who had been removed by Israel in the past? Probably the latter.[18]

The role of Canaan in this list is particularly interesting. It is likely that the relationship between Israel and Canaan was in reality quite different from that described in the Hebrew Bible. The earliest reference to Israel is from the stone victory inscription of the Egyptian Pharaoh Merneptah at the end of the thirteenth century BCE—over two hundred years before the establishment of a kingdom in Israel. Here Merneptah claims to have subdued a number of foreign peoples, including both Israel and Canaan, which appear to be paired as related peoples, occupying adjoining lands.[19] The Egyptians thus connected Israel and Canaan as two similar opponents in the region of Palestine, which is very different from the biblical tradition of an indigenous people (Canaan) that is displaced by migrating tribes (Israel). Even more surprising, on the basis of archaeological evidence many scholars believe that during this period Canaanites and Israelites would have been almost indistinguishable.[20] Many different theories are espoused by scholars about the rise of Israel. For some, Israel may have migrated from Egypt in a way similar to the biblical exodus; for others, Israel arose in Palestine. For some, Israel revolted against Canaanite overlords, while for others Israel merely coalesced in the rural highlands away from the Canaanite cities. Regardless of the political relations of the two peoples, we know that their language and religion were similar. Israel probably came into existence as worshipers of a single male deity, Yahweh, depicted at times like Canaanite El and at times like Canaanite Baal, and the Israelite God was probably also associated with a consort, Asherah. But as Mullen argues, Israel is defined by its creation of its own ethnic awareness, the establishment of boundaries, and the construction of Otherness:

> The pressures to form ethnic boundaries are most strong, I would suggest, *not* in those instances where obvious distinctions among groups, traditions, and practices might be most apparent; rather the compulsion to define and reinforce those identity ascriptors arises most strongly when the similarities among various groups are greatest, and concomitantly, so are the possibilities of absorption.[21]

In other words, the Other is in fact similar to the We (Theorem 3). And as we saw in the introduction, ethnicity is often ascribed based on selective minor and even subjective differences. The objective distinctiveness of ancient Israel and Canaan may have been less than imagined, imposed on a history of peoples who arose from quite similar religious environments.

OTHER NATIONS AND CULTS

It may seem that God's rejection of the pre-Israelite nations is arbitrary—they happen to be lying in the land that was promised to Israel—and also vindictive, but we should nuance this judgment with three observations. First, the nations in the lists above are defined, even invented, *retrospectively*. They were either bygone or fictitious, and not contemporary neighbors. Their role is created to fill a need in a moral history, and to define ethnic and religious boundaries (Theorem 5: Other distorted). The question of "fairness" does not so much apply to those bygone nations as to the nations that were perceived to follow them who were contemporary neighbors of Israel. Second, Israel's origin as "outsiders" meant that only people residing specifically in the promised land were singled out. What other far-off nations did was irrelevant.[22] As much as the Deuteronomistic History may paint a picture of the nations as Other, it is not all other nations, nor even a majority, but only a few who resided on the land who are considered irredeemably wicked. Third, this fairness problem is present whenever we examine *any* religious view that includes determinism or predestination.[23] Believing in determinism or predestination *requires* that the in-group look upon the Other as having been wicked *from the beginning* and *by nature* (Theorem 9: Eternal Other).

Still, the Deuteronomistic History proffers a more specific justification for why these nations were marked for extermination: they have religious practices that are loathsome to God. The abominations of the pre-Israelite nations become the justification for God's expulsion; they practiced a "pure" form of abomination, and in the wrong place: the land that God had promised to Abraham's progeny. The danger of participating in foreign religious cults was viewed as extreme (Theorem 4: Seductive power of the Other). The warning "Do not practice the abominations of the nations" (Deut 18:12) is placed centrally in the Deuteronomistic History, a blueprint for the narrative that follows. And the hold of these cults on people's minds is strong. We are told that even if the legitimate cult of Yahwism were to be taken up by the foreign peoples, they would inevitably revert to their old ways (2 Kings 17:24–41). The practices of the pre-Israelite nations are thus perceived as dangerous because they will crop up—have already cropped up—in the practices within Israel, with disastrous results.

But this raises a question of religious identity that was present in Israel from the very beginning and would remain in Israel into the post-exilic period and after: are *alternative* practices within Israel, perhaps even practices *native* to Israel, suppressed by being *redefined* as foreign (Theorem 8: Origins reassigned)? Cult practices in early Israel may have been quite different from the picture painted by the Deuteronomistic

Historian. The clear word of God that differentiated the cult of Yahweh from the cults of the gods of the land was only imposed on the narrative retrospectively. Morton Smith described a situation of a mixed cultic and ethnic situation in ancient Israel, from the period of the judges down through the exile and after.[24] The diverse practices condemned by the Deuteronomistic History, claims Smith, had in the preceding centuries been accepted as orthodox. The mixture of the cult of Yahweh with the cults of other gods only began to be seriously challenged in Israel in about the ninth century BCE. A Yahweh-alone movement began to arise only then within Israel. Other scholars also emphasize that early in Israel there was a mixture of cults that was only gradually challenged by a Yahweh-alone movement. Saul Olyan:

> Otherwise legitimate symbols and practices (the bull icons of Dan and Bethel, the *bamot* [high places], the asherah [branch symbol of Asherah], Nehushtan [bronze serpent], and *massebot* [pillars]) are judged illegitimate by the deuteronomistic school, who make use of polemical distortion as a technique to eliminate these practices and remove these symbols from the cultus. . . . The evidence of the Hebrew Bible alone suggests strongly that Asherah [the goddess] and the asherah [branch symbol] were considered legitimate in the state cult, both of the north and the south, in Jerusalem, Samaria, and Bethel, and probably in very conservative circles.[25]

Mark Smith concurs: there was a strong overlap between the names and epithets for Yahweh in Israel and names for gods among the neighbors. "Deuteronomy thus appeals to an imagined Mosaic past to legitimate a purity of worship which never existed in fact."[26]

To modern readers, the redefinition of practices may seem a small price to pay in the defense of monotheism; from our distance even repression can seem justified as the weeding process necessary to achieve a coherent monotheistic faith, or at least monolatry, a cultic worship of one god while ignoring the others.[27] But the justification argument implies that monolatry is a religious belief so unappealing that it can only be enforced through religious persecution. As attractive as monolatry may be today as a theological forerunner of monotheism, its role in the eighth and seventh centuries BCE must be seen, first, as an innovation, and second, as a part of a political centralization program that often separated off a vast number of practices and *redefined* them as foreign. Perhaps now it is clear why the Deuteronomistic Historian demonized and mythologized nations of the land more than the more distant nations: if controlling *internal* practices was the goal, it was easier to identify them as practices remaining *on the land,* understood as remnants of the mythologized pre-Israelite peoples.

REAL NEIGHBORS

We have examined the view of the Deuteronomistic Historian concerning the largely invented pre-Israelite nations, but the view concerning those nations contemporary with Israel and Judah was quite different. At Judges 10:6 we find a historical statement about nations supposedly in the past, but it uses *current* names instead:

> The Israelites did again what was evil in the sight of the Lord, worshiping the Baals and Astartes, the gods of Aram, the gods of Sidon, the gods of Moab, the gods of the Ammonites, and the gods of the Philistines.

This list betrays no overlap with the fairly fixed list of pre-Israelite nations in Deuteronomy 7:

Deut 7:1–2: Hittites, Girgashites, Amorites, Canaanites, Perizzites, Hivites, Jebusites
Judg 10:6: Aram, Sidon, Moab, Ammonites, Philistines

The list in Judges is composed solely of peoples bordering on Israel that still existed at the time of the composition of the Deuteronomistic History; one might say, they are what Canaan had become, real-time equivalents to the mythologized pre-Israelite nations. These contemporary nations are treated in various ways in the biblical texts, and that is precisely the point: they do not conform to a single pattern. They are not mythologized as Other in the same way that the pre-Israelite nations are.

If we take the nations listed at Judges 10:6 in order, we find a variety of perspectives reflected in the biblical text. Aram was an ancient people, powerful enough to be mentioned in numerous texts of the great empires. It is interesting that it is an acceptable people of origin for Abraham. Aram, the progenitor of the Arameans, was listed anachronistically as Abraham's grandnephew in Genesis 22:21, and the closeness of their relations is indicated by this. This establishes a kinship in the genealogy, and Isaac and Jacob both return to take wives from Abraham's Aramean kin. Abraham is depicted as breaking with his people to create a new people, and while later Jewish tradition would hold that Abraham left his Aramean family as a rejection of polytheism, that is not stated in the biblical account. In fact, Arameans are not depicted in a consistently negative way. David married an Aramean, the mother of Absalom. Much of the international relations of Israel and Judah in the eighth century was taken up with the Arameans, when positive relationships with this kingdom were often entered into even if sometimes condemned by the prophets (Am 1:5, Isa 7:8; compare 1 Kings 15:18). A particularly arresting example of this is the account of Ben-hadad, King of Damascus in Syria (Aram), who allies first with Israel against Judah, then with Judah against Israel (1 Kings 15:16–24). The king of Judah who engineers an alliance with Ben-hadad is even presented positively by the narrator. Thus, even though Aram was involved in war with Judah, it was not depicted as a *necessary* enemy, only a *contingent* or *occasional* enemy as a result of a political development.

Sidon was a Phoenician city, and Phoenicians are also treated in a mixed way. To be sure, Jezebel was a notorious princess of Sidon and then queen of Israel (through marriage to Ahab), but it was her *actions* that earned her condemnation by the Deuteronomistic History. We see from other passages that Phoenicians are not always viewed so negatively. King Hiram of the Phoenician city Tyre is positive toward David and Solomon (1 Kings 5:1–12, 9:10–14). This fact becomes even more surprising when we realize that "Phoenicians" is simply a later name for the Canaanites! Shockingly, even considering the fact that Jezebel was Phoenician and that Phoenicians were in reality the same as Canaanites, this nation is not presented in a consistently negative way.

The next two nations in the list from Judges, Moabites and Ammonites, were more often viewed as the successors of the Canaanites. According to archaeological evidence, Moab and Ammon (along with Edom and Midian) arose at about the same time as the Israelites (thirteenth century BCE), but with the victories of David, Moab and Ammon became vassal states bordering Israel to the east and south. Moab and Ammon are generally considered bad—recall their supposed origins in the incest of Lot's daughters—but positive relations with Moab are indicated at Deuteronomy 2:9 and 1 Samuel 22:3–4, so positive that the relations apparently reflect a "period of peaceful co-existence between Israel and Moab."[28] One of Solomon's wives was Ammonite (1 Kings 14:21), although it was perhaps presented as a negative association; however, this did not prevent Rehoboam, her son, from succeeding Solomon on the throne. Ruth, the great-grandmother of David, was a Moabite, which is perhaps viewed as an unexpected aspect of the lineage, but Zelek the Ammonite is mentioned without criticism as a member of David's court (2 Sam 23:37). After the Babylonian defeat of Jerusalem, a certain Ishmael, who was in the line of David, allied with the Ammonites against the governor appointed by the Babylonians (Jeremiah 40–41). Throughout Israel's history, then, Moabites and Ammonites are sometimes treated with a sense of *Realpolitik*, even though at other times they are said to have inherited the wickedness of Canaan.

Last in the list of peoples in Judges 10 are the Philistines. They were one of the so-called Sea Peoples—migrating peoples whom the Egyptians had already encountered in the eastern Mediterranean in the centuries before the foundation of Israel. The Egyptians describe the Sea Peoples as marauding warriors who brought chaos and forced migrations of Egyptians and others. They ultimately settled in the area of Palestine in the thirteenth to twelfth centuries BCE (the words Philistine and Palestine are related). They were a dominant people in the land until David won control of much of their territory in the tenth century BCE, but they remained independent of Israel. Much of the dramatic conflict in the Deuteronomistic History involves the Philistines—they captured the Israelites' ark temporarily, and Goliath was a Philistine. They are often referred to as uncircumcised, and the word "Philistine" even remains a pejorative adjective in modern English. Elizabeth Bloch-Smith suggests that the Philistines in particular functioned as the contemporary ethnic group against which Israel defined its own ethnic identity: the Israelites were circumcised, the Philistines were not, the Israelites abstained from pork, the Philistines did not, the Israelites had beards, the Philistines were clean-shaven, and so on.[29] The Canaanites, suggests Bloch-Smith, did not function to define the *outer* boundaries of Israel as the Philistines did, but were a fictionalized Other that defined the *internal* sins associated with the worship of Baal and Asherah. Yet despite the construction of the Philistines as the close ethnic Other, they are, like the other contemporary nations, sometimes treated more neutrally. David enlisted Philistine mercenaries (Gittites, 2 Sam 15:18–23), and there was a covenant with the Philistines reported in Genesis 21:22–34, 26:26–31.

Weinfeld suggests, probably correctly, that this surprising difference in treatment arises because the Israelites considered Philistines to be fellow outsiders to the area, and not native to the land.[30] Weinfeld's theory gains credibility when one also considers the special case of the Gibeonites (Josh 9). By means of a ruse, they trick the Israelites into thinking that they are a people from far away, and not resident in the land. The Gibeonites then exact a vow from the Israelites not to harm them. This act spares them the annihilation to which others are subject, even though according to Deuteronomy 7 they should have been eliminated as well. The Gibeonites remained under the wing of Israel, however, at a price: they were cursed to perpetual slavery as servants in the temple. They became, it seems, an instrumental Other as servants, as their cult site was subordinated to the temple in Jerusalem. Was it the need to reinterpret Others as servants that allowed the ruse to proceed, or the need to reinterpret servants as Others by redefining their origins? Either way, Theorem 7 applies here: Ambiguous groups can be reassigned and adopted.

At times these real neighbors are depicted very negatively, but they are not always treated as a mythological Other; they can be viewed more realistically. This accords with distinctions that are observable in Egypt as well: there were two different discourses for representing foreigners, a stylized, ideologically charged, and essentially mythologized mode, and a more realistic mode.[31] In Israel the neighboring nations were sometimes simply treated as nations competing in war (2 Sam 10). The traditions found in the Deuteronomistic History, whether they are to be attributed to the sources or to the Deuteronomistic editing, can reflect a savvy understanding of the realities of international politics. One can hardly distinguish between the way conflicts with the foreign kings are described and the way conflicts between the kings of Israel and Judah are described. The moral status of all the kings, both internal and external, always depends on the extent to which their actions accord with God's plan. Any king, internal or external, who threatens the existence or religious purity of Israel and Judah could be condemned. The real, contemporary neighbors of Israel could at times be assimilated to their ancestor, Canaan, but at other times were viewed with a sense of *Realpolitik*.

GREAT EMPIRES

In all of this discussion of the small neighboring nations we have not considered how Israel conceived of the great empires that ruled in the ancient near east—Egypt, Assyria, and Babylon (Persia will be treated in chapter three). These nations do not appear in the stereotyped lists of either the pre-Israelite or contemporary nations in the Deuteronomistic History, even though they appear often in other biblical texts. Egypt is depicted negatively in the exodus narrative, but they are all treated fairly realistically in the later history books; they are too great to redefine, and mythologizing their weakness or inferiority would not be believable.[32] Part of this realism is based on the understanding that they are not always negative. The negative tones of the woes against the nations in the prophets should not blind us to the fact that the political leaders in Israel and Judah often negotiated directly with these nations, with or without the prophets' approval, and that the nations were rarely considered *fundamentally* wicked, only contingently or occasionally wicked. The difference between the Pharaoh whom Joseph served and the Pharaoh of Exodus could be considered indicative of the swing between acceptable and evil leaders of the great empires. Isaiah 19 even looks forward to a conversion of Egypt in the future that would be unthinkable in regard to Canaanites. Further, even when they are negative they are not mythologized. Second Kings 17–23 presents Assyria, Babylon, and Egypt simply as overwhelming foreign powers. Isaiah 30–31 opposes an alliance with Egypt, but not as an Other in the manner of the pre-Israelite nations. Despite the destructive role of Assyria and Babylon in defeating first the northern half of Israel and then Judah, they are depicted as nations that arise upon the scene of world politics for these roles, and not as permanently or inherently evil. Thus even though Assyria and Babylon had a negative role in Israelite and Judean history, they are condemned more for their actions, and not for an inevitable status as Other.

Ultimately, then, the Hebrew Bible does not reflect *one* view of other nations; there are at least three different *kinds* of nations in terms of the view of the Other: (1) the mythologized pre-Israelite nations of the authors' *past* which God had commanded should be exterminated; (2) the small surrounding nations of the authors' *present* with whom the kings of Israel and Judah competed and negotiated; and (3) the great empires that dominated international politics. The first group, whom the biblical authors would never have met directly, is rendered as thoroughly evil. They were supposed to be exterminated but were not, and are the bearers of a cult of the gods who, by their ghostly influence, threaten the vulnerable foundations of the centralized cult of God in Israel. There is an ironic contrast between the perceived vulnerability of the cult of God and the language of power and even ruthlessness.[33] The strong Other produces a strong We (Theorem 1), but the identity is also one of vulnerability (Theorem 4: Seductive power of the Other). The great empires are interesting because although their role in inflicting national calamity on Israel was viewed as negative—the enslavement in Egypt, the Assyrian destruction of northern Israel, the later Babylonian destruction of Judah—*they are not consistently mythologized as evil.* If these empires act in an evil way, it is because an evil king has risen up to perform particular actions that are destructive to Israel. Even if this continues over a long period of time, it is not generally considered a permanent and fixed part of their national character.[34]

But it is the smaller surrounding nations that exhibit the most ambiguity. They were ethnically, geographically, and even genealogically more closely related to Israel, and Israel and Judah had to contend with them constantly. They were sometimes treated realistically and even with a practical acceptance. But by the same token it is they who *at times* had to be reconstructed as Other, more like the Canaanites. In reality the boundary between Israel or Judah and the neighboring nations was a porous boundary. There were vassal and slave relations, trade relations, diplomatic relations, marriage relations, and cultic influences. But from time to time the neighboring nations were reinterpreted as equivalent to the pre-Israelite peoples, as *that kind* of Other (Theorem 7: Ambiguous groups reassigned). Thus the intensity and clarity of the polemical language in Deuteronomy 7 and other texts is a reaction to a dangerous ambiguity. The contemporary nations are likened to the unreal pre-Israelite peoples, defined as Other by the myth of Israel's past, but on a daily basis there was probably a set of brisk relations between Israel and these nations.

INTERNAL OTHERS

We have so far considered the construction of the foreign nations as Other in the biblical tradition, but in every culture there are also, from the point of view of the dominant group, internal Others, such as Other races or classes, Other genders, Other sexual orientations, Other levels of ability (Theorem 6). In the Hebrew Bible and in the New Testament, public discourse was almost always from the point of view of the free, propertied, male head of household with a particular kinship lineage; this is generally the voice that speaks in the text, and is almost always the audience who is directly addressed. Thus projecting the woman or slave as Other presumes this arrangement. If there are any exceptions in the Bible, they are rare. We cannot begin here to outline the role of each of these internal categories in Israelite society, but for the purpose of discussion we can briefly note some of the relations between the external Other and internal Other in ancient Israel.

As noted in the introduction, various kinds of external and internal Others are often constructed together, placed in a matrix of Otherness. The construction of a world of Others is handled in an integrated way; that is, the foreign nation as Other is linked with two or three of the internal Others (Theorem 6). The category of Other, seen across several variables at once, is a method of culture, a way of organizing the universe, a map of identity by negation. Consider first Deuteronomy 23:1–3, 6–9:

> No one whose testicles are crushed or whose penis is cut off shall be admitted to the assembly of the Lord. The *mamzer* (offspring of a forbidden union) shall not be admitted to the assembly of the Lord. Even to the tenth generation, none of their descendants shall be admitted to the assembly of the Lord. No Ammonite or Moabite shall be admitted to the assembly of the Lord. Even to the tenth generation, none of their descendants shall be admitted to the assembly of the Lord. . . . You shall not abhor any of the Edomites, for they are your kin. You shall not abhor any of the Egyptians, because you were a *ger* [resident alien] residing in their land. The children of the third generation that are born to them may be admitted to the assembly of the Lord.

In this listing of who can and cannot enter the congregation, we find legally restricted categories defined by (1) disability (mutilated genitals), (2) "mixed" kinship as a result of category violations (*mamzer*), (3) ambiguous nationality (*ger*), and (4) contemporary neighbors as Other (Ammonite, Moabite), and two other nations are not restricted (Edomites, Egyptians).[35] Far from being separate entities, the construction of internal and external Other is closely interrelated. One can easily find passages in other times and places as well in which different categories of Other are intentionally treated together in order to construct a general, integrated ordering of society.

We may pause briefly over the *ger* and the *mamzer*. The *ger* is usually translated "resident alien," while *toshab* is the visiting foreigner or "sojourner" and *nokri* is simply a "foreigner."[36] Somewhere between the *ezrach* or full citizen of Israel and the *nokri* or *toshab*, the *ger* is under the legal protection of an Israelite, and is included in many of the religious festivals as a sort of obligatory guest. Theorem 7 states that ambiguous people may be defined as adopted members, and so it is here, but this does not really tell us where they came from or how they were viewed. It was suggested by Mary Douglas that the *ger* was the Israelite from the north who was forced to migrate to Judah in the south after the Assyrians defeated the northern territory in 722 BCE.[37] According to this theory, they are Israelites, but do not belong to the tribe or extended family structures of the south. Lacking local kinship ties, land, and inheritance, they are socially vulnerable, often listed with the widow and the orphan as special categories cared for by others (Deut 16:11–14).[38] Alternatively, *ger* may have referred to those from the nations of the land who remained after the conquest, that is, who were not annihilated. The role of the *ger* as laborer (Deut 29:11) seems similar to that of the remnants of the pre-Israelite peoples such as the Gibeonites who were said to be adopted as laborers. The benevolent tone found in Leviticus 19:34 ("You shall love the *ger* as yourself") does not preclude the *ger* from being an instrumental Other, like workers in other cultures, just as the concern for the widow and the orphan does not preclude their being treated as Other.

The *mamzer* is also an ambiguous internal Other.[39] Not a bastard in the English sense of that word, that is, a child born out of wedlock who is unable to inherit, a *mamzer* is the child of an incestuous union or a forbidden union, and is severely restricted in Jewish law in terms of marriage. Just as Jewish agricultural laws forbade the mixing of seeds, so also in the human realm there are forbidden categories of mixing for reproduction. Precisely what the forbidden category is, however, is not clear. In rabbinic tradition, the child of a Jewish mother and a gentile father is a *mamzer*, while the child of a Jewish father and a gentile mother is simply a gentile. This meaning of *mamzer*, however, does not appear in the Hebrew Bible. Both *mamzer* and *ger*, then, were socially constructed legal categories of ambiguous persons, now only vaguely understood.

Like Deuteronomy 23, Leviticus 18–20 can also be analyzed as a treatment of the We and a set of integrated internal and external Others. Leviticus 18–20 is a distinct section of the legal codes of the Pentateuch. Found in the so-called Holiness Code of Leviticus 17–26, it is part of the Priestly Source (P). The concluding statement summarizes its themes:

> You shall keep all my statutes and all my ordinances and observe them, so that the land to which I bring you to settle in will not vomit you out. You shall not follow the practices of the nation that I am driving out before you.

Because they did all these things, I abhorred them. . . . I am the Lord your
God; I have separated you from the peoples. (Lev 20:22–24)

Separation and differentiation—the process by which the world was created—is here applied to the nations. A disproportionate number of statements of "I am the Lord" and the command to "be holy" are found here,
defining a We in the same context in which certain categories are also constructed as Other. Listing only a few laws, these three chapters have a summary quality about them. Chapters eighteen and twenty are very similar,
the former providing a list of prohibited practices, most of them sexual
(Theorem 5: Other distorted in a stereotyped list of offenses), and the latter in general repeating them, with the punishments now stipulated:

Lev 18: prohibited practices	*Lev 20: practices and punishments*
Do not do as Egyptians and Canaanites do	Consulting mediums—exclusion
	Cursing father or mother—death
Prohibition of kinds of incest	Incest—death
Prohibition of sex with menstruant	Sex with menstruant—exclusion
Prohibition of sex with kinsman's wife	Adultery—death
Prohibition of sacrificing children to Molech	Sacrificing children to Molech—death
Prohibition of sex between males	Sex between males—death
Prohibition of sex with an animal	Sex with animal—death
Conclusion:	Conclusion:
For these I vomited out the nations	Observe these so you will not be vomited out
Observe these, even the *ger*	I have separated you from the nations
	Do not be like the nations driven out

The ending of chapter twenty repeats what was stated at the beginning
of chapter eighteen: Israel should not be like the nations, for God has separated Israel out for a special, holy identity. At the same time that external boundaries with the nations are to be strictly maintained, Israel is to
observe internal boundaries just as strictly: "You shall therefore make a
distinction between the clean animal and the unclean, and between the
unclean bird and the clean; you shall not bring abomination on yourselves
by animal or by bird or by anything with which the ground teems" (Lev
20:25). Israel is not to confuse categories, not by mixing seeds in the same
field, nor by "mixing" in improper sexual relations—man with kinsman's
wife, man with betrothed slave woman, man with man, man or woman
with animal.

Leviticus 19, the center of this balanced arrangement, focuses on ethical demands, and uses positive and negative commands to express the nature of holiness. It appears at first an odd miscellany, in which we find:

> Echoes of the Ten Commandments
> Make appropriate sacrifice for well-being
> Leave corner gleanings of the field, even for the *ger*
> Help the laborer and the disabled
> Make fair judgments in court
> Love your kinsperson as yourself
> Do not mix animals or seeds
> Do not have sex with a betrothed slave woman
> Allow trees to grow four years as "uncircumcised"
> Do not engage in sorcery or consult mediums
> Do not oppress the *ger*; love the *ger* as yourself
> Use honest measures

As in Leviticus 18 and 20, only a selection of laws is presented, which here pertain mainly to the sanctity of the extended household and the ordering of domestic life. Douglas argues that the balanced structuring of Leviticus 18–20 prioritizes chapter nineteen as the center, with "love your kinsperson (neighbor)" as the center of the center. Says Douglas, "Justice is the apex of the pediment, the conspicuous place of honor."[40]

But if this concern for justice and domestic order defines the We, what particular infractions mentioned in chapters eighteen and twenty would turn the We out of the land, would dissolve the We into the Other? What dangerous image of the Other would be invoked to horrify Israel into obedience? While there are many passages in the legal sections that address the issue of ritual impurity (protecting the sanctity of the altar, eating unclean animals, and so on), the Holiness Code, of which Leviticus 18–20 is a part, speaks mainly of the danger of *moral* impurity attaching to Israel, an impurity so severe that the land will vomit them out. Some scholars hold that moral impurity is only introduced as a metaphor, an extension of the idea of ritual impurity, but Jonathan Klawans argues that they are both ideas of real impurity, treated in different passages and in different ways.[41] Ritual impurity affects the individual; moral impurity affects the land and the temple. Ritual impurity does not make one morally impure (that is, a "sinner"), and moral impurity does not render one ritually impure. Ritual impurity is not "dangerous," if one merely avoids contact with the sacred. It is not sinful, but is a normal occurrence, there is a remedy for it (purification rituals), and it is often unavoidable, as in the case of burying a corpse. The causes of moral impurity, on the other hand, are sexual sins, idolatry, and bloodshed. There is no stipulated purification for moral impurity (other than the Yom Kippur ritual), and how the polluted land is to recover is never stated.

To avoid moral impurity, the internal order of society is maintained as an obsession parallel to the safeguarding of external boundaries. As Douglas has pointed out, in every culture the boundaries of the human body are seen as analogous to the boundaries of the group.[42] A culture that strictly controls the boundaries of the group will also strictly control the boundaries of the body: what foods are pure or impure, under what conditions sex can occur, whether a woman can cut her hair or a man can trim his beard. Anything that happens to be on the boundary between two distinct categories receives special treatment and often becomes either taboo or sacred. Taboo and sacred, as it turns out, are not so different from each other. Both reflect our sense that special power is present and is either dangerous or provokes awe—or both. Thus, although there is often ambiguity in the real world, with its many gray areas, the distinctness of categories can be restored by rendering any ambiguous element as taboo. Leviticus 18–20 is thus not unusual in this regard; it is only unusual in trying to present the whole of the external and internal boundaries in three chapters.

All of this sheds light on a particular case of internal Other found in this passage, that of same-sex love. Leviticus 18 and 20 are the only two places in the Hebrew Bible where this is explicitly mentioned, and to be precise, only sexual intercourse between men is prohibited; sex between women is never condemned in the Hebrew Bible. In Leviticus 18:22 sex between men is declared to be an abomination, and in Leviticus 20:13, the punishment prescribed is death. Sex between males is treated in the context of boundary violations, placed strategically in a list of category violations that, with the punishments listed in chapter twenty, frame the constitution of the We in chapter nineteen. In the present context in Leviticus what is prohibited are those relations that are perceived as threats to the welfare of the extended family and that undermine childbearing, or, perhaps more specifically, threaten the lineage.[43] And yet this may be too practical a way of putting it. It may be more an issue of *symbolic* order, that is, the distinction and separation of categories that order a society.[44] The series of commandments almost all pertain to the protection of the social order through the avoidance of mixed categories. It is not so much that committing any of these actions will threaten effective procreation; they will threaten order. The prohibitions are expressed as very potent cases of ritual impurity, the impurity of improper contacts, and they are so potent that they carry over to a threat of moral impurity which will render the land impure, and for which there is no period or act of purification. In Leviticus 18–20, perhaps more than any other passage, we find at one time the construction of We and Other, and the integration of internal Other and external Other (Theorem 6). It is a creation of an entire grid of boundaries that attempt to define all that is good and all that is bad.

CONCLUSION

Creation in Genesis begins in a state of undifferentiated plasma, and through a process of separation and differentiation gives rise to the first orders of nature. A series of falls results in a more populated and more differentiated world. For the biblical authors, the genealogies of Genesis defined the relationships of peoples of the known world. Early on we find a relationship between marriage rules and external Others: sexual relations too close (violations of incest rules) give rise to perpetual enemies (Canaan, Moab, and Ammon), while sexual relations too distant (exogamy) also give rise to perpetual enemies (Ishmael and Esau). The nations are depicted in three categories. First, the pre-Israelite nations on the land are presented in stereotyped lists, and have an unreal quality about them. In each case they appear to be legendary or from a bygone era and were considered irredeemably bad. The nation whose origin was most closely related to Israel, Canaan, was treated as the very epitome of evil. Second, other nations, contemporary neighbors of Israel, sometimes received the mantle of Canaan, but were at other times treated with a sense of *Realpolitik*. Third, the great empires of the period—Egypt, Assyria, Babylon—were only treated as negative when they rose to oppress Israel.

Central to the narrative of the Primary History are covenant and conquest. The covenant passages establish both the outer boundaries of Israel, marking the people off from external Others, and simultaneously imposing ordered distinctions on the people's practices that define internal Others as well. The covenant is both a legal and a public, communal text that constitutes the We of Israel in relation to God, but the construction of the Other is never very far from this (Theorem 2: From We to Other). The integration of understandings of internal and external Others, and of We and Other, is paramount in these texts. A constant in the covenant narratives is the importance of not making human covenants with the peoples who reside in the land, and in fact their altars must be destroyed (Exod 24:33, 34:12–16; Deut 29:16–28). From the We passages of the covenant we are a short step to the destruction passages of Deuteronomy 7. The land must be purified by the removal of those who are indigenous, somewhat like a great blood sacrifice. The urgency of this theme likely enters into the narrative because these passages were composed or edited during the campaign of King Josiah to centralize the cult in Jerusalem and suppress the variant cults in the land.

The present chapter, covering the Primary History of Israel, has included a whirlwind of kinships and kingships, affinities and animosities, covenants and conquests. From here we turn to address later Jewish and Christian texts, and will take up the question of whether Israel changed, of whether Christianity was different, or indeed of whether any culture is different.

NOTES

1. Susan Niditch, *Chaos to Cosmos: Studies in the Biblical Patterns of Creation* (Chico, CA: Scholars Press, 1985); see also Jon Levenson, *Creation and the Persistence of Evil: The Jewish Drama of Divine Omnipotence* (San Francisco: Harper & Row, 1988).

2. Carol Delaney, *Abraham on Trial: The Social Legacy of Biblical Myth* (Princeton, NJ: Princeton University Press, 1998); Howard Eilberg-Schwartz, *The Savage in Judaism: An Anthropology of Israelite Religion and Ancient Judaism* (Bloomington: Indiana University Press, 1990), 167–68. The history of Israel can also be referred to as a biography of Israel: "The nation is imagined as a person"; see Ilana Pardes, *The Biography of Ancient Israel* (Berkeley: University of California Press, 2000), 1–2.

3. Regina Schwartz, *The Curse of Cain: The Violent Legacy of Monotheism* (Chicago: University of Chicago Press, 1997), 81–82. Her approach to the conquest theme was anticipated by Robert Allen Warrior, "A Native American Perspective: Canaanites, Cowboys, and Indians," in *Voices from the Margins*, ed. R. S. Sugirtharajah (Maryknoll, NY: Orbis, 1995), 277–85. See also R. Christopher Heard, *Dynamics of Diselection: Ambiguity in Genesis 12–36 and Ethnic Boundaries in Post-Exilic Judah* (Atlanta, GA: Society of Biblical Literature, 2001).

4. Albrecht Alt, *Essays on Old Testament History and Religion* (Sheffield, UK: JSOT Press, 1989), 80–86; Yehezkel Kaufmann, *The Religion of Israel from Its Beginnings to the Babylonian Exile* (Chicago: University of Chicago Press, 1960), 221–22; Rainer Albertz, *The History of Israelite Religion in the Old Testament Period*, 2 vols. (Louisville, KY: Westminster/John Knox, 1994), 1:32; Robert L. Cohn, "Negotiating (with) the Nations: Ancestors and Identity in Genesis," *Harvard Theological Review* 96 (2003): 152–58, 161–66; "Before Israel: The Canaanites as Other in Biblical Tradition," in *The Other in Jewish Thought and History: Constructions of Jewish Culture and Identity*, ed. Laurence J. Silberstein and Robert L. Cohn (New York and London: New York University Press, 1994), 78, 86–87.

5. The term was introduced by David Noel Freedman, "The Law and the Prophets," *Vetus Testamentum Supplement 9: Congress Volume* (Leiden, Netherlands: Brill, 1963), 250–65.

6. Moshe Weinfeld, *The Promise of the Land: The Inheritance of the Land of Canaan by the Israelites* (Berkeley: University of California Press, 1993), 1. To be sure, there are partial parallels in other cultures; see K. Lawson Younger, Jr., *Ancient Conquest Accounts: A Study in Ancient Near Eastern and Biblical History Writing* (Sheffield, UK: Sheffield Academic Press, 1990). However, Peter Machinist rightly argues for a quantitative distinction on this point ("On Self-Consciousness in Mesopotamia," in *The Origins and Diversity of Axial Age Civilizations*, ed. S. N. Eisenstadt [Albany: State University of New York, 1986], 183–202, and "The Question of Distinctiveness in Ancient Israel: An Essay," in *Ah, Assyria . . . : Studies in Assyrian History and Ancient Near Eastern Historiography Presented to Hayim Tadmor*, ed. Mordechai Cogan and Israel Eph`al [Jerusalem: Magnes, 1991], 198–212).

The migration of Israel from outside in, what in most other traditions—Mesopotamian or Egyptian, for example—would be viewed as "barbarian invasion," is in Israel cited as one of the mighty acts of God. Outsider status is a "mark of divine chosenness"; see Cohn, "Negotiating," 164–65. See also Robert L. Cohn, "The Second Coming of Moses: Deuteronomy and the Construction of Israelite Identity," in *Proceedings of the Twelfth World Congress of Jewish Studies* (Division A: The Bible and Its World), ed. Shmuel Ahituv et al. (Jerusalem: World Union of Jewish Studies, 1999), 65; Peter Machinist, "Outsiders or Insiders: The Biblical View of Emerging Israel and Its Contexts," in Silberstein and Cohn, eds., *Other in Jewish Thought*, 53; Mu-chou Poo, *Enemies of Civilization: Attitudes toward Foreigners in Ancient Mesopotamia, Egypt, and China* (Albany: State University of New York Press, 2005); Pardes, *Biography*, 4–5, 16; Meir Sternberg, *Hebrews between Cultures: Group Portraits and National Literature* (Bloomington: Indiana University Press, 1998), 189–91; Steven Grosby, *Biblical Ideas of Nationality Ancient and Modern* (Winona Lake, IN: Eisenbrauns, 2002), 15–16. Rome alone of the Mediterranean and near eastern empires also idealized itself as a migrant nation, a beginning memorialized in the *Aeneid*.

7. Anthony D. Smith, *Chosen Peoples* (Oxford and New York: Oxford University Press, 2003), 54–55, and now see also David M. Goodblatt, *Elements of Ancient Jewish Nationalism* (New York: Cambridge University Press, 2006).

8. Michel de Certeau, *The Writing of History* (New York: Columbia University Press, 1988), 319; Robert L. Cohn, *The Shape of Sacred Space* (Chico, CA: Scholars Press, 1981), 7–23; and Pardes, *Biography*, 5, 15.

9. Cf. also Exod 3:7–8, Gen 15, Josh 3:10. Other bloodless descriptions are Exod 34:10–16 and Deut 11:22–25.

10. Weinfeld, *Promise*, 86–87. Marc Zvi Brettler, *The Creation of History in Ancient Israel* (London/New York: Routledge, 1995), 71–76, also argues rightly that the Deuteronomistic History imposes the *herem* on source stories that might not have emphasized it as strongly. John J. Collins, "The Zeal of Phinehas: The Bible and the Legitimization of Violence," *Journal of Biblical Literature* 122 (2003): 3–21, notes the irony of, on the one hand, Deuteronomy's compassion for slaves and the *ger* and the condemnation of child sacrifice, and on the other hand the imposition of the total ban on conquered peoples. See also Marc Zvi Brettler, *The Bible after Babel: Historical Criticism in a Postmodern Age* (Grand Rapids, MI: Eerdmans, 2005), 53–74.

11. Mark Smith, "Anat's Warfare Cannibalism and the West Semitic Ban," in *The Pitcher Is Broken: Memorial Essays for Gösta W. Ahlström*, ed. Steven W. Holloway and Lowell K. Handy (Sheffield, UK: Sheffield Academic Press, 1995), 190.

12. E. Theodore Mullen, *Ethnic Myths and Pentateuchal Foundations: A New Approach to the Formation of the Pentateuch* (Atlanta, GA: Scholars, 1997), 69; *Narrative History and Ethnic Boundaries: The Deuteronomistic Historian and the Creation of Israelite National Identity* (Atlanta, GA: Scholars Press, 1993). See also Schwartz, *Curse of Cain*.

13. Other scholars date the bulk of the composition of this material to the exile in the sixth century, but I follow those who date the main edition of the Deuteronomistic History specifically to the period of Josiah. Some scholars also see in the depiction of Joshua a thinly disguised portrait of Josiah (Lori L. Rowlette, *Joshua*

and the Rhetoric of Violence: A New Historicist Analysis [Sheffield, UK: Sheffield Academic Press, 1996], 13).

14. Cf. Deut 17:2–5. Cohn, "Second Coming," 66, 69 n. 18; Machinist, "Outsiders or Insiders," 53.

15. Deut 7:25, Deut 23:17–18, 1 Kings 14:23–24, Deut 14:3, Deut 18:9–14, Deut 22:5, 14:21. See Kenton L. Sparks, *Ethnicity and Identity in Ancient Israel: Prolegomena to the Study of Ethnic Sentiments and Their Expression in the Hebrew Bible* (Winona Lake, IN: Eisenbrauns, 1998), 259–60; Mullen, *Narrative History*, 71.

16. Robert Oden, *The Bible without Theology: The Theological Tradition and Alternatives to It* (San Francisco: Harper & Row, 1987), 132.

17. Younger, *Ancient Conquest Accounts*, 67–69, 177–78, 233–34, 283 n. 35, 321 n. 127; Poo, *Enemies of Civilization*, 198–205.

18. Edwin C. Hostetter, *Nations Mightier and More Numerous: The Biblical View of Palestine's Pre-Israelite Peoples* (N. Richmond Hills, TX: BIBAL Press, 1995), 62–72, 80–85, 141–42. Sparks, *Ethnicity and Identity*, 257–59, distinguishes the bygone nations—"rhetorical others"—from the real neighbors contemporary with Israel—"objective others," a division which I will modify below. He rightly points out the function of the rhetorical others. It was to be a "destroyed enemy," and suggests that it is *because* the bygone nations no longer existed that the rhetorical power for contemporary Israelites was so strong: the same fate could befall wayward Israelites.

19. G. W. Ahlström and D. Edelman, "Merneptah's Israel," *Journal of Near Eastern Studies* 44 (1985): 59–61.

20. William G. Dever, "How to Tell a Canaanite from an Israelite," in *The Rise of Ancient Israel*, ed. Hershel Shanks et al. (Washington, DC: Biblical Archaeological Society, 1992), 26–60, and Ann E. Killebrew, *Biblical Peoples and Ethnicity: An Archaeological Study of Egyptians, Canaanites, Philistines, and Early Israel 1300–1100 BCE* (Atlanta, GA: Society of Biblical Literature, 2005), 149–96, but see also Israel Finkelstein, *The Archaeology of the Israelite Settlement* (Jerusalem: Israel Exploration Society, 1988).

21. Mullen, *Narrative History*, 53; see also *Ethnic Myths*. My disagreement with Mullen is not on the *process* by which this occurred, but on the *dates* when the various sources were composed.

22. Joel S. Kaminsky, "Did Election Imply the Mistreatment of Non-Israelites?" *Harvard Theological Review* 96 (2003): 398–99. Kaminsky's two-part division, as well as that found in Sparks, *Ethnicity and Identity*, 257–59 (see above), will be modified below.

23. The determinism of the Deuteronomistic History is not so much predestination, especially not individual predestination, as it is the unfolding of the will of God; so rightly Peter Machinist, "Fate, *Miqreh*, and Reason: Some Reflections on Qohelet and Biblical Thought," in *Solving Riddles and Untying Knots: Biblical, Epigraphic, and Semitic Studies in Honor of Jonas C. Greenfield*, ed. Ziony Zevit, Seymour Gitin, and Michael Sokoloff (Winona Lake, IN: Eisenbrauns, 1995), 159–75. See also Marc Zvi Brettler, "Predestination in Deuteronomy 30:1–10," in *Those Elusive Deuteronomists: The Phenomenon of Pan-Deuteronomism*, ed. Linda S. Schearing and Steven L. McKenzie (Sheffield, UK: Sheffield Academic Press, 1999), 171–88.

24. Morton Smith, *Palestinian Parties and Politics That Shaped the Old Testament* (New York: Columbia University Press, 1971), 15–56, 82–98.

25. Saul Olyan, *Asherah and the Cult of Yahweh in Ancient Israel* (Atlanta, GA: Scholars Press, 1988), 73–74; see similarly Michael D. Coogan, "Canaanite Origins and Lineage: Reflections on the Religion of Ancient Israel," in *Ancient Israelite Religion*, ed. Patrick D. Miller (Philadelphia: Fortress, 1987), 115–16; Cohn, "Second Coming," 70, 68; and Susan Ackerman, *Under Every Green Tree: Popular Religion in Sixth Century Judah* (Atlanta, GA: Scholars Press, 1992). Disagreeing is Jeffrey Tigay, *You Shall Have No Other Gods: Israelite Religion in the Light of Hebrew Inscriptions* (Atlanta, GA: Scholars, 1986), 29.

26. Mark Smith, *The Early History of God: Yahweh and the Other Deities in Ancient Israel* (San Francisco: Harper & Row, 1987), 24–26.

27. Schwartz, *Curse of Cain*, focuses more on the central role of monotheism than I have; however, if one were to blame monotheism as the root cause of the quest for a coherent nationalism, that would ignore the fact that polytheistic societies throughout history have found ready at hand many other justifications for killing people and establishing kingdoms. Heroic epic traditions in general, from Homer to John Ford, express the theme of a tentative peace achieved through violence and endurance. The biblical epic is no different.

28. Brettler, *Creation of History*, 83. Despite Schwartz's excellent treatment of these issues (*Curse of Cain*), she overlooks the variety of ways that Israel depicts other nations.

29. Elizabeth Bloch-Smith, "Israelite Ethnicity in Iron I: Archaeology Preserves What Is Remembered and What Is Forgotten in Israel's History," *Journal of Biblical Literature* 122 (2003): 401–25.

30. Weinfeld, *Promise*, 97. See also Machinist, "Outsiders or Insiders," 49; Peter Machinist, "Biblical Traditions: The Philistines and Israelite History," in *The Sea Peoples and Their World: A Reassessment*, ed. Eliezer D. Oren (Philadelphia: University Museum of University of Pennsylvania, 2000), 53–83; Trude Dothan and Robert L. Cohn, "The Philistine as Other: Biblical Rhetoric and Archaeological Reality," in Silberstein and Cohn, eds., *Other in Jewish Thought*, 61–64. Jerahmeelites, Kenizzites, Zerahites, and the Jebusites also remained as a partially assimilated nation; see Saul Olyan, *Rites and Rank: Hierarchy in Biblical Representations of Cult* (Princeton, NJ: Princeton University Press, 2000), 73.

31. Antonio Loprieno, *Topos und Mimesis: Zum Ausländer in der ägyptischen Literatur* (Wiesbaden, Germany: Harrassowitz, 1988); Poo, *Enemies of Civilization*, 59–60, 101–20.

32. F. V. Greifenhagen emphasizes the negative evaluation of Egypt more strongly, and the construction of Egypt as Israel's Other (*Egypt on the Pentateuch's Ideological Map: Constructing Biblical Israel's Identity* [Sheffield, UK: Sheffield Academic Press, 2002]), but see Jonathan Magonet, "The Attitude towards Egypt in the Book of Exodus," in *Truth and Its Victims*, ed. Wim Beuken, Seán Freyne, and Anton Weiler (Edinburgh, UK: Clark, 1988), 11–20; Cohn, "Negotiating," 149, 166. I would argue that the negative view of Egypt is a literary theme of the exodus narrative, and not a constant opposition.

33. Schwartz, *Curse of Cain*; David Biale, *Power and Powerlessness in Jewish History* (New York: Schocken, 1986).

34. Babylon becomes Other like the Canaanites centuries later, when it, like the Canaanites, becomes a legendary evil empire of the past. The same is true to a lesser extent of Assyria; see Peter Machinist, "The *Rab Šāqēh* at the Wall of Jerusalem: Israelite Identity in the Face of the Assyrian 'Other,'" *Hebrew Studies* 41 (2000): 151–68.

35. See Shaye J. D. Cohen, *The Beginnings of Jewishness: Boundaries, Varieties, Uncertainties* (Berkeley: University of California Press, 1999), 248–51. Cohen also compares the exclusion of bastards in the legislation of Solon of Athens. On the analysis of class in ancient Israel, see Gale Yee, *Class Acts: Marginalization in Ancient Israel* (Louisville, KY: Westminster John Knox, forthcoming). On disabilities in the Hebrew Bible, see Saul Olyan, "'Anyone Blind or Lame Shall Not Enter the House': On the Interpretation of Second Samuel 5:8b," *Catholic Biblical Quarterly* 60 (1998): 218–27.

36. For various views, see Christiana van Houten, *The Alien in Israelite Law* (Sheffield, UK: Journal for the Study of the Old Testament, 1991), 19; C. Bultmann, *Der Fremde in antiken Juda* (Göttingen, Germany: Vandenhoeck & Ruprecht, 1992), 93–102; Jacob Milgrom, *Leviticus 17–22* (New York: Doubleday, 2000), 1416–20. In rabbinic literature there is a distinction between a *ger toshab* as a resident alien and a *ger tzadik* as a convert, but that is a later distinction not present in the biblical texts. Julia Kristeva, *Powers of Horror: An Essay in Abjection* (New York: Columbia University Press, 1982), 41–53, discusses the changing definition of "barbarian" in Greece, and also draws in the ambiguous category of metic (*metoikos*), the resident alien in Greece, a category similar to the *ger* in Israel.

37. Mary Douglas, "Who Was the Stranger?" *Archives européennes de sociologie* 35 (1994): 283–98, but also Olyan, *Rites and Rank*, 68–69, 72–80. It is also possible that in an earlier age those who found themselves dispossessed in the kinship system were called "empty men," *anashim reqim*, on which see Gregory Mobley, *The Empty Men: The Heroic Tradition of Ancient Israel* (New York: Doubleday, 2005), esp. 36–38. There may be no direct relation between empty men and *gerim*, but rather a somewhat analogous disconnected status in the kinship system.

38. Sparks, *Ethnicity and Identity*, 238–45, 315. Sparks even suggests that the constant use of "brother" in Deuteronomy for fellow-Israelite is intended to pull dissociated Israelites into a new identity. Sparks's discussion is very informative, but he often romanticizes the role of the *ger*. He inexplicably assumes that the *ger* "assimilates" by being drawn into the cult of Yahweh—why then does he or she remain a *ger*? See, correctly, Olyan, *Rites and Rank*, 80, 96.

39. Michael L. Satlow, *Tasting the Dish: Rabbinic Rhetorics of Sexuality* (Atlanta, GA: Scholars Press, 1995), 56–62. Note that in 1 Enoch 6–11 the offspring of the angels and human women (Gen 6) are *mamzerim*.

40. Mary Douglas "Justice as the Cornerstone: An Interpretation of Leviticus 18–20," *Interpretation* 53 (1999): 345; "Holy Joy: Rereading Leviticus: The Anthropologist and the Believer," *Conservative Judaism* 46 (1994): 10.

41. Jonathan Klawans, *Impurity and Sin in Ancient Judaism* (Oxford: Oxford University Press, 2000).

42. Mary Douglas, *Natural Symbols: Explorations in Cosmology* (New York: Pantheon, 1970), 65–81.

43. Threat to procreation: Mullen, *Ethnic Myths*, 239; David Biale, *Eros and the Jews: From Biblical Israel to Contemporary America* (New York: Basic Books, 1992), 29; threat to the lineage: Howard Eilberg-Schwartz, *The Savage in Judaism: An Anthropology of Israelite Religion and Ancient Judaism* (Bloomington: Indiana University Press, 1990), 183.

44. Stephen F. Bigger, "The Family Laws of Leviticus 18 in Their Setting," *Journal of Biblical Literature* 98 (1979): 187–203; Mary Douglas, *Purity and Danger*, 2nd ed. (Harmondsworth, UK: Penguin, 1970), 54–72; and especially Saul Olyan, "'And with a Male You Shall Not Lie the Lying Down of a Woman': On the Meaning and Significance of Leviticus 18:22 and 20:13," *Journal of the History of Sexuality* 5 (1994): 179–206.

3

❧

The Redefinition of We and Other in Ezra-Nehemiah

The revolutionary changes in the conception of the Other in Ezra and Nehemiah seem to spring up as a totally new phenomenon in the history of Israel, but they have a background in unresolved issues from previous centuries, and we must fill in this background by returning once more to the events covered in chapter two. The kingdom of Israel that David established in about 1000 BCE had, in less than a century, split into two entities: the north, which continued to be called Israel, and the south, where Jerusalem and the temple were located, referred to as Judah (later Judea). When the north fell to Assyria in 722 BCE, the leading citizens were deported and resettled in various parts of the empire. Many likely became refugees and perhaps *gerim* (resident aliens) in Judah. The south continued as an independent kingdom for over a century after that, but in 605 BCE Judah fell as well to the Neo-Babylonians under Nebuchadnezzar. In 597 Nebuchadnezzar quashed a rebellion in Jerusalem and, repeating the practice of the Assyrians, deported many of the leading citizens. A second rebellion arose some years later, but in 586 BCE, Nebuchadnezzar once again wrested control of Jerusalem, deported more of the city's leaders, and this time destroyed the temple. The center of Israel's cultic life for four hundred years now lay in ruins. This initiated the period that is known as the Babylonian exile, when the two main governing institutions of Israel, the temple and the monarchy, were destroyed, and a significant portion of the leaders were led away and resettled in Babylon and elsewhere. Despite the deportation of many of the leading citizens life went on in Jerusalem and environs, and grain sacrifices continued on the site of the temple. Jerusalem was not a ghost town.

Vast changes, however, were about to sweep across the near east. A new king, Cyrus, arose in Persia, and in 539 BCE he quickly defeated the once-powerful Babylonians. Cyrus's policies were very different from those of his predecessors, who ruled other nations by sheer force. His defeat of the Babylonians brought a new, more "rational" administration to the ancient world. First, his empire was much larger, extending from Egypt and Asia Minor in the west all the way to India in the east. It was administered with a more interdependent theory of empire. Cyrus took on the role of benevolent dictator, allowed more local autonomy, and also reestablished temples that the Babylonians had destroyed, including the temple in Jerusalem. The larger empire was divided into a system of provinces called satrapies. Although the residents of the various satrapies were still forced to pay a heavy burden of taxes to the Persian king, there was a much larger degree of local self-rule and interdependent economic activity. The new political theory of Cyrus created the motive, and the roads, postal system, and court administration created the means by which the satrapy courts could become the local realization of the Persian king's court. Compared to the more direct rule of the Egyptians, Assyrians, and Babylonians, the Persians perfected a way to rule subject peoples over vast distances.

This summary description of the Babylonian exile and restoration seems clear-cut, but in reality it was a long, complicated affair, lasting from beginning to end about two hundred years or more. Several factors rendered the situation quite complex. First, there were three different defeats of Judah, in 605, 597, and 586 BCE. The Jerusalem leaders were deported to Babylonia and elsewhere, in what was likely three different deportations. Exiled Judeans began returning in small groups (Jer 40:11–12), followed by more substantial returns described in Ezra and Nehemiah. Thus the picture of a single deportation and a single return is a telescoped view of the situation. In addition, an important question that remains concerns the demographics of those who were in Judah when people began returning from Babylon. Although 2 Chronicles 36:20–21 describes an exile in which the land of Judah lay desolate and vacant, the "myth of the empty land," this may simply reflect the point of view of those who returned to reassert their claims to authority.[1] Were those who remained on the land now simply the poorer Judeans who had never been deported, or deported Judeans who had returned intermittently over the years? Did they include former Israelites from the northern half of Israel who had come south, whether as refugees, deportees, or *gerim*, or were they also people of other nations who had been deported from their homelands by the Babylonians and relocated in Judah? Were the "peoples of the land," as Ezra and Nehemiah call them, all of these groups, an ethnically mixed population? This ambiguity of ethnic identities was an important part of the context of Ezra and Nehemiah, but it is hardly unusual. Ethnic diversity and mixing are more the norm in world history than an aberration, and postcolonial theorists would argue that the myth of a "pure people"—anywhere—is suspect.

The books of Ezra and Nehemiah chronicle part of the process of this restoration. There is an autobiographical aspect to both Ezra and Nehemiah that has given scholars reason to suggest that Ezra-Nehemiah (which originally circulated together) is the earliest example of a non-royal autobiography, and like Herodotus, who wrote in Greece at about the same time, this text is responsible for introducing a new kind of unaffected "realistic" prose.[2] The first-person autobiographical style of much of Ezra-Nehemiah would also lead one to suspect that, in addition to the decrees, letters, and lists, this text was based on separate memoirs by Ezra and Nehemiah. However, as disarming and realistic as the Nehemiah Memoir is in its details, the Ezra material is idealized and unrealistic. It is thus often concluded that there was in fact a Nehemiah Memoir that forms the basis of the second half, but that the Ezra material was not based on a first-person memoir; rather, it was composed with the Nehemiah material as a model.[3] The literary "realism" of this prose is often viewed as a sad decline from the heights of the brilliant literature of the exile and after, such as Isaiah 40–66, Jeremiah, Ezekiel, Job, Ruth, and Jonah, but it is unfair to compare Ezra and Nehemiah to authors such as these. Ezra and Nehemiah are *married* to the language of court and administration, and try to remain faithful to that marriage.[4]

HISTORICAL AND SOCIAL
CIRCUMSTANCES OF EZRA-NEHEMIAH

When King Cyrus of Persia granted some of his subjects the right to rebuild their temples, the exiled Judean Sheshbezzar was among them; he returned to Jerusalem and began to rebuild the temple there. The project stagnated, however, presumably due to a lack of will on the part of the Jerusalemites, and also due to opposition from surrounding leaders who feared a loss of their local control. In 520 BCE, the prophets Haggai and Zechariah managed to rekindle enough support to complete the construction of the temple. By 515 the temple was completed and the meat sacrifices were renewed (grain sacrifices had continued throughout the Babylonian exile), but that was not the end of the story. Two more waves of returnees from Persia were to make their way to Jerusalem, one under Ezra and one under Nehemiah, and these leaders were very dismayed by what they perceived as a degeneration of the cult and religious observance in Jerusalem. Although Ezra and Nehemiah probably never worked in Jerusalem at the same time for their common vision, they are placed together in the tradition, just as many other founding figures were linked as pairs: Moses and Aaron, Elijah and Elisha, Zerubbabel and Jeshua, Peter and Paul, or the paired contrast of Hillel and Shammai. Chapters from each reformer's memoir have evidently been moved and inserted into the memoir of the other in order to accomplish this pairing, and the names of both Ezra and Nehemiah have been inserted at key places (Neh 8:9; 12:26, 36).[5]

A pressing challenge for scholars has been how to describe the social changes in Judean society that are reflected in these texts. Morton Smith introduced a political and sociological explanation for the party politics of Ezra-Nehemiah that is still discussed and debated today, even though a consensus has never formed around it.[6] Smith argued that the struggle between the Yahweh-alone party and the syncretists described in the previous chapter was carried over to the exile and after. Syncretists, from the Greek word for mixing, are often understood as assimilationists, but this is misleading; it suggests that they were content to disappear into the fabric of the surrounding society. Rather, the syncretists may have had a very strong sense of identity, but simply imposed less-rigid boundaries. The elite leaders in Jerusalem who were forcibly exiled to Babylon took with them the stricter boundaries of the Yahweh-alone party, values which likely served them well in defining a minority ethnic status among the Babylonians. They thus returned to Jerusalem with a strong sense of their elite status in the land of their origin, a genealogical connection to the land and the entitlement that derives from that, values of strict separation that helped to maintain ethnic identity, and a sense of ethnic unity that is mirrored and reinforced by the notion of the unity, separateness, and absolute demand of God. Theological norms mirrored social norms.

Building upon Smith's analysis of the situation, other scholars turned to the sociology of religion for categories that might apply to the restoration of Judah. Joseph Blenkinsopp, for example, suggests that the reform parties of Ezra and Nehemiah were a sect within Judean society.[7] Although Ezra and Nehemiah never controlled the high priesthood, they created a movement that challenged the patterns of society espoused by the leading religious authority figures in Jerusalem. Blenkinsopp notes that at key passages these reformers are referred to as those who "quake (*haredim*) before God," (Ezra 9:4, 10:3). Trembling before God is a motif that occurred at Sinai (Exod 10:16), but here in Ezra, as at Isaiah 66:2, 5, a marked group of worshipers seems to be intended. Blenkinsopp argues that these *haredim* or "quakers" were a pietistic reform movement in the post-exilic period. Some modern ultra-orthodox Jewish pietists are called *Haredim* as well, and although there is no *historical* connection between this recent group and the ancient *haredim*, they may share a similar outlook that matches the name.

But whether the reformers were a sect depends also on how one defines the term. According to typical definitions of "sect," members generally have an identity separate from society at large, even if they interact with others on a daily basis. They form a new community of salvation, claim to embody the values of an earlier golden age, limit salvation to those who have chosen to become members and live according to the community's standards, and enforce strict rules of endogamy (that is, marrying within the community). There is a strong consciousness of being a small subset of culture with sharp boundaries, a claim to exclusive access to religious truth, expulsion as a form of punishment, and little distinction between clergy and laypeople. Of all of these traits, the most salient is that sects draw clear boundaries with society at large. If society is imagined as a pie chart, the sect sees itself as a narrow slice, with clearly marked boundaries. The sect even derives its reason for existence from its separatism; the sect *needs* the "unredeemed" larger society to stand for what it is not. The sharper the sense of sin that the sect projects onto the larger society, the greater the sense of redemption for the small number of members within it. Like a sect, Ezra-Nehemiah claimed to have embodied the core traditions of the parent-body, and like a sect they created new boundary markers: endogamy and more precise Sabbath observance. But unlike a typical sect, split off from society, they did not affirm their own minority or marginal status and stay on the sidelines; they tried to gain control of Judean institutions. Ezra and Nehemiah were, after all, commissioned by the Persian king, which renders sect an inapt term.

A different category from the social sciences may fit the situation of Ezra and Nehemiah more accurately, and that is revitalization movement. A revitalization movement can be defined as an organized group that tries to reform the core of society by appealing to a personal commitment to a religious and ethical lifestyle that embodies traditionally shared beliefs. Like the sect, the revitalization movement holds as sacred the same core traditions as the parent-body. But while sects take their self-definition from their minority status—a pure community on the margins of a wicked society—revitalization movements are not content to create a pure sect; they want to bring the parent-body to a new level of observance. These popular movements try to revitalize society by bringing people to a more authentic observance of these traditions.[8] A particularly relevant example might be John Calvin's reform of Geneva, so similar to Ezra and Nehemiah's reform of Jerusalem, but revitalization movements can be as varied as the Women's Christian Temperance Union, Christian Evangelicals, or Muslim fundamentalists. More contemporary to Ezra and Nehemiah, we should consider the Zoroastrians in Persia or, as we shall see in chapter five, the Pharisees. Although revitalization movements may in some cases be "nativist," it should be noted that the Ezra-Nehemiah reform was imposed by Persia and, unlike 1 Maccabees, for example, utilized Imperial Aramaic as well as Hebrew. The extent of the colonial hybridity was not the same in the two cases. One might object that it is often said that the returning Judeans were more like a sect in that they intentionally defined themselves as a pure inner circle.[9] However, although this does describe their self-understanding, we shall see below that it is likely that they actively recruited others to become "returnees" (Theorem 7: Ambiguous groups reassigned) and attempted to control civic institutions. The reform movement reflected in Ezra and Nehemiah, then, was more like a revitalization movement than a sect, although it is possible that the different chapters do not represent identical social situations.

There is a growing consensus of scholars that behind the missions of Ezra and Nehemiah lay the political strategies of the Persian kings. Archaeological evidence suggests that before Ezra and Nehemiah, governors had already been appointed to strengthen Jerusalem as a semi-independent city apart from Samaria, and that Persia had invested in redeveloping the region of Judah and the city itself as a temple city. The Ezra-Nehemiah reform was a revitalization movement in Judea, authorized top-down by a supportive Persian king, just as another Persian king did at a temple-city in Egypt; there a priest named Udjahorresnet composed his own autobiographical inscription that is strikingly similar to Nehemiah's account.[10] The king's permission to rebuild was not so much a benevolent response to the pleas of Ezra and Nehemiah as a proactive strategy to shore up the military capabilities of the region. If that is the case, then searching for subtleties of party or class divisions may be less revealing than simply assuming here the conflicts between favored and less-favored local clients of the imperial patrons. (Compare below concerning 1 and 2 Maccabees.)

CONTENTS AND SOURCES OF EZRA-NEHEMIAH

The differences among the various sections of the text suggest that a number of literary sources and royal edicts were utilized to compose the whole. In some cases, they were also divided and rearranged to create the final text. Here I follow a common, but not universal scholarly view of the sources of Ezra-Nehemiah.[11] We shall focus on three sections (here simplified), which probably represent three different stages in the attempt to restore a purified cult in Jerusalem:

1) Ezra 1–6: first rebuilding under Jeshua and Zerubbabel
2) Ezra 7–10, Nehemiah 8–10: Ezra Memoir
3) Nehemiah 1–7, 11–13: Nehemiah Memoir

One can see from the chapter divisions that sections two and three were broken up and rearranged, presumably to make one unitary account of the "partners" Ezra and Nehemiah. Nehemiah's memoir (section three) may have been composed before Ezra's (section two). At any rate, the three sections are similar in many ways, depicting a series of oppositions to the reform movement by local leaders and the attempts of Ezra and Nehemiah to steel the resolve of the people in the face of opposition, with a repeated motif of opposition-creating-identity. The social memory of the purified community is thus being formed before our eyes. The sections have been brought together under a single vision of the renewal of Judean society, but they reflect significant differences as well; shifting views of the We and Other can be traced.

Section 1: Ezra 1–6

The first section of Ezra-Nehemiah, Ezra 1–6 (which is to be clearly distinguished throughout from section two, the Ezra Memoir) recounts what for Jews was the most important event of this period, the successful rebuilding of the temple. The language of Ezra 1–6 that constitutes the We of the author's community is quite idealized. God's plan for a renewed Judean community is even placed, ironically from our point of view, in the mouth of King Cyrus of Persia:

> The Lord stirred up the spirit of King Cyrus of Persia so that he sent a herald throughout all his kingdom, and also made a declaration in a written edict . . . : "Any of those among you who are of his people—may their God be with them!—are now permitted to go up to Jerusalem in Judah, and rebuild the house of the Lord, the God of Israel—he is the God who is in Jerusalem. . . ." The heads of the families of Judah and Benjamin, and the priests and the Levites—everyone whose spirit God stirred—got ready to go up and rebuild the house of the Lord in Jerusalem. (Ezra 1:1, 3, 5)

Although Ezra 1–6 concerns the efforts of Jeshua and Zerubbabel to bring a band of returnees back to Jerusalem and rebuild the temple, the focus is actually more on God, the Persian kings, and the people as a whole divided into their respective orders (Ezra 3:8–13). The impetus to return and rebuild the temple comes from God, who has stirred up the spirits of the reestablished community, but it comes also through the actions of Cyrus of Persia.

But interestingly, placed *before* the temple officials in the passage quoted above are the "heads of the families" (*roshei ha`avot*), or later in Ezra, "elders" (*savim*), who *lead* the return. They are not leaders *in the temple*, as are the priests and Levites, but *tribal* leaders. The heads of the families are very prominent here and elsewhere in Ezra-Nehemiah as leaders in their own right. Thus there appears to be a distinction between priestly leadership and lay leadership in Ezra-Nehemiah. Upon the return of some of the exiles from Babylon, the importance of these aristocratic authority figures was once again invoked in Jerusalem. Blenkinsopp suggests that part of the conflict between the returnees and those who remained revolved around the hereditary rights to the plots of land to which the "heads of families" now laid claim. We shall return to this question below.

In Ezra 1 the action is centered on the first foundation of the altar for sacrifice (1:2–3), and immediately after that the Judeans observe the festival of Sukkot. Just as the covenant renewal ceremonies in the Primary History were understood to have brought the people into existence, we should also expect the commitment rituals in Ezra-Nehemiah to provide a constitutional moment for the We, and that is what we find. Ezra 1–6 emphasizes the foundation of the temple, the institution of the meat sacrifices, and the liturgy of the priests and Levites. The temple and its liturgy is the locus of the Judeans' identity, but the construction of the Other cannot be far behind. The first positive scenes of community building are followed by another in which it is said that the returnees were "in dread of the peoples of the land" (3:3). This drama continues at 4:1–3:

> When adversaries of Judah and Benjamin heard that the returned exiles were building a temple to the Lord, the God of Israel, they approached Zerubbabel and the heads of families and said to them, "Let us build with you, for we worship God as you do, and we have been sacrificing to him ever since the days of King Esar-haddon of Assyria who brought us here." But Zerubbabel, Jeshua, and the rest of the heads of families in Israel said to them, "You shall have no part with us in building a house to our God, but we alone will build for God, as King Cyrus of Persia has commanded us."

The We and Other are stated simply: the We are identified as "all the people" (Ezra 3:11), and the Other as "peoples of the land" (Ezra 4:4) and "adversaries of Judah and Benjamin." These adversaries are described as worshipers of God who are nevertheless newcomers, those from other nations who were forcibly deported to Samaria and only then took up the worship of God (compare 2 Kings 17:24–41).

The term "people [or peoples] of the land" is found in rabbinic literature, where it refers to those Jews who are not sufficiently observant of Jewish law, and this is how the term is known in later Jewish tradition, but that is not its original meaning. The phrase was used in a more positive sense as powerful rural landowners in Israel (for instance, 2 Kings 11), but in Ezra 1–6 and the Ezra Memoir (though *not* in the Nehemiah Memoir) it is used negatively to refer to people who reside in the vicinity of Jerusalem but who are not considered true Judeans, that is, those who are deemed "foreign." How the meaning of "people of the land" changed so dramatically from a positive to a negative meaning is not clear, but there may be a natural development that transforms terms for the rural periphery into terms of derision. "Heathen," "pagan," and "savage" are all terms that originally referred to people from the uncultivated countryside, not quite civilized, and in the construction of a new Christian identity came to mean those outside of the boundaries of Christendom.[12] "Gentile" is similar in origin. Those on the outer periphery of the We are like those who reside on the heath just outside the cultivated lands surrounding the city, and are "heathen." The geographically dangerous margin becomes a symbolic margin. The perspective of the Judeans returning from Babylon, shaped by the urbane worldview of the world capitals, may have relegated the residents they encountered to an "earthy" status. They are heathen, "outlandish," "people of the land."

Whatever the true origins of this group, the author of Ezra 1–6 sees their offer to help build as an insincere gesture to join the cult of Jerusalem. The author suggests there is malice in their intent by calling them "adversaries" (*tsarim*), but they are in no way violent, and this has led some scholars to speculate that the reform party has overreacted. Lester Grabbe points out that in many of these opposition scenes a menacing motive is attributed to the opponents even though there is no evidence for it.[13] In chapter two we observed the irony that Israel was not so much afraid of foreigners who were distant as those people who had actually inhabited the same space. Whereas God's former command was to exterminate all of those on the land, the new directive is simply not to worship with them. The definition of the identity of Israel is no longer expressed as a military domination of the land, but in terms of a coherent identity that can coexist with other peoples in an international urban setting without dissolving around the edges. The need for a sharply defined identity must replace military might. What will define this group is correct cult at the temple, a sanctified city, and a pure endogamy. To accomplish this, the author of Ezra 1–6 has divided the landscape into two distinct groups: Judeans returning from the exile (*golah*) and the foreign nations or people of the land who were newcomers to the worship of God. Conveniently ignored are two other groups: Judeans who were not exiled but had remained on the land, and those people who were descended from the Israelites in the north. These two groups may have been part of the "people of the land" who thwarted the building plan (Ezra 4:4–5), but the text before us pushes aside these middle categories and presents the world as two extreme alternatives: Judean returnees on the one hand and adversaries who were only pretenders to be Israelites (Theorem 7: Ambiguous groups reassigned). Only those who had been exiled and returned were seen to have experienced, in Hindy Najman's words, "the purifying power of the exile."[14]

Sara Japhet suggests that the adversaries were northern Israelites who remained on the land when their leaders were deported by the Assyrians. Rather than foreigners, they might have been authentic Israelites continuing their long-held practice of making pilgrimages to Jerusalem to worship there.[15] Such a pilgrimage might have even been a staple of the religious life of Ezra's and Nehemiah's opponents, and considered by the latter to be quite "orthodox." Further, in Jeremiah these pilgrims are said to be engaged in practices such as shaving which were probably penitential rituals. As Japhet says, there is an "undoubtedly deep emotional involvement and national self-identity of these people."[16] She adduces a broad range of references to different groups on the land, all laying claim to an authentic identity as "Israel": the Judean leaders who had been carried away into exile in Babylon; their number who had returned to reassume control in Judea; Judeans who had not been exiled and remained on the land; the leading citizens of the northern Israelites who had been deported under the Assyrians; the Israelites who had escaped that deportation, remaining on the land in the north, and who came to Judah at the pilgrimage festivals; northern Israelites who may have come south to Judah as refugees or *gerim*; Judeans who had settled in Egypt at the military colony in Elephantine; and Judeans who had settled in other areas such as Ammon. But the returning Judeans, the *golah* community, had a simpler view of the situation:

> According to Ezra-Nehemiah only one Israelite community exists in the land of Israel: that of returned exiles! . . . The dichotomy is sharp: the "exiles" are Israel, all others—"the peoples of the land." . . . What then, is the book's attitude to those Israelite groups who did not belong to the returning exiles, those who remained in the land, in Judah and Samaria? The answer is very simple: according to Ezra-Nehemiah there are no such people at all![17]

Japhet could hardly have stated Theorem 7 more clearly. Opponents of the reformers were being redefined as inauthentic—even those northern Israelites who had worshiped God for centuries. In later sections of Ezra-Nehemiah, as we shall see, even fellow-Judeans who were not true to the reformers' program were likely redefined as foreigners.

Our attention should be particularly drawn to the Judeans who remained on the land—who were never exiled—as they probably constituted the core of those opposed to Ezra's and Nehemiah's reforms. As Japhet points out, this group would have had a theologically oriented justification for their position, and a strong sense that they were the true remnant of pre-exilic Israel. The Judeans who had been exiled to Babylon, however, developed an equally strong theological understanding of their own sense of belonging to God's true mission. The idea that these Judeans could successfully deny the social reality and redefine many as illegitimate may seem implausible or even bizarre, but this is not an unusual practice. Groups may be redefined as inside or outside a social body almost arbitrarily. For the Essenes at Qumran outsiders, even Jews, were considered gentile, and the members spoke of themselves as having been gentile before entering the sect. Although it is hard to imagine how the Judeans from Babylon could supplant the Judeans still in residence, the former would have carried the authority of the Persian king.

But is there no trace of a middle category? Are there no northern Israelites now residing in Judea who are acceptable, or Judeans who were not exiled and yet allied themselves with the reformers? Ezra 1–6 makes one passing reference to such people; note especially the italicized portion:

> The people of Israel, the priests and the Levites, and the rest of the returned exiles [*golah*] celebrated the dedication of the house of God with joy. They offered one hundred bulls, two hundred rams, four hundred lambs, and as a sin offering for all Israel, twelve male goats, according to the number of the tribes of Israel. Then they established the priests and Levites in the temple in their divisions as it is written in the book of Moses. . . . The Passover lamb was eaten by the people of Israel who had returned from exile, *and also by all who had joined them and separated themselves from the pollutions of the nations of the land to worship the Lord, the God of Israel.* (6:16–19, 21)

While it appears that Ezra 1–6 grants primary authority to the returnees, it is also noted here that some local people joined the movement. Such a group is not even mentioned in the Ezra Memoir, nor in most scholarly discussions of Ezra-Nehemiah. The Ezra Memoir that follows will not entertain a positive role for Judeans who were not returnees, but Ezra 1–6 does—once—and the Nehemiah Memoir appears to mention them positively once as well (Neh 1:2–3).[18] Although on an ideal level Ezra-Nehemiah (or at least the Ezra Memoir) eliminated from true Israel the Judeans who remained on the land, Japhet suggests that on a practical level they were incorporated by being recruited and redefined as returnees, just as certain others were redefined as foreigners.

Another complexity of the situation is also often missed. We are told at Ezra 3:7 that the craftsmen of Tyre and Sidon, nearby Phoenician cities, were welcomed in the city, even though Phoenicia was simply the later name for Canaan, and Tyre and Sidon were Canaanite cities! While it is true that the positive relations with Tyre and Sidon described here are meant to re-create the relations between Solomon and King Hiram of Tyre in building the first temple (1 Kings 5), it is remarkable that the *Realpolitik* found there should be repeated here as well, and it only becomes more pronounced in the course of Ezra and Nehemiah. Even though these craftsmen are Canaanites, they are well received while other "neighboring peoples"—which include Israelite and Judeans?—are spurned.

Thus the conclusion of Ezra 1–6, like the beginning, contains some of the most idealized language of Ezra and Nehemiah. It continues:

> Then, according to the word sent by King Darius, [the Judean leaders] accomplished with all diligence that which King Darius had ordered. So the elders of the Jews built and prospered through the prophesying of Haggai and Zechariah. They finished their building by command of the God of Israel and by the command of Cyrus and Darius of Persia, and this house was finished on the third day of the month of Adar, in the sixth year of the reign of King Darius. (6:13–15)

As at the beginning of Ezra 1–6, so here at the end the word of God is seen as revealed in positive edicts from foreign kings, and they are likened to prophetic inspiration. The temple is joyously reconstructed by command of God and command of the king of Persia—the same Aramaic word, *te`em*, is used for command in both cases. There is a fundamental harmony of mission between God, the prophets Haggai and Zechariah, Cyrus and Darius of Persia, and the renewed community of returnees in its proper orders: elders and heads of families, priests, Levites, and all Israel. It is argued by Tamara Cohn Eskenazi that the passage just quoted is the central, thematic affirmation in Ezra-Nehemiah,[19] but these verses are the conclusion and climax of only one part of Ezra-Nehemiah. The other parts will have different theological centers.

Ezra 1–6 expresses the most idealized conception of the Judean community in all of Ezra-Nehemiah, and limits conflict and Otherness to those who are presumed to be from the mixed nations neighboring Judah to the north. The difference between Ezra 1–6 on the one hand and the Ezra and Nehemiah Memoirs on the other may be likened to the stages of other reform movements. At the beginning there is one external division, but no internal divisions within Judah, nor conflict between returnees and those who were not deported. In fact, the latter "who separated themselves from the abominations of the land" are welcomed into the Passover celebration. In the next two sections clouds will gather that reveal bitter divisions within the returnee community, and more strident means of community definition will be introduced.

Section 2: Ezra Memoir (Ezra 7–10, Nehemiah 8–10)

Although the Nehemiah Memoir was probably based on that reformer's own first-person account, it is debated whether the Ezra Memoir was derived from Ezra's narrative or was composed by a follower of Ezra with the Nehemiah Memoir as a model. We shall continue to refer to this section as the Ezra Memoir to distinguish it from Ezra 1–6 and the Nehemiah Memoir even though it is not clear who wrote it.

The Ezra Memoir begins with the introduction of Ezra, a priest in the high priestly family (descended directly from the first priest, Aaron), and a "scribe highly skilled in the law of Moses." His priestly status will be an important guarantee of his authority, but he was never the high priest and it is his role as scribe of the law of Moses that will be far more central. Ezra's knowledge of the law of Moses empowers him to teach the stricter observance to those from Judah who now reside throughout the province Beyond the River (Ezra 7:25); the leaders are all instructed by him (Neh 8:13). This section of the Ezra Memoir creates an image of Ezra and an image of the law as the constitution of the Judean people that remains in Judaism to this day. In the Ezra Memoir he is depicted as a figure parallel to Moses (Ezra 7:10), who teaches law to the people of Israel, and as a figure parallel to Joshua leading the conquest. Ezra reenacts Joshua's reading of the law at the covenant renewal ceremony (Josh 8:30–35), but grants an even stronger centrality to an expanded law. The idealization of Ezra's mission is sometimes carried to the point of unbelievability. The king of Persia not only authorizes Ezra to return to restore Jerusalem; he also sends along a fantastic amount of gold and silver without any armed guard (7:22). The Nehemiah Memoir will be told with much more verisimilitude, and Ezra and Nehemiah are honored differently—and separately—in Jewish tradition.

After the very romanticized introduction, Ezra's arrival in Jerusalem brings to light the realization that there is trouble in paradise:

> The officials approached me and said, "The people of Israel, the priests and Levites have not separated themselves from the peoples of the lands with their abominations (*to`evot*), from the Canaanites, Hittites, Perizzites, Jebusites, Ammonites, Moabites, Egyptians, and Edomites. For they have taken some of their daughters as wives for themselves and for their sons. Thus the holy seed has mixed itself with the peoples of the lands, and in this faithlessness the officials and leaders have led the way." (Ezra 9:1–2)

This passage is one of the most important in the Hebrew Bible in terms of the construction of the We and Other; the definition of the boundaries of Israel is altered in a fundamental way. Many prominent people in Jerusalem had married women from foreign nations, nations that are arranged in a stereotyped list typical of the lists found in the earlier biblical texts. However, based on what we found in the last chapter, it is surprising to find that this list includes nations from three different categories: legendary pre-Israelite nations (Canaanites, Hittites, Perizzites,

Jebusites), contemporary neighbors (Ammonites, Moabites, Edomites), and great empires (Egyptians).[20] Ezra's reaction reflects a separation much stronger than was previously the case in Israel. Earlier biblical texts allowed for the possibility of marriage with captured women from the other nations (Deut 21:10–14). It is also specified in Deuteronomy 23:2–9 that Ammonites and Moabites were not allowed to join the congregation, implying that others were; Deuteronomy 23 explicitly allows for the acceptance of Edomites and Egyptians. Is there a new notion in Ezra 9:1–2 that *all* gentiles are polluting? Probably not as such. The list in Ezra 9:1–2 does encompass all gentiles, but the prohibition applies strictly to *marriage*. We have seen that Canaanite/Phoenician craftsmen from Tyre and Sidon were welcomed in Jerusalem to ply their trade, so long as they did not engage in business on the Sabbath. What is imposed is a new restriction on marriage, even though Nehemiah 10:28–30, 13:1–3 later incorrectly refers to it as an already existing part of Moses' law.

Throughout much of Jewish history, religious affiliation has been assumed to be passed through the mother, not the father. It might be suggested, then, that opposition to intermarriage with foreign women arose out of fear that the affiliation of the children would automatically follow that of the mother. However, this aspect of Jewish practice only arose much later, in the second century CE.[21] Religious affiliation before that was traced through the father, and therefore Ezra 9:1–2 must associate intermarriage with some other threat to Judean life. The reasons given in the text are two: the threat of the abominations of the peoples of the land, and the fact that intermarriage was considered the mixing of holy seed with the peoples of the land. In regard to the first, it was assumed that the foreign peoples committed idolatry and morally offensive acts which actually polluted the land, and joining in this activity would lead to moral impurity— it was this moral impurity of the land that had supposedly given rise to the exile.[22] Earlier biblical texts did not attribute an inherent impurity to gentiles *in general*, and marriage with gentiles was not prohibited. The pre-Israelite nations on the land were singled out for condemnation because of their supposed abominations, and later neighbors of Israel were deemed to be like them, but gentiles in general were not considered impure or in any way inferior. The fact that intermarriage was permitted and that the great empires were treated more neutrally is evidence of this.

Many scholars argue, however, that Ezra-Nehemiah introduces a new notion of racial or ethnic purity, a separation between ideal Israel and foreigners that is maintained by a strict endogamy. But Christine Hayes emphasizes that the reform of Ezra-Nehemiah is not racial in the modern sense of the word.[23] The concern of Ezra-Nehemiah is for the purity of the families that returned, a genealogical purity, as one might find with priestly families in ancient Israel or elsewhere. This is in fact what is new in Ezra-Nehemiah's concept of identity: *all the returning families are treated like priestly families*. This comparison with priestly lineages will be relevant to the rest of the discussion. The returnees' families are the ones that God supposedly chose, and it is for this reason that the genealogical lists in Ezra-Nehemiah are carefully kept. By this theory, genealogical purity would be more akin to the concern for aristocratic bloodlines than a distinction between races, and Ezra 9 introduces the evocative concept of the people as holy seed. However, here and in regard to Paul's "inclusiveness" (which we turn to in chapter seven), we shall raise the problem of the ambiguity of the terms "race," "ethnic group," "kinship," and "genealogical purity." The difference may be more one of degree than a clear qualitative distinction.

To understand the divisions that Ezra is introducing, one must remember that there are not just two categories in ancient Jewish purity law, sacred and polluting, but three: sacred (such as the temple), polluting (such as a corpse), and common or mundane, the neutral category of most things. Some mundane items, such as seeds, were not considered intrinsically sacred or polluting, but it was a violation of the laws of purity if different seeds were mixed in the same field, just as in biblical law one could not mix wool and linen in the same garment or yoke an ox and a donkey together, even though none of these things is polluting by itself. As a result, some scholars have concluded that Ezra-Nehemiah does not relegate all gentiles to a *polluting* status, in the same way that corpses or lepers were considered polluting, but to a mundane or non-sacred status, that is, not holy enough to mix with the holy seed of Israel.[24] In terms of marriage rules, "all Israel," and not just the priests, have moved from mundane to sacred, even if "all Israel" is now understood as including only returnees. And yet we can imagine that the *opponents* of the returnees would have understood "Israel" to mean "Greater Israel," the people who lived in the land of Judah and Samaria and worshiped God. Michael Fishbane suggests that the author of the Ezra Memoir arrived at the stricter prohibition of intermarriage by interpreting two different biblical passages in light of each other:[25]

Deut 7:1–6 (summarized):
    Do not intermarry with the Hittites, Girgashites, Amorites, Canaanites, Perizzites, Hivites, and Jebusites.

Deut 23:3–8 (summarized):
    No Ammonite or Moabite shall be admitted to the congregation of the Lord.

Two different commands prohibiting interaction with *specific* gentile groups are brought together and expanded to arrive at a prohibition of intermarriage with *all* gentiles (Theorem 8: Origins of practices reassigned). It is clear now why the list of nations in Ezra 9:1 contains all three categories. Ezra-Nehemiah is not simply forbidding marriage to the pre-Israelite peoples or to contemporary neighbors who are like them, but to *all* non-Judean peoples, including those of the great empires; they are *equally* ineligible for marriage. Like seed, they must remain in their own fields. Below we shall examine the possible economic and sociological background of this aspect of the reform.

Ezra 1–6 had constructed the Other in a fairly simple way. The Others were the external nations on the northern periphery of Judah. They may come knocking and claim to worship God, but in response they are simply relegated to the category of outsiders, opponents of the returnees' community. The Ezra Memoir, on the other hand, reflects a more complicated inner division, in which the Other on the horizon has been discovered among us, in the form of foreign women and their children. The external Other is also the internal Other (Theorem 6). Unlike Ezra 1–6, the opponents in the Ezra Memoir are not the northern governors and their minions—here they *help* the returnees (Ezra 8:36)!—but those on the inside who act like the foreign nations of the past. In addition, the idealized and clearly embellished mandate from the Persian king is not to protect the city re-building project from outsiders; rather, Ezra is to set up judges and enforce the law of Moses with a very heavy hand:

> All (says the Persian king) who will not obey the law of your God and the law of the king, let judgment be strictly executed on them, whether for death or for banishment or for confiscation of their goods or imprisonment. (Ezra 7:26)

Renewed Worship for a Renewed Community

The covenant renewal chapters of the Ezra Memoir present a long series of communal liturgies that include celebration and penance, ritual and Scripture study, confession and covenant, and the reconstitution of the returnees as ideal Israel. The covenant renewal ceremonies in the Hebrew Bible were said to follow upon some crisis in the history of the patriarchs; the restatement of the covenant served to reconstitute society (see also in Ezra 9). Just as Josiah's reform in 621 BCE was carried out with a newly discovered Book of the Law in hand, here there is an explicit use of the "Torah of Moses" as a constitutional text to which the reformers swear allegiance.[26] Over the course of the five chapters (Ezra 9–10, Neh 8–10), the Ezra Memoir conducts the reader through an experience of sin, repentance, and redemption for the community. The constitution of the We by means of this complex covenant renewal ceremony reads like a long liturgy, a service for the purification of the community. The result seems run-on and muddled, but the liturgical aspect is clear nonetheless, and that is what is important. Ezra transformed Judean observance; the sacrifice in the temple was complemented by a gathering outside the temple of a confessional community oriented around the law. The revitalization of religious life in Jerusalem became a model for the religion of Judah, or Judaism, elsewhere. It is ironic that Ezra's obsession with purifying the geographical center of Judah would give rise to a kind of religious experience that would function so well in the spread of Judaism through many parts of the world. As Shaye J. D. Cohen says, "Ezra 'published' the Torah by making it accessible to the masses. . . . [He] tried to remove the priest as the intermediary between the people and the sacred traditions by giving the people direct access to 'the Book of the Torah.'"[27]

Corresponding to the revitalized liturgical life, therefore, is a growth of discourse about ritual and personal piety. The Ezra Memoir couples a separation from the Other with a new, more intense religious discipline for the We:

> When I heard this, I tore my garment and my mantle, and pulled hair from my head and beard, and sat appalled. Then all who trembled (*haredim*) at the words of the God of Israel, because of the faithlessness of the returnees' community, gathered around me while I sat appalled until the evening sacrifice. (9:3–4)

It is in the context of the sharper prohibition of marriage that Ezra focuses on those who tremble (*haredim*) at the words of God. Ezra's experience in chapters nine and ten provides a model of a penitential discipline that is partially experienced in the reading of these chapters aloud in a communal setting:

> While Ezra prayed and made confession, weeping and throwing himself down before the house of God, a very great assembly of men, women, and children gathered out of Israel. The people also wept bitterly. (Ezra 10:1)

> [The people respond]: So now let us make a covenant with our God to send away all these wives and their children, according to the counsel of Ezra and of those who tremble [*haredim*] at the commandment of our God. (Ezra 10:3)

> All the people of Judah and Benjamin assembled at Jerusalem. All the people sat in the open square before the house of God, trembling [*haredim*] because of this matter and because of the heavy rain. (10:9)

As Blenkinsopp notes, the references to trembling do not stand alone; they correspond to other aspects of religious experience. Ezra is often depicted as fasting, and whereas fasting was often a sign of protest or grief in the

Hebrew Bible, the Ezra Memoir is unusual in describing fasting as more of a spiritual discipline, occurring numerous times:[28]

> I proclaimed a fast there, that we might fast before God, to seek from him a safe journey. . . . So we fasted and petitioned our God for this, and he listened to our entreaty. (Ezra 8:21, 23)

When Ezra enters into another prayer of confession and covenant renewal in Nehemiah 9 (also part of the Ezra Memoir), fasting is again an important preparatory aspect. Once the danger of the foreign wives is made clear, the returnee community must act to purify itself. The reconstitution of the community is not simply accomplished through a hurried divorce, but Ezra models for them a new spiritual life. The special piety and fasting of those who quake before God—like the Puritans, Quakers, and modern *Haredim* who followed them—must also be accompanied by a strict endogamy and maintenance of boundaries that is at the same time both expansive—all members of ideal Israel, not just priests, must be pure in marriage practices—and restrictive—very few are ideal Israel.

Section 3: Nehemiah Memoir (Nehemiah 1–7, 11–13)

Nehemiah 1–7, 11–13 is probably expanded from Nehemiah's own memoir of his attempts to continue the reform begun by Ezra. We encounter a realistic description of the process of reform—realistic in the sense that countless unexpected details of the encounters are included in a blunt, un-idealized style. It is not the idealized account that we encountered in the Ezra Memoir.[29] Instead of the edicts and letters from the great Persian kings, we find only letters to local leaders (Neh 6:5–7). And on a personal level, there is an un-idealized quality to the depiction of the conflicts between Nehemiah and others; Nehemiah comes off as more steely and obsessive than heroic. Even in his own first-person narrative he reveals the grandiose personality of the reformer. He has no interest in humanizing or idealizing himself, only in affirming that his reform comes from God.

The Nehemiah Memoir begins with his gradual awareness of the problems in Judah:

> While I was in Susa, the capital of Persia, I asked those who returned from Judah about the Judeans who survived, those who had escaped the exile to Babylon, and about Jerusalem. They replied, "They are in great trouble and shame. The wall of Jerusalem is broken down and its gates have been destroyed by fire." (Neh 1:2)

Nehemiah's opening introduces two motifs that will characterize his entire memoir: first, it is the *walls* of Jerusalem that must be secured, not the temple as in Ezra 1–6, or the community itself as in the Ezra Memoir, and second, it is a matter of honor and shame. The reason for the focus on the city walls is clear enough. Once the temple was erected and established, it was now up to the returning Judeans to secure a temple-city. The second motif requires more explanation. Non-western societies, and especially those in the ancient Mediterranean and ancient near east, focused much more strongly on public honor and its opposite, public shame, than do modern westerners. While modern capitalist economies focus on individualism, rational market activities, innovation, acquisition of wealth, and *internalized* self-esteem and guilt, societies in the ancient west emphasized tradition and the acquisition of *public* honor and status. This discourse of public honor and shame is particularly evident in the Nehemiah Memoir. Nehemiah explicitly associates the decrepit walls with shame (note italicized words):

> When Sanballat the Horonite heard that we were building the wall, he was enraged, and he *mocked* the Judeans. He said *in the presence of his associates and the Samarian army*, "What are these *feeble* Judeans doing? Will they restore things? Will they sacrifice? Will they revive the stones out of the *heaps of rubbish*?" Tobiah the Ammonite said, "*Any fox* going up on the wall would *break it down!*" Hear, our God, for we are *despised*. Turn their taunt back *on their heads*, and give them over as *plunder* in a land of *captivity*. (4:1–3)

The taunt of Nehemiah's opponents seems almost ritualized, like taunt-songs and dances that one finds in many cultures. Unlike the modern cognitive view of words as merely descriptive, in the ancient world words of honor were perceived as actually building others up and words of shame as tearing them down. Nehemiah's Memoir as a whole can be seen as his account of the resolution of the issues of honor and shame. Further, the building up of the Judeans' honor *reversed* their own shame, and simultaneously cast shame upon their adversaries (note italicized words):

> So the wall was *finished*, . . . and when our enemies *heard of it*, *all the nations around us were afraid and fell greatly in their own esteem*, for they *saw* that this work had been *accomplished* with the *help of our God*. (Neh 6:16; compare 5:9)

Nehemiah's autobiography emerges out of his vision of the grand scale of his mission. In a series of statements he recounts his achievements, calling to mind the language of Psalms and royal inscriptions, and also the Egyptian reformer Udjahorresnet's autobiographical inscription mentioned above. In addition, the combination of urgency, outrage, and a sense of personal burden for the deliverance of others can be compared to figures like Paul. In fact, the self-images of Nehemiah and Paul are surprisingly similar (Neh 13:10–31). Nehemiah assumes the authority of the

true believer and acts with absolute conviction that he is God's chosen in-
strument. Says Japhet: "Even the struggle between the people of Judah
and their adversaries becomes in the story of Nehemiah a struggle between Nehemiah himself and his enemies. . . . "[30] Likewise, when Nehemiah discovers that Tobiah the Ammonite was living in quarters in the
temple, he says:

> I returned to Jerusalem and discovered the wrong that the high priest had
> done on behalf of Tobiah. . . . I became very angry, and threw all the house-
> hold furniture of Tobiah out of the room. Then I gave orders and they
> cleansed the chambers, and I brought back the vessels of the house of God
> and the offerings. (13:7–9)

Nehemiah's methods are strident and intense, even violent. When he condemns the men who had married foreign women, he reports: "I con-
tended with them and cursed them and beat some of them and pulled out
their hair" (Neh 13:25). The difference in tone between the Ezra Memoir
and the Nehemiah Memoir can be summed up in this: Ezra pulls out his
own hair; Nehemiah pulls out the hair of others.[31] But in each of Nehemiah's conflicts, one wonders whether the threat is magnified in order
to justify his own response.

Part of the believable, realistic detail of the Nehemiah Memoir lies in
the fact that his power struggle is no longer with nameless groups on the
periphery of Judah. There is more specificity to his descriptions of conflict. His main battles are with three named men who would seem *at first*
to represent the foreign nations to the north, the east, and the south: Sanballat the Horonite, Tobiah the Ammonite, and Geshem the Arab. But despite Nehemiah's insistence on constantly referring to them by these foreign ethnic markers, the first two have strong Judean connections.
Sanballat was governor of Beyond the River (or Samaria), and was evidently an Israelite who worshiped Yahweh; his children had names compounded with Yahweh, and his daughter married the grandson of the
Jerusalem high priest (Neh 13:28). Yet Nehemiah contemptuously refers
to him in almost every instance as a "Horonite," which probably means
one from Beth-horon, just north of the boundary between Israel and Judah, ten miles from Jerusalem. His use of the title Horonite has the effect
of pushing Sanballat over an imaginary border as well. To Nehemiah, he
is not Sanballat the Israelite or Sanballat the Samarian or even Sanballat
the governor of Beyond the River; he is Sanballat the Horonite. An ambiguous figure is redefined as Other (Theorem 7).

The same redefinition of ethnic identity likely occurred with Tobiah.
This figure has a name compounded with Yahweh ("My good is Yah,"
that is, "My welfare is with Yahweh"), and was related by marriage to

several Judean leaders (Neh 6:18). He was evidently the head of a wealthy Jewish trading family that moved between Jerusalem and Ammon—thus "the Ammonite." We hear about this family in later texts, records, and inscriptions, and in all of these later references the family is considered quite "Judean" and continues using names compounded with Yahweh.[32] Thus Nehemiah has pushed this figure as well over an imaginary border to give him a foreign, rather than Judean identity, which Nehemiah insists on mentioning constantly. Of the three foreign-sounding opponents of Nehemiah, therefore, only Geshem the Arab, the governor or puppet king of Kedar in Arabia, is truly a foreigner. While Ezra may have redefined some worshipers of God as foreign, Nehemiah almost assuredly does so in the case of Sanballat and Tobiah.

Nehemiah, like Ezra, attempted to purify the body of the Judean community by forbidding marriage with non-Judeans, and provides a much more specific picture of his activities. Rather than associate the wives broadly with a mythologized list of nations as Ezra did, Nehemiah provides details of the women's ethnic origins:

> I saw Judeans who had married women of Ashdod, Ammon, and Moab, and half of their children spoke the language of Ashdod, and they could not speak the language of Judah. . . . I made them take an oath in the name of God, saying, "You shall not give your daughters to their sons, or take their daughters for your sons or for yourselves." (13:23, 25)

To be sure, Ammonites and Moabites had become bywords for contemporary neighbors who were like the pre-Israelite peoples, but Ashdod was not used in the stereotyped lists, and it is mentioned here first. The Ashdodite accents of the children resonate as an authentic detail in the picture. Nehemiah also recognizes the *Realpolitik* of foreign traders and officials. As was the case in Ezra 1–6 (but not in the Ezra Memoir), people from Tyre and Sidon here conduct trade in Jerusalem. Later a concern will be raised that they are entering into the gates to sell their wares on the Sabbath, but no objection is raised to the presence of these people on days other than the Sabbath, and the relations actually seem quite businesslike. Further, there is no sense that it is *their* abomination for violating Judean law, but rather the Judeans' for allowing it. At Nehemiah 5:17 the author also mentions, without any reservation or embarrassment, that he hosts foreign visitors at his table. Thus a double distinction can be drawn between the Nehemiah Memoir and the Ezra Memoir. First, the Nehemiah Memoir defined the foreign women in terms of real foreign groups and not in terms of a mythologized list of foreign nations, and second, the potentially ambiguous category of craftsmen of Tyre and Sidon and visiting foreigners appears in the Nehemiah Memoir, but not in the Ezra Memoir.

The Ezra Memoir could construct the Other in an ideal state and omit any reference to acceptable foreigners, but the Nehemiah Memoir describes both the acceptable and unacceptable foreigners in a more realistic way.

THE EXPULSION OF FOREIGN WOMEN:
ECONOMIC AND SOCIOLOGICAL BACKGROUND

A number of scholars have attempted to reconstruct the sociological factors that led to the prohibition of intermarriage and the expulsion of the foreign women and their children. There are two aspects of inheritance that are sometimes adduced to explain the motivations of the returnees' reform program. If women who married inherited family property, then the potential loss of property to the foreign women might have been significant, but that is probably not the case here. In biblical law women could only inherit under exceptional circumstances, and property could not be alienated from the tribe (Num 36:1–12). Yet it is possible that inheritance through the male line, the traditional practice in Judah and Israel before the exile, was not universal in post-exilic Judah. Surrounding peoples might therefore have been opposed to Ezra's and Nehemiah's reforms precisely because the alliances they had forged through marriage with Judean leaders were being dissolved. This remains a faint possibility, but another economic dynamic is somewhat more likely. A century earlier, when the leaders of Judean society were first exiled, their land rights would have likely been forfeited to those who remained.[33] This latter group entered into marriage alliances with people of "Greater Israel," alliances that were considered acceptable at the time. In insisting that these alliances be severed, the returnees were trying to dissolve the hold on power, wealth, and land rights that those who remained had amassed, and reassert their own claims to the land.

It is also possible that the expulsion of foreign women is not itself an economic issue, even if economic and political concerns drive the larger party conflicts. In times of crisis, anxiety over group identity gives rise to more rigid boundary definitions through strict endogamy. The reforms of Ezra and Nehemiah attempted to clarify group boundaries as a response to anxiety over identity.[34] The "foreign women" may in fact have not been foreign at all. Eskenazi and Eleanore Judd consider a number of possibilities of the women's identity: non-exiled Judeans, northern Israelites, foreign women, or Judean women with foreign practices.[35] They compare the situation of the ancient *haredim* to modern ultra-orthodox *Haredim*, and point out that in the sectarian culture of the modern *Haredim* marriage to a non-*Haredi* Jew is considered a mixed marriage. We are in the end left without enough data to determine the ethnic identity of the foreign women in Ezra-Nehemiah. Be that as it may, however, there is still the underlying problem that strict endogamy based on religious group sounds offensive to many modern readers, exclusive and not inclusive. But strict entrance requirements are typical of the demand for perfection found in most religious movements, and they are part of early Christianity as well (Matt 18:17, 1 Cor 5:11, 2 Cor 6:14–7:1, *Barnabas* 4:2). One might counter that preferential marriage based on behavior is not the same as that based on race or ethnic group, but *any* community that practices preferential endogamy for *any* reason will, after a generation or two, become an ethnic group, and Christianity very quickly took on the terms and ideals of an ethnic group.[36] "Marrying within the faith" is the preferred endogamy of most religious groups, certainly sectarian religious groups. Baptists would not be Baptists without preferred endogamy.

Many scholars have also condemned the divorce and exclusion of the foreign wives and children because it would have left these people vulnerable. The prohibition of intermarriage in Ezra 9:1–2 might have looked different if it were merely a law for all subsequent marriages and did not involve the dissolution of existing marriages and the expulsion of women and children. If the 113 wives expelled were wealthy—and Ezra would not have been likely to scrutinize their status if they were poor—they may have been re-assimilated into their fathers' houses. We have no way of knowing what became of the wives and children, although their exposure to a very vulnerable existence is quite possible. This has called forth searching reflections by scholars, two of which may be considered here. First, Tamara Cohn Eskenazi:

> Recent studies of the postexilic Judahite community link religious concerns with socioeconomic ones. . . . [M]arriage with outsiders spells loss of land to the Jewish province. . . . An opposition to foreign women is thus understood not as a misogynist restriction but rather a defense of the rights of women in the community against outside competition and therefore a matter of maintaining communal cohesiveness and continuity.[37]

Second, D. J. A. Clines:

> Many modern readers . . . will be appalled by the personal misery brought into so many families by the compulsory divorce of foreign wives, and will be outraged at Ezra's insistence on racial purity, so uncongenial to modern liberal thought. . . . Is there not . . . a strong "racialist" motive behind the divorce of foreign wives? That can hardly be denied, but the defense of the "holy race" is engaged in more strictly on religious grounds than has been the case with most so-called "religious" persecutions and wars. . . . But when all is said and done, there is no denying that the breaking up of families was a horrible thing.[38]

In both cases there is an admirable effort to weigh both sides of the moral judgment carefully, and yet they each ultimately emphasize different conclusions. What may lie behind the difference is the minority religion/ majority religion perspective of the Jewish and Christian authors respectively. The greatest threat to minority religions is often not persecution but assimilation through intermarriage. For people of the majority religion, however, such as Christians in North America and Europe, intermarriage is not generally perceived as a threat. Since the majority religion is the default value of a society, intermarriage is even a boon in terms of the "market share" of their religion in society as a whole. Over time intermarriage cancels out minority religions, but not the majority religion. The moral interpretation of Ezra-Nehemiah, then, becomes a referendum on the question of inclusiveness/exclusiveness in the present world, where the inclusive mission of Christianity has traditionally been understood to mean that other religions, including Judaism, will disappear in God's good time (Eph 2:15–16). The inclusiveness of Christianity is achieved only through the erasing of other religions.[39]

In addition to Eskenazi, other scholars have defended the reforms of Ezra-Nehemiah. Paul Hanson argues that this reform and clarification of boundaries was necessary at a time of crisis to reestablish integrity within Judean society. Without these reforms, Judah would have "been assimilated to its religiocultural environment, much like the Jewish community of Elephantine (a Jewish military colony in Egypt)."[40] But this presumes that the authentic core of Judean identity was the one that emerged victorious from the political struggles in Jerusalem, and that the "religiocultural environment" was a sort of background static into which Israelite religion was on the verge of dissolving (Theorem 6: Other distorted, ironically in this case in a "typical" direction). The Samarian Israelite community, however, survived as Samaritans alongside Judeans, and has continued until today. Throughout history, in every religion, orthodox definitions arise out of elements that originally entered through mixing, yesterday's mixing becoming today's orthodoxy. Further, the returnees themselves *had already mixed* with their environment in Babylon and Persia. It is probable, for example, that the returnees' emphasis on law and purity results, not from native Judean tradition, but from the centrality of these very elements *in Persian theology* (Theorem 8: Origins of practices reassigned). Nativist revivals, a subset of revitalization movements, often unknowingly redefine the colonizer's culture as native. This irony of identity is stated well by Esther Benbassa and Jean-Christophe Attias:

> Is there a single period in Jewish history when the Jews did not embrace, in one way or another, openly or covertly, the achievements of an essentially

"foreign" wisdom? . . . What is more "Spanish" than Spanish Judaism? What, in a later period, was more "Italian" than Italian Judaism, more "French" than French Judaism, more "German" than German Judaism?[41]

Jews around the world today are different precisely because they have evolved in response to their environments, and it is the Persian values in Ezra-Nehemiah that contributed so much to the rise of a new Jewish identity. If we consider also the Persian values brought by the returnees—state literacy, immutable law, loyalty to the Persian king—we may imagine the returnees bringing an ideal of "civilization" to a region that was "tribal," people of the land.

TERMS FOR WE AND OTHER

In each of the three sections, the Other and We are recast in a way that privileges the perspective of those returning from exile in Babylon, but there are significant differences among the sections as well. We may examine this more closely by considering the terms that are used to describe We and Other (see table 3.1).

Although some terms for We and Other appear in different sections, each of the sources remains surprisingly distinct. Ezra 1–6 uses a variety of terms for We and Other, but none of them often enough to take on any special significance.[42] The Ezra Memoir, on the other hand, emphasized

Table 3.1.   Significant Occurrences of Terms for We and Other in Sections of Ezra-Nehemiah

	Terms for We	Terms for Other	Are Outsiders Recognized?
Ezra 1–6	Israel *golah* (rarely) people of Judah	adversaries people of the land	those who join recognized (Ezra 6:21)

Ezra Memoir	Israel
	golah (often)
	kol ha`am
	   "all the people"
	qahal
	   "congregation"
	haredim
	   "quakers"
		list of nations
		people of the land
		"to separate" (*bdl*)
			outsiders not recognized

Nehemiah Memoir	Israel Judah Judeans	*goyim* "nations" named individuals	craftsmen from Tyre and Sidon accepted

particular terms for We and Other to such an extent that they become fixed expressions here and in later Judaism. This leads us to an important observation: *many of the themes that are traditionally associated with Ezra-Nehemiah as a whole are actually found almost entirely in the Ezra Memoir.* This is especially the case with three of the most important terms for the We: "those who tremble" (*haredim*), the "exiles" (*golah*), and "congregation" (*qahal*). The Ezra Memoir invests *golah* with a significance beyond what is found in Ezra 1–6: "children of the *golah*" sometimes become simply "the *golah*" (Ezra 9:4, 10:6). The community that was formed *outside* the land of origin becomes stronger than the one that remained in the land. For the We the Ezra Memoir also often uses the phrase "all the people" (*kol ha`am*); it is found in the covenant renewal ceremony in the Ezra Memoir, especially in Nehemiah 8. The fixed phrase is used as a liturgical term for the congregation gathered to hear and respond to the worship of God, and is also a constitutional term—the people as a whole standing in covenant with God. *Qahal*, which had already been used in earlier biblical texts for the congregation of Israel (Deut 23:3–8), likewise takes on an even stronger significance in the Ezra Memoir as a special term for the congregation of Israel, come together in worship before God. Those who are part of the *golah* or returnee community are gathered into a *qahal* or congregation, which is constituted by covenant renewal ceremonies in which all returnees sign on and promise to keep the law of Moses. One particular verse sums up the ideology of community formation in the Ezra Memoir:

> And whoever would not come within three days [to expel his foreign wife], by order of the officials and elders, all his property would be placed under the ban [*herem* root], and he himself expelled from the congregation [*qahal*] of the exiles [*golah*]. (Ezra 10:8)

Thus the ones who do not join the redefined community and expel their foreign wives will in turn be expelled and treated like the nations on the land at the time of the conquest: their property will be placed under the ban (*herem*). Similarly, the fixed phrase "peoples of the land" also provided a potent label for the Other, played out in a list of nations in three categories: legendary nations of the land, contemporary neighbors, and great empires (Ezra 9:1). The source that has the most idealized constitution of the We, the Ezra Memoir, also has the most mythologized definition of Other.

The Nehemiah Memoir introduces its own vocabulary. It does mention Jerusalem often, even obsessively, but never with a fixed phrase; it is much more likely to mention the walls, gates, or physical aspects of the city. Above all the terms that the Nehemiah Memoir prefers for the reform group are "Judah" and "Judeans." The term "Judah" is used sparingly in Ezra 1–6 and the Ezra Memoir, and "Judean," *Yehudi*, is never used by them. This gives rise to another important observation: *these most obvious of terms, Judah and Judean, the terms used by later Jews and scholars alike to describe the insiders, were not the self-identifier of the community in Ezra 1–6 and the Ezra Memoir. In the Nehemiah Memoir, however, Judah and Judean occur over thirty times.* There is a heightened sense of the term that *affirms* group identity. The first usages in the Nehemiah Memoir are particularly telling, in that they are introduced both in the mouth of the opponents *and* Nehemiah as a rallying identity marker, in the very chapter (Neh 4) we have noted earlier as obsessed with honor and shame. The terms "Judah" and "Judean" are also used very pointedly in this chapter as a contrasted identity to the series of itemized and ethnicized enemies, Sanballat the Horonite, Tobiah the Ammonite, Arabs, Ammonites, and Ashdodites (compare also 12:31, 44; 13:12). The same sort of heightened sense of Judean, an identity affirmation over and above a merely ethnic-geographical marker, may also be reflected in a text written at about this time, Zechariah:[43]

> In those days ten men from nations of every language shall take hold of a Judean, grasping his garment and saying, "Let us go with you, for we have heard that God is with you." (8: 23)

So whereas the use of "Judah" may be expected—after all, "Israel and Judah" were old terms for the north and south—its use here together with *Yehudi*, Judean, takes on a stronger sense: the "temple community." The heightened sense of identity may signal the rousing of the revitalization movement that lies behind these texts. In the introduction we saw that concepts of nation begin with a *Volk* and posit a primordial people as ancestors. In the Nehemiah Memoir and Zechariah 8, "Judah" is coupled with a new term, "Judean," to construct before our eyes a social memory of something that, in postmodernist terms, was later assumed to be "always already there."

The difference is subtle but significant. Cohen argues that the word that we translate "Judean" or "Jew" (Hebrew *Yehudi*, Greek *Ioudaios*) originally only bore a geographical sense of "one from Judah."[44] As such, it could also be an ethnic marker; outsiders would see one from Judah as belonging to a different ethnic group, a Judean. Later, in the aftermath of the Maccabean Revolt in the second century BCE, it developed in addition a "cultural-religious" meaning to connote a believer in the religion centered in Judah or Judea, that is, a "Jew." Although I agree in general with his conclusions, he actually says little about the early uses of *Yehudi* in the Hebrew Bible. I would modify his distinction in this way: at times the earlier usage can include, in the mind of a reformer like Nehemiah or a prophet like Zechariah, a heightened ethnic sense or a communal identity before God that has meaning as a group-identifier beyond a strictly geographical sense. This ethnic sense is so heightened and so associated specifically with the reversal of shame that it approaches the cultural-religious; the *strength* or *emotive* nature of the affirmation trumps the cognitive reference of the word; it means "Judean!" If we may call Cohen's two meanings Judean-1 (ethnic-geographical) and Judean-2 (cultural-religious), then the term in Nehemiah 4 and Zechariah 8 is perhaps Judean-1b: ethnic-geographical as a heightened expression of community identity that reverses shame.[45] Thus, Nehemiah's construction of Judean as We against the outsiders was so strong that it takes on a more powerful communal resonance. And yet, we should not be tempted to push the meaning of Judean here from 1b to 2, a cultural-religious confession. The motive force in Nehemiah's heightened sense of Judean identity is still "ethnic."

The terms for Other in the Nehemiah Memoir correspond to this. Unlike the Ezra Memoir, the Nehemiah Memoir never uses the generalized and mythologized phrase "peoples of the land" for the Other. In addition to the older term *goyim*, "nations," opponents of Nehemiah, are listed as individuals, Sanballat, Tobiah, Geshem, and as we saw, he *ethnicizes* these figures, calling them the Horonite, the Ammonite, and the Arab. Further, he also brings to grief another named ethnic group, the Ashdodites. As a result, Nehemiah does not evoke mythologized categories for Other, but opposes Judeans to specific, named individuals and ethnic groups.

CONCLUSION

The three sections of Ezra-Nehemiah have much in common in terms of the construction of the We and the Other. Following the cataclysmic changes of the defeat and deportations of the exile, these sections are all written from the point of view of those who see the core of God's restored community as those who returned from captivity. In addition, all three sections present a narrative arc of opposition-and-identity. The We of ideal Israel is constituted in response to the Other. Each of the three sections of Ezra-Nehemiah also culminates with the institution of an important aspect of Judean religious life. Ezra 1–6 concludes with the construction of the temple, the Ezra Memoir with the reading of the law and the establishment of the newly constituted congregation, and the Nehemiah Memoir with the construction of the walls of Jerusalem. Further, in each case one or more religious rituals are enacted to celebrate the achievement. We may thus posit some unity of vision to Ezra-Nehemiah as a whole, but it appears that the three different sections do not use the same terms for the in-group and out-group, and when they do use the same terms, it is often in different ways. Each of the three sections seems to reflect a slightly different period in the reform process and a different emphasis in regard to who the Other is and how the We will be named. In Ezra 1–6, the more utopian section, the opponents are limited to those from the Samarian province of Beyond the River, and there is no sense that the community in Jerusalem needs to be purged. In the Ezra Memoir, however, this is reversed; there is no mention of external elements at all, and the officials from Beyond the River seem to be *supportive* of the reform. All of the conflicts in this section appear to be between the reformers and those in Jerusalem who resist reform, the "people of the land." The Ezra Memoir uses language of divorce and separation from the internal Other (using the *bdl* root, "to separate"), and borrows the language of abominations from the Holiness Source.[46] The newly defined We is named in a new way, as *haredim* (quakers), *golah* (returnees), and *qahal* (congregation). The third section, the Nehemiah Memoir, also gives expression to a polarized point of view, but with more realistic detail and with less reliance on mythologized categories. The Other is identified with a series of named individuals and more clearly demarcated groups, and to name the We the Nehemiah Memoir uses the terms "Judah" and "Judean" with a new emphasis that reverses shame. It is only in the Ezra Memoir that we find two of the most significant identifiers of We and Other, *qahal* (congregation) and "people of the land," but the Nehemiah Memoir gives us the most common group-identifier of all: Judean.

NOTES

1. Hans M. Barstad, *The Myth of the Empty Land: A Study in the History and Archaeology of Judah during the "Exilic" Period* (Oslo/Cambridge: Scandinavian University Press, 1996). Yehezkel Kaufmann, *History of the Religion of Israel IV: From the Babylonian Captivity to the End of Prophecy* (New York: Ktav, 1977), 197–201, argues that the land actually was decimated, and therefore virtually empty at the time of the return. A less-extreme position is defended by David Vanderhooft, *The Neo-Babylonian Empire and Babylon in the Latter Prophets* (Atlanta, GA: Scholars Press, 1999), and Charles E. Carter, *The Emergence of Yehud in the Persian Period: A Social and Demographic Study* (Sheffield, UK: Sheffield Academic Press, 1999).

2. Tamara Cohn Eskenazi, *In an Age of Prose: A Literary Approach to Ezra-Nehemiah* (Atlanta, GA: Scholars, 1988), 1–2; Sara Raup Johnson, *Historical Fictions and Hellenistic Jewish Identity: Third Maccabees in Its Cultural Context* (Berkeley: University of California Press, 2004); Sara Raup Johnson, "Novelistic Elements in Esther: Persian or Hellenistic, Jewish or Greek?" *Catholic Biblical Quarterly* 67 (2005): 571–89.

3. Wilhelm Th. In der Smitten, *Esra: Quellen, Überlieferung, und Geschichte* (Assen, Netherlands: Van Gorcum, 1973), 88, although Joseph Blenkinsopp,

Ezra-Nehemiah (Philadelphia: Westminster, 1988), 45–46, still maintains that the Ezra material is based on a memoir.

4. Eskenazi, *In an Age of Prose*; Lawrence M. Wills, *The Jew in the Court of the Foreign King: Ancient Jewish Court Legends* (Minneapolis, MN: Fortress, 1990), passim; Jon L. Berquist, *Judaism in Persia's Shadow: A Social and Historical Approach* (Minneapolis, MN: Fortress, 1995).

5. The order and date of the missions of Ezra and Nehemiah are not certain, but here I follow the order of Ezra in 454 BCE and Nehemiah in 446.

6. Morton Smith, *Palestinian Parties and Politics That Shaped the Old Testament* (New York and London: Columbia University Press, 1971).

7. Joseph Blenkinsopp, "A Jewish Sect of the Persian Period," *Catholic Biblical Quarterly* 52 (1990): 5–20; Blenkinsopp, *Ezra-Nehemiah*, 178–79; Blenkinsopp, "The 'Servants of the Lord' in Third Isaiah: Profile of a Pietistic Group in the Persian Period," *Proceedings of the Irish Biblical Association* 7 (1983): 1–23; and Albert I. Baumgarten, *The Flourishing of Jewish Sects in the Maccabean Era: An Interpretation* (Leiden, Netherlands: Brill, 1997).

8. Anthony F. C. Wallace, "Nativism and Revivalism," *International Encyclopedia of the Social Sciences*, ed. David L. Sills (New York: Macmillan and Free Press, 1968), 11:75–80; Anthony F. C. Wallace, "Revitalization Movements," *American Anthropologist* 58 (1956): 264–68; Kenelm Burridge, "Revival and Renewal," *Encyclopedia of Religion*, ed. Mircea Eliade, 16 vols. (New York: Macmillan, 1987), 12:368–74; James A. Beckford, "New Religions," *Encyclopedia of Religion*, 10:390. The broad term "revitalization movements" includes some millenarian groups, utopian communities, revivalist movements, and also nativist movements that reject alien or colonial cultures. Kenneth D. Tollefson and H. G. M. Williamson, "Nehemiah as Cultural Revitalization," *JSOT* 56 (1992): 41–68, look for more specificity than the sources allow. Here I have distinguished sect from revitalization movement, but one might also define sect somewhat differently. Bryan Wilson, *Magic and the Millennium: A Sociological Study of Religious Movements of Protest among Tribal and Third-World Peoples* (London: Heinemann, 1973), 18–30, has divided sects into seven types, one of which, the reformist sect, is similar to the revitalization movement.

9. Shemaryahu Talmon, "The Emergence of Jewish Sectarianism in the Early Second Temple Period," in *King, Cult and Calendar in Ancient Israel: Collected Studies* (Jerusalem: Magnes, 1986), 165–201.

10. Joseph Blenkinsopp, "The Mission of Udjahorresnet," *Journal of Biblical Literature* 106 (1987): 409–10; Joseph Blenkinsopp, "The Nehemiah Autobiography," in *Language, Theology and the Bible: Essays in Honor of James Barr*, ed. Samuel Balentine and John Barton (Oxford: Clarendon; New York: Oxford University Press, 1994), 199–212. On the Persian political developments, see Berquist, *Judaism in Persia's Shadow*; Kenneth G. Hoglund, *Achaemenid Imperial Administration in Syria-Palestine and the Missions of Ezra and Nehemiah* (Atlanta, GA: Scholars Press, 1992); and David Vanderhooft, "New Evidence Pertaining to the Transition from Neo-Babylonian to Achaemenid Administration in Palestine," in *Yahwism after the Exile*, ed. Rainer Albertz and Bob Becking (Assen, Netherlands: Van Gorcum, 2003), 219–35.

11. On literary sources, see Blenkinsopp, *Ezra-Nehemiah*, 41–47; H. G. M. Williamson, *Ezra, Nehemiah* (Waco, TX: Word, 1985), xxiii–xxxv; H. G. M.

Williamson, "The Composition of Ezra i–vi," *JTS* 33 (1983): 1–30; Sara Japhet, "Sheshbazzar and Zerubbabel—Against the Background of the Historical and Religious Tendencies of Ezra-Nehemiah," *ZAW* (Part 1) 94 (1982): 66–98, esp. 88; (Part 2) 95 (1983): 218–30.

12. Jonathan Z. Smith, "Differential Equations: On Constructing the Other," in *Relating Religion: Essays in the Study of Religion* (Chicago: University of Chicago Press, 2004), 236–37. See also Edmund Leach, "Anthropological Aspects of Language: Animal Categories and Verbal Abuse," in *Reader in Comparative Religion: An Anthropological Approach*, ed. William Lessa and Evon Vogt (New York: Harper & Row, 1979), 153–65. Mu-chou Poo, *Enemies of Civilization: Attitudes toward Foreigners in Ancient Mesopotamia, Egypt, and China* (Albany: State University of New York, 2005), 41, points out that in both Akkadian and ancient Chinese the word for geographically marginal people is generalized to become a negative adjective.

13. Lester Grabbe, *Ezra-Nehemiah* (London/New York: Routledge, 1998), 162–63.

14. Hindy Najman, "Ezra," in *The Jewish Study Bible*, ed. Adele Berlin and Marc Zvi Brettler (Oxford: Oxford University Press, 2004), 1669–70.

15. Sara Japhet, "People and Land in the Restoration Period," in *Das Land Israel in biblischer Zeit*, ed. Georg Strecker (Göttingen, Germany: Vandenhoeck & Ruprecht, 1983), 105. See Jer 41:4–10, Tobit 1–2.

16. Japhet, "People and Land," 105.

17. Japhet, "People and Land," esp. 112–15. See also Blenkinsopp, *Ezra-Nehemiah*, 52; Smith, *Palestinian Parties and Politics*, 113–14.

18. Blenkinsopp, *Ezra-Nehemiah*, 133, is more positive on the openness to converting outsiders.

19. Eskenazi, *In an Age of Prose*, 37.

20. See also Japhet, "People and Land," 114–15. The only place in the earlier biblical texts where this combination of three categories appears is 1 Kings 11, which is an insertion that counters and corrects the positive portrayal of Solomon in 1 Kings 3–10. Not present in the parallel section of 2 Chronicles, this section could have been a very late addition to the Deuteronomistic History. See Michael Fishbane, *Biblical Interpretation in Ancient Israel* (Oxford: Clarendon; New York: Oxford University Press, 1985), 125–26; and Blenkinsopp, *Ezra-Nehemiah*, 175. Following the lead of most commentators, I prefer the reading of Edomites (from 1 Esdras) to Amorites as found in the Masoretic Text; see Japhet, "People and Land," 124 n. 55, and Blenkinsopp, *Ezra-Nehemiah*, 174.

21. Shaye J. D. Cohen, *The Beginnings of Jewishness: Boundaries, Varieties, Uncertainties* (Berkeley and Los Angeles: University of California Press, 1999), 203–307.

22. Jonathan Klawans, *Impurity and Sin in Ancient Judaism* (Oxford: Oxford University Press, 2000), 44–45.

23. Christine Hayes, *Gentile Impurities and Jewish Identities: Intermarriage and Conversion from the Bible to the Talmud* (Oxford: Oxford University Press, 2002), 7–8, 27, 30–34, 68: gentiles are not polluting but mundane, while true Israelites— "Judeans"—are now as holy as priests. See also James Kugel, "The Holiness of Israel and the Land in Second Temple Times," in *Texts, Temples, and Traditions: A Tribute to Menachem Haran*, ed. Michael V. Fox et al. (Winona Lake, IN: Eisenbrauns, 1996); Martha Himmelfarb, "'A Kingdom of Priests': The Democratization of the Priesthood in the Literature of Second Temple Judaism," *Journal of Jewish Thought*

and Philosophy 6 (1997): 89–102. Saul Olyan, *Rites and Rank: Hierarchy in Biblical Rep-resentations of Cult* (Princeton, NJ: Princeton University Press, 2000), 40, 48–51, 67–68, 82–84, 93–94, disagreed, but see Olyan's later discussion, "Purity Ideology in Ezra-Nehemiah as a Tool to Reconstruct the Community," *Journal for the Study of Judaism* 35 (2004): 1–16.

24. Hayes, *Gentile Impurities*, 30–31; Olyan, *Rites and Rank*. I have greatly sim-plified the searching arguments of Olyan, Klawans, Hayes, Kugel, and others, and chosen what to me seem to be more intuitive English words for the categories. Note that Daniel Boyarin ("The *Ioudaioi* in John and the Prehistory of 'Judaism,'" in *Pauline Conversations in Context: Essays in Honor of Calvin J. Roetzel*, ed. Janice Capel Anderson, Philip Sellew, and Claudia Setzer [London: Sheffield Academic Press, 2002], 216–39) follows Talmon ("Emergence") in describing the reformers' endogamy quite differently. While the scholars above argue that (1) formerly, priests could not marry women from non-priestly families, but (2) now "all Israel" is held to the standard of priests, Talmon and Boyarin argue that (1) formerly all marriages of Israelites with non-Israelites were forbidden, but (2) now non-returnees count as non-Israelites. It appears that the former scholars are outlining an etic (outsider's perspective) theory of what was actually going on, and Talmon and Boyarin an emic (insider's perspective) theory of how it must have been in-terpreted by the reforming party.

25. Fishbane, *Biblical Interpretation*, 115–19, 143. Fishbane's more detailed analy-sis also brings in Leviticus 18:24–30.

26. See Paul D. Hanson, *The People Called: The Growth of Community in the Bible* (San Francisco: Harper & Row, 1986), 293, on the constitutional aspect of Ezra's reform, and cf. the reception of the Book of the Law or Book of the Covenant in 2 Kings 22–23.

27. Shaye J. D. Cohen, *From the Maccabees to the Mishnah* (Philadelphia: West-minster, 1987), 138; see also Kugel, "Holiness of Israel"; Hanson, *People Called*, 293; Tamara Cohn Eskenazi, "Ezra-Nehemiah," in *Women's Bible Commentary*, ed. Carol A. Newsom and Sharon H. Ringe (Louisville, KY: Westminster/John Knox, 1992); and Lawrence M. Wills, "Ascetic Theology before Asceticism? Jew-ish Narratives and the Decentering of the Self," *JAAR* 74 (2006): 902–25. But Marc Zvi Brettler can also assert that "Judaism" predates Ezra: "Judaism in the Hebrew Bible? The Transition from Ancient Israelite Religion to Judaism," *Catholic Biblical Quarterly* 61 (1999): 429–47.

28. David Lambert argues rightly that fasting is originally a visible sign of grief to attract God's attention, and is not a sign of contrition or penitence; it is expres-sive rather than reflective ("Fasting as a Penitential Rite: A Biblical Phenomenon," *Harvard Theological Review* 96 [2003]: 477–512). This is the case in Neh 1:3–4, but in the Ezra Memoir there is a connection between fasting and confession. See also Blenkinsopp, *Ezra-Nehemiah*, 168, 177, 179; Wills, "Ascetic Theology." This issue will re-emerge in chapter five.

29. In der Smitten, *Esra*, 69–74; Grabbe, *Ezra-Nehemiah*, 160.

30. Japhet, "Sheshbazzar and Zerubbabel," 87.

31. I am indebted to a former student, Alexis Berko, for this observation.

32. Lawrence M. Wills, *The Jewish Novel in the Ancient World* (Ithaca, NY: Cornell University Press, 1995), 72, 187–93.

33. Paula McNutt, *Reconstructing the Society of Ancient Israel* (London: SPCK; Louisville, KY: Westminster/John Knox, 1999), 198. Cf. Exod 11:15.

34. Olyan, *Rites and Rank*, 160 n. 78, notes that it is not just ambiguity in marriage that is eliminated. The *ger* or resident alien is never mentioned in Ezra-Nehemiah because this would imply that there are shades of gray in the definition of We and Other. See also Jon L. Berquist, *Controlling Corporeality: The Body and the Household in Ancient Israel* (New Brunswick, NJ, and London: Rutgers University Press, 2002), 135–61. It is also likely that the old preferred endogamy based on the *mishpachah* or extended family was dissolved by Ezra and Nehemiah in favor of a new endogamy of those recognized as Judeans; see Berquist, *Controlling*, 157, and Herbert Niehr, "The Changed Status of the Dead in Yehud," in Albertz and Becking, eds., *Yahwism after the Exile*, 152.

35. Tamara Cohn Eskenazi and Eleanore Judd, "Married to a Stranger in Ezra 9–10," in *Second Temple Studies: 2. Temple and Community in the Persian Period*, ed. Eskenazi and Kent H. Richards (Sheffield, UK: JSOT Press, 1994), 266–85; cf. also Esther Benbassa and Jean-Christophe Attias, *The Jew and the Other* (Ithaca, NY, and London: Cornell University Press, 2004), 106; Duane L. Smith-Christopher, "The Mixed Marriage Crisis in Ezra 9–10 and Nehemiah 13: A Study of the Sociology of the Post-Exile Judaean Community, " in Eskenazi and Richards, eds., *Second Temple Studies*, 243–65."

36. See the discussion in chapters five to seven, especially concerning the contributions of Denise Kimber Buell and Caroline Johnson Hodge. Gerd Lüdemann, *The Unholy in Holy Scripture: The Dark Side of the Bible* (Louisville, KY: Westminster John Knox, 1997), 74–75, misstates the situation drastically when he draws a line between the expulsions in Ezra-Nehemiah and the Nazis. A more meaningful comparison might be drawn between Ezra-Nehemiah and the reforms of Calvin, or any other strongly defined religious movement.

37. Eskenazi, "Ezra-Nehemiah," 120–21.

38. D. J. A. Clines, *Ezra, Nehemiah, and Esther* (Grand Rapids, MI: Eerdmans, 1984), 116. Even social-science approaches may reveal a condemnation of these texts. David Janzen applies the sociologically derived term "witch-hunt" to Ezra, even though the women and children do not have to be uncovered, and they are not executed (*Witch-Hunts, Purity and Social Boundaries: The Expulsion of the Foreign Women in Ezra 9–10* [Sheffield, UK: Sheffield Academic Press, 2002]). Would Calvin's purging of Geneva, in which people were actually executed, be called a witch-hunt? Janzen is to be congratulated for applying Mary Douglas' theory of grid and group (pp. 59–62), but whereas Janzen assumes that Ezra reflects a low-grid, strong-group outlook, I would argue that as a revitalization movement, the Ezra reform was more likely high-grid, strong-group.

39. It is this disturbing element that is overlooked in Steven McKenzie's otherwise excellent book, *All God's Children: A Biblical Critique of Racism* (Louisville, KY: Westminster John Knox, 1997). McKenzie brings forth as examples of inclusiveness the texts of Luke, Acts, and John, which are among the most dangerous texts in the New Testament in terms of preaching the error or even demonic nature of Judaism, and he also adds Ephesians 2, in which Judaism is said to disappear—although, to be fair, it should be noted that gentile religions either disappear or worship at Jerusalem in Jewish eschatology as well.

40. Hanson, *People Called*, 294–95. See also Smith-Christopher, "Mixed Marriage."

41. Benbassa and Attias, *Jew and the Other*, 52–53. See also Gerd Baumann, *Contesting Cultures: Discourses of Identity in Multi-Ethnic London* (Cambridge, UK, and New York: Cambridge University Press, 1996), 192–93; David M. Carr, *Writing on the Tablet of the Heart: Origins of Scripture and Literature* (Oxford and New York: Oxford University Press, 2005), 253–72.

42. "Israel" is an ideal term more than a nation with clear boundaries. It is never used in any section to refer to the ten northern tribes; that group is never named as such, even where we may suspect that they are present—Sanballat, for example. They have been written out of history, the "ten lost tribes of Israel."

43. Japhet, "People and Land," 110–11.

44. Cohen, *Beginnings of Jewishness*, 104–6; consider the earliest uses of *Yehudi*: 2 Kings 16:6, 25:25 and Jer 32:12, which all refer to those from Judah *while outside of Judah*; that is, it is an ethnic-geographical marker. See also John J. Collins, "Cult and Culture: The Limits of Hellenization in Judea," in *Hellenism in the Land of Israel*, ed. John J. Collins and Gregory E. Sterling (South Bend, IN: University of Notre Dame Press, 2001), 39.

45. Boyarin, "*Ioudaioi* in John," would also emphasize the heightened identity of Judean from the days of Ezra-Nehemiah, but although I agree with much of his reconstruction, I disagree with some of his conclusions. He applies Talmon's analysis ("Emergence") in the following way: the returning Judeans understand themselves as an inner group, a subset, even a sect within Israel, and this meaning continues down to the second century CE. This is conceivable, but I think unlikely. Above I argued that the reformers were trying to expand their influence to take over Judah, or actually, "Benjamin and Judah" (Samaria was not possible). Sect implies a consciousness of having been set apart, and Ezra-Nehemiah reflects a consciousness of taking over. Even if Boyarin's and Talmon's distinction holds for Ezra-Nehemiah, I question its applicability to later texts in chapters four and six.

46. Olyan, "Purity Ideology," 13–16.

4

❧

Judaism and Hellenism in 1 and 2 Maccabees

We have witnessed great changes in the construction of We and Other in Israelite and Judean texts; in 1 and 2 Maccabees new circumstances and new responses gave rise to even further changes in how the We and Other were conceived. These texts are the partisan accounts of the Maccabean Revolt, composed one or two generations after the events. When Alexander the Great, a Greek-Macedonian general, swept through the near east in 333–331 BCE, he ended the rule of the Persians, the empire that played such a strong role in supporting the activities of Ezra and Nehemiah. The Jerusalem temple administration was now under the wing of a western rather than an eastern empire, but why should life be any different? At first, there was little change. The Greek empire recognized local religions and political entities much as the Persians had before them. Jews seemed reconciled to the rule of the powerful Greek ruler, but by the beginning of the second century BCE things began to degenerate under Alexander's successors. Alexander's great world empire, which extended all the way from Greece in the west to India in the east, and southward to Egypt, could not remain under the control of one ruler. After his premature death at age thirty-three, his kingdom splintered into a number of parts, each under a different successor. For the region of Judah, now called in Greek *Ioudaia*, or Judea, the important successor kingdoms were the Seleucids in Asia Minor and the Ptolemies in Egypt. Judea lay at the boundary of these two competing kingdoms, under the rule of first one and then the other.

The reasons for the Maccabean Revolt must ultimately be sought in the new dimensions of Hellenistic colonization and empire. Some contextualizing will help. Before the Greeks, imperial domination meant that the conquered people had to pay taxes, remain loyal, and help fight wars, but they could maintain their own religious and cultural identity. Mode of worship was simply not an issue. The Greek ideal of rule, however, was also based on a model of Greek colonization. Greek city-states founded numerous colonies that were ruled according to the *nomima* or customs of the parent-city: the tribal structure, laws and constitution, rituals and religious calendar, and, increasingly, Greek education as a means of transforming local elites. The high ideals of Greek education slowly changed the upper classes of the ruled peoples and began to assimilate them to a new Hellenistic ideal, and they had to come to terms with Hellenistic culture. The transformation did not have to be thorough; it was only necessary for it to extend to public institutions. As Seth Schwartz argues, Hellenization could succeed across such a large area in so short a time because it "produced temporarily a gulf between public and private. . . . The prevailing definition of 'Greek' now became formal: a citizen of a city with a Greek constitution was Greek." Under Hellenistic rule, "being Greek changed."[1] When Alexander the Great and his successors established a large number of new cities in the east, or resettled old ones, they followed a set pattern for the creation of new city institutions. Each city was required to declare a *dēmos*, a list of aristocratic free male citizens; establish a *boulē* or city council of the leading citizens; and found a gymnasium and an ephebeum for the education and physical training of the aristocratic boys. Cities around Judea, such as Samaria and Scythopolis, were thus transformed, as were Paneion and Hippus, and Gadara to the east. Extracting taxes and soldiers was not enough for this new empire; altering the landscape by creating Greek cities was also required. It is no coincidence that Greek interest in ethnography precedes this transformation of foreign cultures. Greek "openness" to examining the meaning of others' cultures went hand-in-hand with a more thorough transformation of cultures than had been the case with previous empires, a relation of anthropology and colonization similar to that of the modern West.

The transformation of some eastern cities into Greek cities had produced economic boons, and enterprising aristocrats in Jerusalem had noticed this. There were aristocratic Jewish power brokers in Jerusalem who wanted to make sure that their city came into the modern age. An ambitious member of the Jerusalem priestly establishment, Jason, paid the Seleucid king Antiochus a huge sum of money for the right to become high priest, and then proceeded to initiate a necessary step for Jerusalem to become a Greek city: he built a gymnasium for the physical training of boys. Since the exercises were conducted in the nude, Jewish boys underwent operations to remove the signs of circumcision. The leading citizens of Jerusalem began to wear the broad-brimmed Greek hat associated with the god Hermes, and Jason also appealed successfully to Antiochus to enroll a group of the important men in Jerusalem as citizens of Antioch, the Seleucid capital. Just as myriad cities had formerly become colonies of the Greek city-states, Jerusalem became a colony of Antioch (2 Macc 4:9). The *nomima*, or customs and practices, of Antioch would become the *nomima* of Jerusalem. Throughout this period the new practices were not only imposed top-down by the Seleucid Greeks, but were readily adopted by many Jews eager to become citizens of a Hellenized Jerusalem (1 Macc 1:11, 43, 52). "Hellenism" represented an attractive, civilized model for society which many Jews embraced enthusiastically, and it proffered economic benefits on the city within the context of the Hellenistic empires. Those who embraced the institutions of the Greek polis were among the wealthiest citizens; those who did not would remain "metics" (*metoikoi*), or sub-citizens in the new order. (Compare the *ger* in the previous chapters.)

This gradual Hellenization would have probably progressed further had it not been for a new development. In 170 BCE the Seleucid Antiochus IV Epiphanes, who now ruled Judea, was threatened by the new world power arising in the west, Rome, and raised money by looting the Jerusalem temple of many of its gold furnishings. When he was rebuffed and humiliated by the Roman army, he returned and took even more extreme measures to curtail Jewish practices. The formerly voluntary program of Greek worship was now imposed violently, with much slaughter; Antiochus commenced one of the first religious persecutions in history. He banned the practices of Judaism—circumcision, study of Torah, Sabbath observance, Jewish holidays. He erected a fortress for his troops called Akra on the very edge of the temple grounds, and rededicated the temple to Zeus. He also instituted pig sacrifices and offerings to other deities in the temple, and set up altars in many of the cities for Greek sacrifices. The "positive" ideal of Antiochus Epiphanes should be noted; imposing Greek culture was understood as civilizing people and bringing different cultures into one interdependent world culture, a form of Greek universalism. The later Roman historian Tacitus would say that Antiochus had tried to improve Jerusalem, but failed (*Histories* 5.8).

The Hellenistic reform was to reconstitute the city as a Greek city, specifically a colonial city of Antioch, the Seleucid capital (2 Macc 4:9); the Mosaic constitutional elements were banned, the Greek imposed. The typically Greek elements of city government changed the constitution of the city, the new sacrifices initiating as citizens those who participated. Thus the symbols that were exchanged in the reform were not only cultural and religious but constitutional (2 Macc 4:9–11). Constitutional issues had, of course, previously been understood by Jews in terms of the covenant with God. First Maccabees describes the new development as a *reversal* of the covenant process that the earlier biblical texts had emphasized:

> Lawless men came forth from Israel and misled many, saying, "Let us go and make a covenant with the gentiles round about us, for since we separated from them many evils have come upon us." (1 Macc 1:11)

In biblical tradition God had promised that blessings would come to those who kept the covenant, but these lawless men assert that it had brought evils. Only Mosaic constitutional language is used here, but in 2 Maccabees we also find terminology from Greek constitutional discourse:

> Antiochus sent an Athenian senator to compel the Jews to forsake their ancestral laws [*patrioi nomoi*] and cease to live [*politeuesthai*] in accordance with the laws of God. (2 Macc 6:1)

"To live [*politeuesthai*] in accordance with ancestral laws [*patrioi nomoi*]" is a common phrase in Greek political discourse.[2] The fundamental tension in both 1 and 2 Maccabees, then, concerns the constitution of Jerusalem, but it is expressed in Mosaic concepts in 1 Maccabees (composed in Hebrew) and in Greek concepts in 2 Maccabees (composed in Greek).

To sum up, then, every aspect of Antiochus' reform mentioned here relates to the notion of *constitution*. Cultural or religious symbols may indeed be involved, but they are also directly related to the constitutional definition of the city—who rules, and under what political and legal system. The practices prohibited by Antiochus—Torah study, Sabbath observance, circumcision—were all part of the law of Moses, which had been the constitution of Jerusalem since the Persian kings had re-constituted it in the days of Ezra and Nehemiah. The only conceivable motivation for Antiochus Epiphanes to try to eradicate the distinctive practices of the Jews was that the existing constitution of Jerusalem stood in the way of the creation of a Greek colonial city with a Greek constitution.

Resistance to this reform arose, not surprisingly, in the more conservative rural area of Modein, north of Jerusalem. A rural priest named Mattathias refused to offer Greek sacrifices on a makeshift altar, and when he killed the Jew who stepped forward to perform the sacrifice, he set in motion the armed opposition to both the Seleucids and the Jewish Hellenizers who sided with them. Mattathias died soon after, but his five sons, John, Simon, Judas, Eleazar, and Jonathan, continued the revolt as guerrilla warriors. They are called Hasmonean from Hasmon, the family name of Mattathias, but the nickname of Judas, Maccabee (probably from "hammer" in Aramaic), has been applied to the brothers as a whole. Through a series of guerrilla actions the Hasmoneans were able to take the city of

Jerusalem, rededicate the temple to God, and ultimately enter into a settlement with the Seleucid kings wherein they could rule the affairs of Jerusalem. Later the dynasty was able to extend its control of the area around Judea until its borders approximated those of biblical Israel. Although this chain of events is usually seen as quintessentially Jewish, reflecting a tenacious religious identity that would brook no compromise with Greek idolatry, it is not unique. A series of rebellions against the Ptolemies occurred around Thebes in Egypt. And like the Jewish example, apocalyptic texts circulated (*Oracle of the Potter, Demotic Chronicle*) which predicted the transformation of the evil age into a native-ruled golden age. In addition, there were other local deities who inspired nationalistic resistance: Edomite Cos and Tyrian Melkart, in addition to Egyptian Osiris. We should think of the response not just as "Jewish" but as part of a much broader colonial resistance. It is part of the propaganda of 1 and 2 Maccabees, in fact, that only Jews resisted.[3]

WE AND OTHER IN 1 AND 2 MACCABEES

Written originally in Hebrew at the end of the second century BCE or the beginning of the first, 1 Maccabees mimics the style of biblical histories such as the Deuteronomistic History. Intended as a court history of the Hasmonean dynasty, it focuses on three of the Hasmonean brothers: Judas, Jonathan, and Simon. It begins by situating the revolt in a political and moral context:

> After Alexander the Great . . . had defeated King Darius of the Persians and the Medes, he succeeded Darius as king. He had previously become king of Greece. He fought many battles, conquered many strongholds, and put to death the kings of the earth. He advanced to the ends of the earth and plundered many nations. When the earth became quiet before him, he was exalted, and his heart was lifted up. (1 Macc 1:1–3)

The text moves quickly from Alexander the Great to his successors:

> Then his officers began to rule, . . . and they caused many evils on the earth. From them came forth a sinful root, Antiochus Epiphanes. . . . (1:8–10)

That the author of 1 Maccabees finds the origins of the Maccabean Revolt in the victories of Alexander the Great suggests but does not state that Alexander and the Seleucid successors were considered worse than the Persians. But the fact that this same author asserts that Judeans and the Greeks of Sparta descended from a common ancestor (Abraham! Theorem 8: Origins of practices reassigned) and the fact that the author envisioned friendly relations with Rome imply that the Other is not gentiles in general, nor even Greeks in general, but the Seleucid opponents of Israel in particular. The author of 1 Maccabees also recognized that the villains in this scenario were not just foreign rulers, but also Judeans who wanted to erase the distinctive markers of Jewish practice and become more like the nations. It is they who proposed to Antiochus that Jewish practices be suspended (1:13).

Second Maccabees was written in Greek in about 100 BCE, and is not as indebted to the biblical histories. Focusing on only one of the Hasmonean brothers, Judas, it covers a shorter span of history. An earlier history by Jason of Cyrene provided a source, and both the source and the editing were imbued with Hellenistic conventions of history-writing. The differences between 2 Maccabees and 1 Maccabees are in some ways quite significant. As Robert Doran points out, 1 Maccabees opens with hostility toward Alexander the Great and his Seleucid successors, while 2 Maccabees opens with praise for both Seleucid and Ptolemaic kings. Doran explains this difference by suggesting that 2 Maccabees is written at a slightly later point in history than 1 Maccabees, when Rome came to dominate the Seleucid and Ptolemaic empires, and when Judeans were integrating more into the social world of elites in different cities. The outlook in 2 Maccabees, as opposed to 1 Maccabees, "is one of the maintenance of ethnic identity within the framework of an imperial power which can restrain, not unleash, anti-Judean sentiment in various cities."[4]

There is indeed some question as to whether 1 and 2 Maccabees depict a life-and-death conflict between "Judaism" and "Hellenism." Despite the fact that the western intellectual tradition takes it as dogma that the Hebraic and Hellenic worlds must be opposed to each other as dualistic opposites, this is much too simplistic a view, and ignores the other cultures of the ancient Mediterranean. The need for a dualistically opposed Judaism and Hellenism arose from the early Christian belief that the emerging orthodox church achieved a perfect synthesis of the two opposites; without opposites, there could be no perfect synthesis. One of the more interesting recent challenges to this stereotyped view comes from Erich Gruen, who argues that the Jewish authors of this period do not at all define the We and Other as the culture war between Jewish identity and the onslaught of Hellenism. In his reading, the theorems of Otherness apply to 1 and 2 Maccabees only in a very limited way. The Hasmoneans, for example, were not opposed to Hellenism as such, but the policies of one particular Seleucid ruler, Antiochus IV Epiphanes. It is not difficult to see in the opening words of 1 Maccabees the view that the enemies are limited to a single lineage of kings that runs from Alexander the Great down to Antiochus IV Epiphanes. But in Gruen's view, these kings are no more representative of a general Hellenistic threat than the evil Pharaoh at the time of the exodus was a representative of all Pharaohs. The bad Seleucids do indeed have an identity as the Other, but it is not the *Greek* Other; they are likened to the surrounding nations from the Deuteronomistic History, the Ammonites, Moabites, and so on. "Insofar as Judas rallied his forces against the foe, he hoisted a biblical standard directed at the indigenous dwellers of the region, not the Greeks themselves."[5] Gruen suggests that when the author of 1 Maccabees refers to the Seleucid oppressors as "gentiles" (*ta ethnē*), they are being assimilated to the older, biblical concept (Theorem 9: Eternal Other). The surrounding nations are the real Other, and the social memory of biblical history has provided the model for the invective; bad kings were not bad because they were Greek. They were bad because they were like the Canaanites. The mere fact that they are often plural—nations, kings—rather than singular—Seleucid empire—suggests the assimilation of the new opponent to the old. The conclusion: Jews were not opposed to Hellenism and did not perceive it as presenting only the two alternatives of destruction or assimilation. Jews, rather, were confidently *engaged* with Hellenistic culture, confident that their tradition was superior and capable of holding its own in a wider world. Gruen's argument, then, is that both 1 Maccabees and 2 Maccabees share a similar perspective. There is not a simple dichotomy between Judaism and Hellenism, but the opposition is between Israel and *certain* Seleucid rulers, specifically Antiochus IV Epiphanes, understood on the model of the Canaanites.

But Seth Schwartz and other scholars also point out that the differences between 1 Maccabees and 2 Maccabees must be considered.[6] The depiction of the Maccabean Revolt in 1 Maccabees does not depend upon an opposition of Judaism/Hellenism, and as far as we know neither did the Hasmonean leaders see it this way, but by the time of 2 Maccabees, a new construction of We and Other may have developed. Although Gruen is correct that 1 Maccabees assimilates the negative attitude toward Antiochus IV Epiphanes to the older biblical view of the surrounding nations, the author of 2 Maccabees believed that Judas Maccabee was indeed opposed to Hellenism *as such* for Jews.

TERMS FOR WE AND OTHER IN 1 AND 2 MACCABEES

Two terms for the We in 1 and 2 Maccabees, "Israel" and "Hebrews," are derived from earlier biblical parlance, but these terms are not used in the same way in the two texts. In 1 Maccabees "Israel" is an important identity term, used sixty-five times, and is understood as those descended from the patriarchs, while in 2 Maccabees it appears only five times, restricted to stereotyped formulas.[7] "Hebrews," on the other hand, is not used at all in 1 Maccabees, but occurs three times in 2 Maccabees with a decisive affirmation of identity (7:31, 11:13, 15:37). "Israel" is thus a charged identity term in 1 Maccabees, "Hebrews" in 2 Maccabees. This suggests that there is some distinction between the way the two authors name Jewish identity, a distinction that becomes much more significant when we turn to the word "Judean." Judean is found forty-one times in 1 Maccabees, but in 2 Maccabees, which is much shorter, sixty-five times, an emphasis in numbers that corresponds to an extremely important development in meaning. As noted in the previous chapter, Shaye Cohen has argued that the word "Judean" underwent a significant change in the period we are addressing.[8] The Hebrew word *Yehudi*, translated into Greek as *Ioudaios*, originally meant one from the tribal province of Judah, where Jerusalem was located. Judean was an ethnic-geographical term, but did not yet connote a separate *religious* devotion and identification that one could convert to or convert from. This new cultural-religious meaning, Cohen argues, is first found in some Jewish texts just after the period of the Maccabean Revolt. It was the revolt that likely gave rise to a new consciousness of the cultural-religious identity of Judeans, qualitatively and cognitively different from the heightened sense of Judean identity found in Nehemiah 4 and Zechariah 8. This term began to emphasize confessional as well as ethnic-geographical connotations, what modern people would mean by "Jew."[9] Thus, as noted in the previous chapter, we may call the two stages that Cohen identifies Judean-1 and Judean-2. The two meanings are not mutually exclusive, nor does one replace the other; rather, the semantic field of the term broadens to include in some instances new connotations of confessional affirmation.

Cohen is right to distinguish between the uses of Judean in 1 and 2 Maccabees. Judean-2, as I have called it (cultural-religious meaning), does not occur in 1 Maccabees at all, but a clear shift has occurred in 2 Maccabees 6:6 from Judean-1 to Judean-2. After the new laws of Antiochus, "a person could not keep the Sabbath, nor observe the ancestral festivals, nor so much as confess to being a Jew." "Confess to being a Jew" is no longer simply a reference to ethnic origins, but to religious commitment. It can encapsulate constitutional "citizenship," but it also includes personal commitment as well. In 2 Maccabees 9:13–17 it is stated that on his deathbed Antiochus actually repented of his evil deeds in suppressing Jewish practices and promised that if he should live he would "become a Jew" (*Ioudaion esesthai*) and proclaim the power of God. Here also the revolutionary possibility is held out that a person could *choose* to identify as a worshiper of God. Second Maccabees also uses the word "transfer," *metabainō* or *methistēmi*, for the change of identity (2 Macc 4:10; 6:1, 9, 24).[10] Although we encounter the motif of choice and signing on in the covenant tradition and in Ezra-Nehemiah, there it is always understood as the corporate body of Israel, not as a choice of individuals who might transfer their allegiance.

In keeping with the new meaning of "Judean" in 2 Maccabees, we also find here the first use of the abstract term "Judaism" (*Ioudaismos*), as well as the first use of the abstract term "Hellenism" (*Hellēnismos*) to refer to Greek culture.[11] The modern practice of placing an -ism at the end of words originated in a particular innovation in Greek; Herodotus 4.165 (written about 440 BCE) refers to the support of the Medes as "Medism" (*Mēdismos*). The -ism thus created came to be used in other contexts, as in *Hellēnismos* to mean Greek cultural qualities and *Ioudaismos* as well in 2 Maccabees. "Judaism" the term and Judaism the confession were invented simultaneously. Thus in 2 Maccabees 4:13 the most important offense of the Hellenistic reformers, the construction of the gymnasium, is the "height of Hellenism [*Hellēnismos*] and the means of increasing foreignism [*allophylismos*]." In 2:21 it is said that "signs came from heaven to those who were striving zealously on behalf of Judaism" (compare also 8:1, 14:38). These abstract uses of *Ioudaismos* and *Hellēnismos* appear to be naming opposite ideologies.

To be sure, the terms "Hellenism" and "Judaism" are not used often in 2 Maccabees, nor in the same passages, and as a result Gruen minimizes the power of these terms to represent an opposition between two ways of life.[12] They may simply be ways of referring to tendencies or loyalties to one group or the other; that is what "Medism" means in Herodotus. But they may also reflect more than that. Hellenism and Judaism are new abstractions, used here for the first time, which communicate separate and conflicting allegiances. Further, Hellenism is associated with another new -ism, "foreignism" (*allophylismos*). It is especially significant that in 2 Maccabees 6 it is said that the Seleucids demanded of the Jews that they "transfer over" (*metabainō*, 6:1, 9, 24) to foreignism and Greek ways. Although Gruen would argue that the older meaning of *allophylos*, "foreigner," is implied in 1 Maccabees (that is, the foreigner is a member of the surrounding nations), in 2 Maccabees it is *only* used in regard to *Greeks*, and only in this text is the abstract *allophylismos* used (4:13, 6:24). In the hands of the author of 2 Maccabees, it is Hellenism that first gives "Judaism" its clear profile as a cultural-religious marker, in the same context in which "Judean" takes on a new meaning. The We is constructed by the Other (Theorem 1).

Thus in 2 Maccabees and some other texts from this period we find evidence of a fundamental shift from a definition of "Judean" based on an ethnic-geographical identity to a definition based on personal commitment. It may be argued that this is not a qualitative distinction between the two, but a quantitative distinction of emphasis—a people's identity is always defined by a number of aspects: geography, politics, traditions, practices, and theological beliefs—yet it is a significant change nonetheless. Two other motifs in the Jewish texts of this period confirm this. First, there is in the contemporary texts of the Greek Old Testament an increased use of the words "confess" or "proclaim" (*homologeō/exomologeō* and related words).[13] Second, the ethnic-geographical Judean might worship God and observe God's commandments, but in the new cultural-religious meaning the element of personal commitment comes to dominate and is *transportable*. It is ironic that the constitutional developments, first by Ezra and Nehemiah under the Persians and then by the Maccabees under the Seleucids, which focused intensely on Jerusalem, created a "package" of practices and beliefs that had to be confessed by the citizens and was fully transportable to all parts of the world. "Judeanism"—orientation toward Judah—became "Judaism." The result was a more pronounced affirmation of a personal commitment to a set of beliefs and markers that would maintain a far-flung community, even those away from the temple, and later even those whose temple had been destroyed. As Cohen notes, the Egyptian worship of Isis was also at this time spilling out of Egypt and creating its own diaspora of followers; formerly called "Egyptian worshippers of Isis," they were now "Isiasts"[14]— or we may designate the two as Isis worshipers-1 and Isis worshipers-2. It is also no accident that at about the same time that the meaning of "Judean" shifts from a reference to geographical origin to a reference to religious commitment there also arises talk of conversion to Judaism, both positive and negative. Conversion became a positive option in Judith 14:10, but strong reactions against intermarriage with gentiles are voiced in *Jubilees* 15:26. The possibility of *becoming* a Judean is viewed by some as a promise and by others as a threat, but they all now engage the new possibility.

But there is an irony in all this: 2 Maccabees constructs an opposition between Judaism and Hellenism that is argued using Greek terms for the constitution of cities, Greek abstractions of ethnic identities, Greek virtues, and perhaps even broader Hellenistic notions of personal religion (Theorem 5: Other similar to We). Second Maccabees opens the valves of anti-Greek rhetoric at certain points, while at other points it lauds Greek rulers, both Seleucid and Ptolemaic. One of the references to "Judaism" (2:21) goes on to state that the partisans of Judaism repulsed the "barbarian hordes," meaning in this case the Greeks. "Barbarian" was the standard word in Greece for the non-Greek Other; 2 Maccabees ironically appropriates a Greek perspective to malign Greeks (Theorem 8: Origins of practices reassigned).

How are we to make sense of this ambivalent relationship with Greek tradition? Steven Weitzman suggests that Jews under colonial rule use the "arts of the weak" as strategies: appeasement, symbiosis, flattery, mimicry, diplomacy:

> In some cases . . . what might look like assimilation to a foreign culture can be placed within an alternative narrative of cultural persistence, one in which Jews poach resources from the *other* for use in sustaining their own culture.[15]

Anthony Smith sees the Jewish struggle against the Seleucids as "ethnicism," the colonized people's assertion of their own native identity *using the language* of the colonizers.[16] But is this really what we would call "resistance"? Gruen may be correct after all that the author of 2 Maccabees does not see Judaism as pitted in a life-and-death struggle with Hellenism. To be sure, Jewish identity is constructed in opposition to "Hellenism," but in 2 Maccabees it is ultimately a mild opposition. Weitzman suggests that this author highlights diplomatic solutions to the conflict with the Seleucids, not military ones. Although 2 Maccabees is normally read as a strident opponent of Hellenism, its tone is actually much more restrained. Gruen does not see this as ambivalence, but as a sort of Jewish confidence with respect to the greater world powers. For postcolonial theorists, however, there is a debate about whether colonized peoples merely internalize the tensions of living under foreign powers, or also in some cases "digest" the colonial tradition and assert an indigenous cultural identity.[17] The author of 2 Maccabees is at the same time both smitten by Greek literary and cultural tradition and also concerned about the power and the appeal of it, expressing the hybridity and ambivalence of the colonized more than does the author of 1 Maccabees.

CONCLUSION

First and Second Maccabees agreed in describing the choice between Greek and Jewish constitutions for the city of Jerusalem as a fundamental tension, but they described it differently. First Maccabees follows biblical historical models and defines the constitutional crisis from the traditional Israelite side: lawless men are deserting the covenant with God. Second Maccabees uses Greek historical models and describes the constitutional crisis in Greek terms: the ancestral laws (*patrioi nomoi*) were abrogated and Jews ceased to live (*politeuesthai*) according to the laws of God. Despite the constitutional crisis at the center of events, the stark contrast between Hellenism and Judaism was probably not present in 1 Maccabees, introduced instead by the author of 2 Maccabees. Further, the author of 2 Maccabees, in keeping with the religious transformations in the Greek world, began a new stage in the definition of the We by shifting the meaning of the ideal term "Judean" to someone who chooses Judaism over Hellenism.

One might have assumed that in the aftermath of the Maccabean Revolt Jews would have defined their identity in opposition to the religious persecution that had been instigated by the Hellenistic kingdom of the Seleucids. This is precisely how the situation is understood by many today, including scholars who study this period. The situation, however, was apparently much more complex. Gruen argues convincingly that in 1 Maccabees the Other is understood as the surrounding nations as they had been described in the earlier historical books of the Bible, and that any polemic against the oppressive Seleucids assimilates them to this concept. But despite Gruen's tendency to describe 1 and 2 Maccabees in similar ways, the latter moves in an altogether new direction. Some Greek rulers were viewed positively, and the author's Greek pretensions would already indicate a readiness to take up the best of Greek culture, but the author identifies oppressive Greek rulers as a form of Hellenism and foreignism that, *if taken up by Jews*, threatens the very existence of Judaism. Although it is reported as a struggle for the political constitution of the city of Jerusalem, it is more than that. The word "Judean" takes on a new meaning, and Judaism—named here as such for the first time (*Ioudaismos*)—becomes a way of life that one could confess or reject. Conversion also became a significant literary motif, even if the possibility of Antiochus' conversion is considered ludicrous; it came in this period to be considered both an accepted option (Judith) and a rejected option (*Jubilees*).

The meaning of "Judean" in Ezra-Nehemiah and in 2 Maccabees is different, and that difference partly lies in what "Judean" is contrasted with. In Ezra-Nehemiah "Judean" is contrasted with the various non-Israelite (and Israelite?) peoples who were resident in or near Judea at the time that the returnees from Babylon reestablished a presence in Jerusalem. In the Maccabean period "Judean" is contrasted to the external empire that ruled over Judea and threatened to supplant the Mosaic constitution with a Greek constitution. From this point, Juda-*ism* is first named, in opposition to Hellen-*ism*. Thus, the meaning of "Judean" in Ezra-Nehemiah on one hand and 1 and 2 Maccabees on the other must ultimately be sought in the question: *as opposed to what?* We could hardly ask for a more convincing instance of Theorem 1, or for Fredrik Barth's theory that ethnic identity is formed by the definition of boundaries and contrasts.[18]

NOTES

1. Seth Schwartz, "The Hellenization of Jerusalem and Shechem," in *Jews in a Graeco-Roman World*, ed. Martin Goodman (Oxford: Clarendon, 1998), 37–46; Seth

Schwartz, *Imperialism and Jewish Society, 200 BCE to 640 CE* (Princeton, NJ: Princeton University Press, 2001), 27–32.

2. Shaye J. D. Cohen, *The Beginnings of Jewishness: Boundaries, Varieties, Uncertainties* (Berkeley: University of California Press, 1999), 3–4, 92; Elias Bickerman, *The God of the Maccabees: Studies on the Meaning and Origin of the Maccabean Revolt* (Leiden, Netherlands: Brill, 1979), 38–42; Schwartz, "Hellenization of Jerusalem"; and John J. Collins, "Cult and Culture: The Limits of Hellenization in Judea," in *Hellenism in the Land of Israel*, ed. John J. Collins and Gregory E. Sterling (South Bend, IN: University of Notre Dame Press, 2001), 55.

3. S. K. Eddy, *The King Is Dead: Studies in the Near Eastern Resistance to Hellenism, 334–31 B.C.* (Lincoln: University of Nebraska Press, 1961), 135–36, 163–64, 327–31.

4. Robert Doran, "Independence or Coexistence: The Responses of 1 and 2 Maccabees to Seleucid Hegemony," *Society of Biblical Literature Seminar Papers 38* (2 vols.; Atlanta, GA: Society of Biblical Literature, 1999), 1:102–3. See also Seth Schwartz, "Israel and the Nations Roundabout: 1 Maccabees and the Hasmonean Expansion," *Journal of Jewish Studies* 42 (1991): 16–38, and Daniel R. Schwartz, "The Other in 1 and 2 Maccabees," in *Tolerance and Intolerance in Early Judaism and Christianity*, ed. Graham N. Stanton and Guy G. Stroumsa (Cambridge, UK: Cambridge University Press, 1998), 30–37.

5. Erich Gruen, *Heritage and Hellenism: The Reinvention of Jewish Tradition* (Berkeley: University of California Press, 1998), xiv, 5–6, 12–40; Erich Gruen, *Diaspora: Jews amidst Greeks and Romans* (Cambridge, MA, and London: Harvard University Press, 2002), 219–31. Some passages, such as 1 Macc 8:18, remain troublesome for Gruen's thesis. On the dichotomization of Jewish and Greek, see Zhang Longxi, *Mighty Opposites: From Dichotomies to Differences in the Comparative Study of China* (Stanford, CA: Stanford University Press, 1998), 1–54.

6. Schwartz, "Israel"; Schwartz, *Imperialism*, 35. For a slightly different perspective, see Steven Weitzman, *Surviving Sacrilege: Cultural Persistence in Jewish Antiquity* (Cambridge, MA: Harvard University Press, 2005), 42–46.

7. For example, 2 Macc. 9:5, 10:38. See Daniel Schwartz, "The Other."

8. Cohen, *Beginnings*, 14, 69–106; Christian Habicht, "Hellenismus und Judentum in der Zeit des Judas Makkabäus," in *Jahrbuch der Heidelberger Akademie der Wissenschaften für 1974* (Heidelberg, Germany: Carl Winter/Universitätsverlag, 1975), 98.

9. In a similar way, it is often suggested that Greek identity became much more defined in the aftermath of the Persian War, and this was reflected in the development of history writing. Cohen, *Beginnings*, 132, argues that "Hellene" changed from an ethnic-geographical designation to one based on cultural education (Thucydides 1.3.3). See also Schwartz, "Hellenization of Jerusalem."

10. Judith Lieu, *Neither Jew nor Greek? Constructing Early Christianity* (London and New York: Clark, 2002), 58–59, notes Helena's conversion, *metakomizesthai eis tous nomous*, Josephus, *Antiquities* 20.35. Cohen, *Beginnings*, also notes passages from other texts of this era that reflect the possibility of this new meaning, for instance, Bel and the Serpent and Judith 14:10. Daniel Boyarin, *Dying for God: Martyrdom and the Making of Christianity and Judaism* (Stanford, CA: Stanford University Press, 1999), 187–91, limits his discussion to 2 Macc 6:6. He also insists ("The *Ioudaioi* in John and the Prehistory of 'Judaism,'" in *Pauline Conversations in Context: Essays in Honor of Calvin J. Roetzel*, ed. Janice Capel Anderson, Philip Sellew, and

Claudia Setzer [London: Sheffield Academic Press, 2002], 216–39) that conversion by itself does not register a significant shift in the understanding of Judean, but I would argue that combined with the confession motif treated below, it does.

11. *Hellēnismos* had only been used up to this point to mean an unobjectionable command of Greek language; see Habicht, "Hellenismus und Judentum," 97–98.

12. Gruen, *Heritage and Hellenism*, 3–4. Arguing for an intentional opposition of Hellenism and Judaism in 2 Maccabees are Habicht, "Hellenismus und Judentum," 97–98, and Martha Himmelfarb, "Judaism and Hellenism in 2 Maccabees," *Poetics Today* 19 (1998): 19–20.

13. Lawrence M. Wills, "Ascetic Theology before Asceticism? Jewish Narratives and the Decentering of the Self," *Journal of the American Academy of Religion* 74 (2006): 902–25, and on later Christian *exomologēsis* and *exagoreusis*, or public confession of the sinner, see Michel Foucault, "Technologies of the Self," in *Ethics: Subjectivity and Truth*, vol. 1 of *Essential Works of Foucault, 1954–1984*, 3 vols. (New York: New Press, 1997), 223–51; Michel Foucault, "About the Beginning of the Hermeneutics of the Self," in *Religion and Culture: Michel Foucault*, ed. Jeremy R. Carrette (New York: Routledge, 1999), 169–81.

14. Cohen, *Beginnings*, 80–81, 110–19, 125–28. See also Christine E. Hayes, *Gentile Impurities and Jewish Identities: Intermarriage and Conversion from the Bible to the Talmud* (Oxford: Oxford University Press, 2002), 47–57. The shift in Judaism was likely only a local instance, indeed a colonial reaction, to the much broader phenomenon of Greek "universalism." Seth Schwartz's suggestion that Hellenization succeeded by addressing the public and constitutional aspects of urban life and leaving the private side to the cultivation of native traditions must be modified in respect to a second stage, the rise of personal religion ("Hellenization of Jerusalem").

15. Weitzman, *Surviving Sacrilege*, 9 (see also 42–46), using the critical insights of Michel de Certeau, *The Practice of Everyday Life* (Berkeley: University of California Press, 1984), esp. 35–39.

16. Anthony Smith, *The Ethnic Origins of Nations* (Oxford: Blackwell, 1986), 56–57.

17. See Homi Bhabha, *The Location of Culture* (London and New York: Rutledge, 1994), 85–92, on "mimicry": the colonized person translates empire by reproducing it *"almost the same, but not quite."* Mimicry is an *"ironic* compromise," and reflects ambivalence. Mary Louise Pratt, *Imperial Eyes: Travel Writing and Transculturation* (London and New York: Routledge, 1992), 7, 9, describes a more explicit and self-conscious form of mimicry in what she calls "autoethnography," declaring native consciousness using the genres and ideas of the colonial powers, which is what 2 Maccabees does.

18. Fredrick Barth, "Introduction," in *Ethnic Groups and Boundaries: The Social Organization of Cultural Differences*, ed. Fredrick Barth (Boston: Little, Brown, 1969), 5–38.

5

⁓

"Scribes and Pharisees, Hypocrites!" in the Gospel of Matthew

We now turn to New Testament texts, but will find that the issues remain nearly the same. The construction of the Other in the Gospel of Matthew, for instance, is closely related to the construction of the We; they are mutually reinforcing processes. We will examine closely the principal passage that constructs the Other in Matthew, chapter twenty-three, the list of woes against the "scribes and Pharisees, hypocrites," and the main passage that constructs the We, the Sermon on the Mount, chapters five to seven.

Some historical background is necessary at this point. Although Herod the Great was king of Judea and a puppet of Rome when Jesus was born, he died soon afterward, and by the time Jesus was crucified in about 30 CE, Judea was a province of Rome with a Roman governor, Pontius Pilate, rather than a Jewish king. Jewish opposition to Roman rule broke out into open rebellion in the bloody Jewish War of 66–70 CE. The rebellion was put down by the Romans and the temple was destroyed, which eliminated central Jewish political and religious institutions as well. Thus before 70 CE, Jews and the followers of Jesus were under the dual authority structures of the Roman provincial government and the Jewish temple in Jerusalem. To say that one was secular and the other religious is to impose a modern separation of church and state that would have been foreign to ancient worldviews. Both the Roman government and the Jewish temple administration were religious *and* political institutions, but Jews retained dual loyalties and a dual set of obligations. Further, the high priest in Jerusalem held office at the pleasure of the Roman government, and therefore the temple in Jerusalem was part of the colonial administration of the Romans. After 70 CE, even this aspect of Jewish self-rule was gone, but Jews continued as a religious and ethnic body, and new institutions evolved. Rabbinic Judaism emerged over the next few centuries and eventually became the predominant form of religious life for Jews, but this was not the case in the first century.

Most New Testament scholars hold that Mark was the earliest gospel, and that Matthew and Luke used Mark as their main source. Yet there are clusters of sayings found in both Matthew and Luke that are not present in Mark, and most scholars attribute these to a collection of Jesus' teachings now otherwise lost, called Q (from the German word *Quelle*, "source"). By closely comparing these sections of Matthew and Luke, scholars have reconstructed an approximation of the text of Q.[1] In addition, Matthew and Luke each contain material that is unique to that gospel. It could be ascribed to the hand of the author, but in each gospel some of this material hangs together in form and content, and is somewhat at odds with other passages. It is likely that Matthew and Luke each had an additional source unique to that gospel, called respectively M and L. Thus a diagram can be drawn of the probable relations of Matthew, Mark, Luke, and their sources (see Figure 5.1):

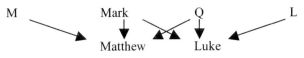

Figure 5.1

Thus most, but not all, scholars assume that Matthew used Mark, and for that source we have a text. Most, but not all also assume that Matthew used Q, but for that the actual words of the text can only be reconstructed from a comparison of Matthew and Luke. Most, but not all scholars assume that Matthew had a source that we call M, but here as well the text can only be partially reconstructed.[2] Here I will be following this consensus, which will be crucial for the discussion that follows.

BOUNDARIES AND DIFFERENCES IN MATTHEW

During the course of the first two centuries, followers of Jesus, who had begun as members of a Jewish sect, soon found the gap widening between their group and the parent-body. Increasing numbers of followers of Jesus were gentile converts and, following the lead of missionaries like Paul, no longer felt that this group was obligated to observe Jewish law. The divorce between Judaism and Christianity occurred slowly, and in different ways in different geographical areas. Although the break with Judaism was read back into events in Jesus' life, it actually only began to be manifested decades after his crucifixion. During the 50s Paul argued that gentiles could be "in Christ" without observing Jewish law, but this view was not readily accepted—note the opposition Paul meets from Jesus' own disciples (Gal 1–2). Thus followers of Jesus who observed Jewish law, both those born Jewish and also gentile converts, might have been in the majority well into the second century. Matthew probably retained a concern for Jewish law and observance that was much greater than that of the other gospels and, unlike Paul, never relaxed the demands of *halachah*: "Do not think that I have come to abolish the law or the prophets. I have not come to abolish them but to fulfill them" (Matt 5:17). Many scholars now agree that Matthew meant exactly what these words seem to say: Matthew's Jesus was not only Jewish, but an observant Jew.[3] Although Christian tradition chose to harmonize Paul and Matthew, and read Matthew's sharp rebuke of "scribes and Pharisees, hypocrites" as Jesus' rejection of Jewish legalism, it is more likely that Matthew did not see the young sect as a new religion or truly separate from Judaism, but as "true Judaism" at the end of time. We would not say, for instance, that the Dead Sea sect had rejected Judaism; in their own minds, they had perfected Judaism. Nowhere in Matthew, for instance, does Jesus refer to "your law," as he does in John; Jewish law is still Matthew's law.

The Gospel of Matthew became the catechetical gospel of the church because it was so well suited for the education and spiritual formation of members. The teaching function of Matthew's gospel can be seen in its five-part structure, modeled on the five books of Moses; the alternation in each section of narrative followed by a teaching discourse; an emphasis on teaching (5:19, 28:20); the development of Jesus as the personified Wisdom of God;[4] and similarities to other early Christian teaching manuals such as the *Didache*. Further, Matthew alone of the gospels contains positive references to scribes within the community of believers in Jesus. Ezra's "scribe of the law of the God of heaven" is similar to Matthew's "scribe trained for the kingdom of heaven" (13:52). That Matthew was or had been a scribe seems likely. Matthew is a gospel that emphasizes, on the one hand, Jewish observance and, on the other, formation-through-education. This is presented in the context of an apocalyptic worldview which held that the end of the world was near, and a judgment between those who were righteous and those who were not was imminent (Matt 10:15, 23; 24:1–44; 25:31–46).

Our next step will be to discern how Matthew defines the boundaries between the community of true followers of Jesus and others. Matthew introduces many people who are outside the community, listed here in order of appearance:

Figure:	First key passage:
People (*laos*)	1:21
Herod	chap. 2
Magi	chap. 2
Chief priests (and priests)	2:4
Scribes	2:4
Archelaus, Herod's son	2:22
John the Baptist	3:1–15
Sadducees	3:7
Diseased, etc.	4:24
Crowds (*ochloi*)	4:25
Pharisees	5:20
Sanhedrin (council)	5:22
Toll collectors	5:46
Gentiles	6:7
Centurion and servant	8:5–13
Herodias and her daughter	14:3–6
Elders	15:2
Canaanite woman	15:21
Herodians	22:16
Pilate	27:2
Pilate's wife	27:19

It is surprising to find here so many groups and figures from outside the Jesus movement. Like the texts in the Hebrew Bible treated in the previous chapters, Matthew constructs a world consisting of different categories, some of which are We, some of which are Other, but many of which, such as the Magi, are external but positive or at least neutral. Not all outsiders are Other. Which categories in Matthew are then the truly *conflicted* boundaries, that is, the boundaries that Matthew most wants to emphasize as representing the duality of We and Other? The evaluation of outside groups is not as clear as one might expect. The fact that Matthew, unlike the other gospels, begins with a genealogy from Abraham to Jesus is significant. Jesus and his followers are among the offspring of Abraham; the affirmation of the Jewish pedigree of Jesus is matched by negative judgments about gentiles. In none of the gospels does Jesus ever eat with gentiles, and in Matthew they are at times treated with contempt: "Let such a person be to you as a gentile or a toll collector" (18:17). The prospect of including gentiles is not raised explicitly until the very end of the gospel. But what, then, do we make of the Roman centurion's servant or the Canaanite woman (8:5–13, 15:21–28)? How can the Magi from the east acclaim the birth of Jesus? References to gentiles remain ambiguous.

The Jewish figures are also ambiguous. Some are presented negatively, but are also relegated to the past. Herod is certainly negative in Matthew 2, but the king himself and his sons were long dead by the time Matthew wrote, and the narrative of Herod slaying the newborns appears to have a legendary function only, evoking Pharaoh and Moses. And whereas Mark and Q wrote while the temple was still standing, Matthew likely wrote twenty years after the fact. Therefore, for Matthew the chief priests and the Sanhedrin were institutions that had not existed for a generation, gone the way of Herod. The negative characters in Matthew's gospel, then, must be divided into those who still had contemporary significance (Pharisees), those who did not (chief priests, Sadducees, Sanhedrin), and those who might have varied roles (scribes). After the destruction of the temple, all of these groups lost their power base except for the scribes and Pharisees, precisely the groups to which we turn next.

MATTHEW, SCRIBES, AND PHARISEES

Scribes are often mentioned in Matthew but are not consistently depicted as Other, and there are scribes among the followers of Jesus. Regarding Pharisees, however, Matthew is always negative. Matthew contains significantly more references to Pharisees than does Mark, and expresses polemical condemnation of this group much more sharply. The Pharisees were one of the prominent groups in Jewish life in the first century, although the number of Pharisees and the exact nature of their movement are not clear. It is sometimes suggested that by the time that Matthew was writing Pharisees were more of a caricatured projection by Christian authors than a real group in contact with them, but this seems unnecessarily skeptical. They are described by the contemporary Jewish historian Josephus, and Matthew, unlike some other followers of Jesus, appears to continue to be enmeshed in Jewish struggles. But be that as it may, a strong image of the Pharisees remains in some quarters in the late first century. They were not a party or a regular part of the governing aristocracy; they are described by Josephus as being in and out of favor with the governing authorities in Jerusalem while the temple was still standing. They were not a separate philosophy, even though Josephus sometimes describes them in that way. From what we can gather, Pharisees were also not a sect in the sense of a group that intentionally defined itself in sharp tension with society at large, as Matthew and the Qumran sect did. Rather, the Pharisees constituted the same sort of group as the returning

Judeans in Ezra-Nehemiah, a revitalization movement.[5] Revitalization movements attempt to transform society by means of renewing the common core of revered traditions (even if some of those are actually new practices now understood as ancient, Theorem 8), and as a result, part of their influence derives from the appeal to conscience. Pharisees pressed for a greater attention to observance of Jewish law in everyday life: Sabbath observance, fasting, tithing (paying one-tenth of produce to the temple), and especially ritual purity. Specifically, the purity that was associated with the offerings in the Jewish temple in Jerusalem was to be applied to purity rules for table fellowship in Jewish homes. Table fellowship was to be sanctified by the washing of hands, cups, and dishes, and the tithing of grain so that the proper Jewish offering for the food had been paid to the temple. Pharisaic revitalization was thus the application of temple purity to the sanctification of everyday life. It is possible, even probable, that the Pharisees, who had never been tied directly to the temple administration, allied themselves after 70 CE to the local scribes and city councils (synagogues), creating a stronger presence at a local level, and advocating a revitalization of Jewish observance there.[6] Just such a coalition may have been responsible for slowly reconstituting a new Judaism without a temple, supporting the practices and beliefs later collected as rabbinic Judaism.

There are several ways of describing the difference between the Pharisees and the early followers of Jesus. In chapters two and three we discussed the theory of Jonathan Klawans, who traces a continuing distinction in ancient Israel and Judaism between an emphasis on ritual impurity (the effect of impure contacts) and moral impurity (the effect of serious sins).[7] Matthew is not indifferent to ritual impurity (compare Matt 23:23 below), but in general emphasized moral impurity while the Pharisees emphasized ritual impurity. Moral impurity for Matthew, however, was not just a way of defining righteousness (as it was, for instance, in Leviticus 18–20); it also covers all the aspects of inner intention: one must have the right inner disposition in order to avoid moral impurity, and the Pharisees' strong emphasis on ritual impurity did not, in Matthew's eyes, protect from moral impurity. Corresponding to these divisions there was likely a difference in class as well. While the temple was still standing the Pharisees were likely members of the retainer class, that is, those who held intermediate positions for the Jerusalem temple administration, and they remained an ascendant social group afterwards.[8] They would have enjoyed some degree of public honor. They were certainly important enough to be affirmed by the aristocrat Josephus, and were probably influential beyond their numbers, as revitalization movements often are. But ambiguities remain. To say that the Pharisees were members of the retainer class makes them sound like bureaucrats, while to call them a revitalization movement makes them sound like pietists and idealists. Both characterizations may have a kernel of truth. More to the point, to describe Pharisees as retainers implies that their power and status was bestowed from above, while describing their movement as a revitalization movement implies that their role came about as a result of their popular appeal. Again, both characterizations are probably true. The Pharisees were a religious revitalization movement that championed everyday Jewish observance, especially Sabbath observance, fasting, tithes, and ritual purity. In addition, their social role was probably that of retainers of the temple authorities before the destruction of the temple, and they remained allied with landowners, scribes, and the remnants of the priestly class afterward.

Matthew, on the other hand, though probably a scribe, writes to a community that was likely from the urban artisan and merchant classes. Christian literacy, where it occurs, and especially Matthew's idealization of the Christian scribe make sense among urban merchants, many of whom probably managed with a functional literacy. In the social hierarchy of the ancient world, artisans and merchants lacked the security of class and were often, though not always, poor and struggling classes. Matthew and other New Testament texts reflect the attributes of the urban merchants—flexible, independent, entrepreneurial, mobile, insecure, literate in greater numbers than the rest of the population. Although not among the lowest classes, they were universally looked down on by aristocrats. Cicero, for example, refers at one point in passing to "artisans, shopkeepers, and all the dregs of a city" (*In Defence of Lucius Flaccus* 18). But the status of all these social levels must be seen on a relative scale. Pharisees, as retainers, would have been far beneath Cicero, but elevated compared to most followers of Jesus in the first century, and the urban merchants and artisans that most likely made up Matthew's community would have been higher in wealth and status than rural peasants.

There is one other aspect of the Pharisees in Matthew that makes them different from the other Jewish groups, and which is often ignored even by scholars: they are often contrasted with toll collectors. Pharisees loom large and menacing as the opponents of Jesus, and toll collectors have an important role as those whom Jesus joins in fellowship. To understand the role of the Pharisees in the narrative, one must understand why they would be constructed as Other *in explicit contrast to the toll collectors*.[9] Ambiguous groups have been reassigned (Theorem 7). The word for toll collector in the gospel, *telōnēs*, is often translated as "tax collector" (or in the King James Version, "publican"), but that misrepresents their role in society. They did not collect the direct taxes of Rome or the various puppet kings, nor were they the wealthy "tax farmers" who bid for the rights to collect taxes from a specified region. Toll collectors served the Roman tax system, but at the lower levels only. They were charged by the Roman administration with the collection of indirect taxes, that is, duties and tolls. They were evidently viewed by aristocrats as unscrupulous members of an unsavory profession, busybodies who had to look through people's possessions to assess the proper tolls. They were also viewed by Pharisees as lax in terms of purity, creating a very practical problem for ritual purity in that they had to touch many people's possessions. In addition, since the Pharisees were focused on tithing, or the tax on grain and produce that was commanded by biblical law to be paid to the temple before its destruction, the toll collectors in fact worked for competing tax systems. (After the destruction of the temple, tithes were still paid to the priests and Levites, and only much later to rabbinic scholars.) Even if the two systems were both under the indirect control of the Romans, as a revitalization movement within Judaism the Pharisees would have argued that one of these taxes was commanded by God. Pharisees before the destruction of the temple were probably retainers of the Jerusalem temple administration and toll collectors were members of the merchant class. Thus the class distinction between Pharisees and toll collectors may have been the same as that between Pharisees and Matthew's community. Yet it is still difficult to imagine why in the gospels toll collectors would receive special acceptance into the kingdom over observant Jews like the Pharisees. Is it a simple case of "the enemy of my enemy is my friend"? Does it reflect the unexpected reversals at the end of time, the acceptance of those normally considered undesirable? Attempts to see the toll collectors as slaves who worked for the tax-gathering aristocrats, or alternatively as the very poor are not convincing.[10]

This digression on toll collectors allows us to develop a theory of how the Pharisees are constructed *in relation to toll collectors*. There are a number of surprises when one examines the function of Pharisees and toll collectors in the earliest Christian texts. It is commonly assumed that Pharisees were the typical opponents of Jesus and dominated early Christian discourse. When we look, however, at the New Testament texts composed up to the time of the Jewish War and the destruction of the temple (69 CE), we find that Pharisees occur *in only one passage in Q, once in Paul's letters, and in only six passages in Mark*. But after the Jewish War, the numbers increase sharply: Matthew has thirty references to Pharisees, Luke-Acts thirty-six, and John twenty. In the period up to the time of the Jewish War, then, when the Pharisees would have been retainers for the temple administration, they are rarely mentioned; in the period after the Jewish War, however, when they are no longer retainers for the temple authorities, but have likely moved into coalitions with surviving aristocrats outside of Jerusalem, they take on a much more pronounced role as foil for the piety of the followers of Jesus. The posttemple role of the Pharisees in

Jewish society may have shifted significantly, and it is this to which Matthew, Luke, and John are probably reacting.

And just as remarkably, the appearance of the toll collectors in the New Testament follows precisely this pattern. Up to the time of the Jewish War, toll collectors appear in only two passages in Q, do not occur at all in Paul, and appear in only one passage in Mark. After the Jewish War, when the number of references to Pharisees increases, so do the references to toll collectors. Matthew mentions them nine times and Luke eleven. In this passage from Luke the Christian image of the Pharisee and the Christian image of the toll collector are co-constructed (Theorems 1, 2):

> Two men went up to the temple to pray, one a Pharisee and the other a toll collector. The Pharisee prayed, "God, I thank you that I am not like other people—thieves, rogues, adulterers, or even like this toll collector. I fast twice a week, I tithe." The toll collector, however, would not even look up to heaven, but beat his breast and said, "God be merciful to me, a sinner!" I tell you, this man went down to his home justified rather than the other; for all who exalt themselves will be humbled and all who humble themselves will be exalted. (Luke 18:9–14; compare Luke 7:29–30)

The toll collector is here "justified," but note that he is described *as the Pharisee would view him*, a sinner who could not look up to heaven. Toll collectors are also grouped positively in Matthew in one passage with sinners (11:19), and in another passage with prostitutes (21:31). Stated simply, the Jesus movement, which preached the forgiveness of sins, also constructed an account of its founder in which the sinner is welcomed, even championed. This situation did not last (1 Cor 5:11, 2 Cor 6:14–7:1, *Barnabas* 4.2, 5.9), but the myth of origins did: the *practice of forgiving sins* among early followers of Jesus was sanctioned in the gospels by the *inclusion of sinners* (Theorem 7: Ambiguous groups reassigned).[11]

The self-understanding of early followers of Jesus on this point can be illuminated by studies in the sociology of deviance and "self-stigmatization." Sectarian movements often affirm their separate and deviant status in society by flouting convention. It is not considered a problem for early followers that Jesus is accused of being "a glutton and drunkard, and friend of toll collectors and sinners" (Matt 11:19). Just as members of the Society of Friends gladly took over society's derogatory description of themselves as "Quakers," and the American youth movement of the 1960s took on the self-appellation "freaks," so also the affirmation of toll collectors (along with sinners and prostitutes) by early followers of Jesus takes on significance as the self-definition of a deviant and sectarian group.[12] A symbolic contrast of Pharisees and toll collectors is beginning to emerge in the gospels after 70 CE, and it is no accident that it is specifically toll collectors who appear very significantly and negatively in early rabbinic texts as a dualistic contrast to the *haverim,* "comrades," a group often identified with the Pharisees. Thus, just as the New Testament texts contrast Pharisees and toll collectors as the negative and positive poles of a dualistic contrast, so also early rabbinic texts utilize the same dualistic contrast, now reversed: Pharisees (or *haverim*) are We, and toll collectors are an internal Other. The Pharisees, then, stand out in Matthew as the group that is truly Other, and toll collectors move to a favored status because they are Other to the Other, and can be used as a symbol of the doctrine of forgiveness. Toll collectors and sinners also serve to self-stigmatize followers of Jesus as a deviant group.

CONSTRUCTING THE WE: THE SERMON ON THE MOUNT (MATTHEW 5–7)

As noted above, Matthew's gospel can be divided into five major sections, an analogy to the five books of Moses, each section composed of a narrative followed by a discourse. The Sermon on the Mount, which emphatically defines the We, is the discourse of Matthew's first section. The placement of the Sermon on a mountain rather than a plain (as in Luke) also renders Jesus a figure like Moses. The parallel between Jesus' new pronouncement and Moses' law is intended. The mountain also connotes other things as well. As K. C. Hanson notes, it is on sacred mountains that the "divine and the human meet."[13] The Sermon is not just a presentation of Matthew's theological beliefs; it is a ritual initiation of the disciples, and by extension the later audience as well, into Jesus' activities: teaching, healing, seeing God, and so on. Utilizing the theories of Victor Turner, Hanson points out the similarities to rituals of initiation: the separation of the disciples from their familiar settings, the liminal period in which special knowledge or status is imparted, and the reintegration of the disciples into society at the end with a changed status.

The Sermon itself can also be divided into five parts, each of which has a different character:

(1) beatitudes (5:1–16)
(2) Jesus' new presentation of the law (5:17–48)
(3) instructions on charity, prayer, and fasting (6:1–18)
(4) general instructions on community (6:19–7:12)
(5) concluding sayings on two ways (7:13–29)[14]

Matthew's Sermon is very similar to Luke's Sermon on the Plain (6:17–49), and so is probably based first of all on Q, but parts of it are probably derived from M, and it is in these sections that we also find similarities to the early Christian teaching handbook *Didache*.[15] By comparing Matthew's words here with the probable sources, it is possible to see what Matthew has introduced into the text, and also to see more clearly what each of the different voices brings to the discourse of We and Other.

The Beatitudes

The beatitudes introduce the Sermon. The differences between Matthew's beatitudes and Q's seem minor at first, but on closer analysis, are very significant. Matthew has nine beatitudes to Q's four, and the latter are shorter, more concrete, and address the recipients of the blessings more directly in the second person. Note the italicized differences in these beatitudes:

Matthew 5:3, 6	*Q 6:20, 21*
Blessed are the poor *in spirit,* for *theirs* is the kingdom of heaven.	Blessed are *you* poor, for *yours* is the kingdom of God.
Blessed are those who hunger and thirst *for righteousness,* for *they* shall be filled.	Blessed are *you* who hunger, for *you* will be filled.

Q here is directly concerned with the physical needs of the poor, and addressing them directly in the second person, states that their needs will simply be met—how it is not said—while Matthew speaks of those blessed in the third person and transfers the concerns from physical needs to spiritual attributes: poor *in spirit,* hunger and thirst *for righteousness.*[16] Matthew also contains other beatitudes not found in Q whose main point corresponds to the changes noted here: blessed are the meek, the merciful, the pure in heart. Yet although Matthew changed Q's beatitudes from second-person address ("Blessed are you poor") to third-person ("Blessed are the poor in spirit"), this section as a whole is concluded with two sayings from Q that are shifted by Matthew to an emphatic second-person address:

Matthew 5:13–15	*Q 14:34*
You [plural] are the salt of the earth, but if salt has lost its flavor, how will its saltiness be restored?	Salt is good, but if salt has lost its flavor, how will it be seasoned?
You [plural] are the light of the world. People do not light a lamp and put it under a bushel basket.	No one lights a lamp and puts it in a cellar but on a lamp stand.

Matthew has a reason here for switching the address to second person. The exact meaning of salt of the earth is not clear, or how salt can lose its flavor, but the important word in Matthew's sayings is "you," here in the plural. The proverbial sayings in Q become virtual naming ceremonies in Matthew: "*You members* are the salt of the earth! *You members* are the light of the world!" Matthew's emphasis is a strong affirmation in the face of the blame of outsiders; like Nehemiah 4, it is a reversal of public shame.

Jesus' Intensification of the Law

If the Sermon on the Mount is a rite of initiation in which new teaching is bestowed upon those initiated and they become the salt of the earth, then the understanding of the law in the following section (5:17–48) will constitute the new teaching. It is introduced by a constitutional statement on the place of the law in the new messianic community:

> I have come not to abolish the law and the prophets, but to fulfill them. . . . Whoever then relaxes one of the least of these commandments and teaches people to do so will be called least in the kingdom of heaven; but the one who does them and teaches them shall be called great in the kingdom of heaven.

Matthew states categorically a principle—the continuing validity of Jewish law—which was in the process of being rejected by others in the early church. Contrary to Mark, Luke-Acts, John, and Paul on the one hand, Matthew, James, and the author of Revelation on the other believed that Jewish law remained binding on both Jewish and gentile followers of Jesus. Does Matthew's constitutional statement invoke the Jewish covenant? Although the word for "blessed" is not the term used for covenant blessings, Matthew pushes wisdom terminology in the direction of covenant blessings and curses; doing and teaching are the criteria by which one is included or excluded in regard to the kingdom of heaven.[17] Matthew concludes the constitutional statement with the following demand: "Unless your righteousness exceeds that of the scribes and the Pharisees, you will never enter the kingdom of heaven" (5:20). Matthew evidently means that the righteousness of Jesus' followers should exceed that of the scribes and Pharisees in observance of Jewish law as well as in internal disposition. This greater righteousness does not come through Pharisaic concerns of ritual impurity; rather, righteousness in Matthew lies in avoiding moral impurity by observing the law with a perfect inner disposition, one that does not look to a public display.

These verses are a preamble to a series of six paragraphs (5:21–48), each of which compares a commandment from Jewish law with Jesus' new revelation of its significance. They each take the form, "You have heard it said *x*, but I say to you *y*." The first one reads:

> You have heard that it was said to our forefathers, "You shall not kill, and whoever kills shall be liable to judgment." But I say to you that anyone who is angry with his brother or sister shall be liable to judgment.

In Christian tradition these six comparisons are called antitheses or antinomies (meaning opposing laws or even negations of laws), and have been viewed as a replacement of Jewish law by a new Christian righteousness not based on law. However, this judgment reflects Paul's influence on Christian theology, and not Matthew's meaning. As the previous constitutional statement assures the audience, Jewish law is still binding on followers of Jesus, and a close reading of these paragraphs confirms this. Despite the language of contrast, the Jewish law of the first half is not negated in the second half; the contrast is that in the second half of each declaration the law is *stronger*; Jewish law is now *even more demanding*, not null and void. The sayings are intensifications, not antitheses or antinomies.[18]

By summarizing them we can follow the logic of their intensification of the law:

1. You have heard it said: murder leads to judgment
   Now: even anger leads to judgment

2. You have heard it said: you shall not commit adultery
   Now: you shall not even look at a woman lustfully

3. You have heard it said: divorce is possible with a bill of divorce
   Now: divorce is not permitted (except for adultery)

4. You have heard it said: you shall not swear falsely
   Now: you shall not swear at all

5. You have heard it said: retaliation is limited to an eye for an eye and a tooth for a tooth
   Now: do not retaliate at all

6. You have heard it said: you shall love your neighbor and hate your enemy
   Now: you must love even your enemy

In each case, following Jesus' new, more demanding requirement does not violate the older one, but sanctifies social relations above and beyond the everyday life of pious Judaism. It is super-law, and also eschatological law, for the end of time has begun. Just as the Pharisees were "building a fence around the Torah" by creating more specific observances, and the Qumran sect was requiring heightened demands of purity, Matthew expanded the claims of the law. Jewish law is not relegated to the past; it has been perfected in Jesus' role as the new Moses. Such eschatological renewal of old institutions is typical of apocalyptic sects. As one sociologist of religion puts it, in such sects "the new dispensation will be no mere improvement on the present, but perfection itself."[19] Jesus' words also turn the discussion very intensively in the direction of inner dispositions: do not be angry, do not commit adultery in your heart, turn the other cheek, love your enemy. The audience is asked to change from a pious, observant Jew into a *perfect* brother or sister who fulfills all the law, both in external observance *and in inner inclination*. If "perfect" seems too strong a word here, note that it is at the conclusion of these paragraphs that Jesus says, "Be therefore perfect as your heavenly Father is perfect" (5:48).

The analysis of Matthew becomes even more interesting at this point if we note the sources of the six intensifications and Matthew's changes. The third, fifth, and sixth find parallels in Q or Mark, but the substance of the other three do not. It is likely that the latter—on anger, lust, and swearing—are derived from the Matthean source M, and served as a model for the others. The intent in M is not to silence the body through discipline, as later Christian ascetics would advocate, but to silence the wrong inner dispositions. This will be achieved in part by enjoining the correct attitude in the Sermon on the Mount, but also by constructing the "hypocrites" below as the representatives of the wrong approach. This is where the bitter polemic against the Pharisees arises, for in Matthew's view, they focus too much attention on correct external actions. The distinction found in M between a showy, external practice of piety and a heartfelt internal experience of devotion may reflect Klawans' distinction between ritual purity and moral purity, but may reflect a class friction as well. M and Matthew both advocate patterns of religious life that correspond to a class level below that of the Pharisees, much as the Quaker movement was opposed to the show of high church practices, or the Sufi movement in Islam sought a direct relationship with God that did not require intermediary clerics. This raises the question, which will be taken up again below, as to whether M's and Matthew's program for inner integrity actually *began* as a reaction against the Pharisees' program for outer integrity.

Who Are the Hypocrites?

The Sermon on the Mount next moves from a new understanding of the law—meant, perhaps, to shock the audience into an abrupt shift in awareness—to a description of three different aspects of religious practice: almsgiving, prayer, and fasting. Within this broad topic of Jewish piety, Matthew presents a clear message (6:1–2):

> Do not practice your religious devotion in public in order to be seen by others, for then you will have no reward from your Father who is in heaven. Thus, when you give alms, do not sound a trumpet before you, as the hypocrites do in the synagogues and in the streets in order to receive the praise of others.

It is emphasized that the followers of Jesus *must not* make a show of their acts of charity. Further, the honor that one would have sought from others should be sought instead from "your Father who is in heaven." In Matthew's reversal of shame, outward human honor becomes a shroud that blocks the view of God.[20] Matthew's pattern in the three practices, charity, prayer, and fasting, is the same:

> Do not do x publicly, for public approval, as the hypocrites do, but secretly for your Father who is in heaven.

We may wonder what "hypocrites" means precisely in Matthew. They are not identified here, although in Matthew 23 they will be matched with scribes and Pharisees.

In modern English the word "hypocrite" generally refers to people who say one thing but do another, whether the inconsistency is conscious or unconscious. The Greek word *hypokritēs*, however, is more ambiguous. In the Greek translation of the Hebrew Bible it means a godless or wicked person (translating Hebrew *honef*), but in the larger Greek world it meant the actor in a play, and therefore the sense of pretense or acting and the two-part personality of an actor who plays a part come to the fore. Thus in early Christian texts, the exact nuance of the word is not always clear, but it may have as many as three meanings: (1) one who is godless or wicked; (2) a person who pretends to be one thing but *consciously* acts contrary to that; and (3) a person who believes one thing but *unconsciously* acts contrary to that. Does the sin of hypocrisy in Matthew consist in consciously deceiving others or in being in denial about one's own sin?

The word also reflects an important development in Hellenistic psychology. At the same time that there was an evolution from hypocrisy as simple vice or deceit (Job 34:30, 2 Macc 6:25) to a focus on inner, even subconscious lack of integrity, other terms also arose in Jewish and Christian literature to express this same notion of having a double perspective: divided heart (*kardia dissē*, Sir 1:28), having a divided mind (*dignōmōn, Didache* 2:4), double-tongued (*diglōssos*, Sir 5:9, *Didache* 2:4), and double-minded (*dipsycheō*, James 4:8). Among some Jews and followers of Jesus, a vocabulary was developing to describe the psychology of dishonesty and lack of integrity, mirroring contemporary developments in Stoicism. There was increasing interest on interior states, in addition to exterior actions. During this period the term *haplotēs*, "simplicity," also came to mean integrity, sincerity, and liberality, or one might say, the opposite of hypocrisy (Col 3:22, 1 *Clement* 23:1; compare Matt 6:22), or the "unhypocritical love" (*agapē anupokritos*) of Romans 12:9. The adjective form is used in some places in the Greek Old Testament to translate the same Hebrew word that is translated "perfect," *teleios*—similar, therefore, to Matthew's sense of "perfect" in the Sermon on the Mount.[21] Matthew is thus not alone in examining inner intentions; it is a staple of Jewish and Christian texts. But Matthew pushes it much further than they do: hypocrisy is an extreme form of being double-minded, and it is the opposite of perfect. We and Other could not be more distinct. This new development will be even more in evidence in Matthew 23.

General Instructions in the Sermon on the Mount

The beatitudes, a constitutional statement on the law, and the intensifications of the law become a necessary preamble to wisdom in the Sermon on the Mount. In Q, wisdom sayings are authoritative simply because Jesus, the envoy of the figure of personified Wisdom, is uttering them. Matthew begins with this structure but expands each section, rendering the whole Sermon double the size of the Q sermon. The radical reorientation demanded in the preamble means that the wisdom is now understood differently. It is absolute. Jesus is not an envoy of personified Wisdom, but wisdom embodied as the new Moses. The Sermon on the Mount is thus a formational text that constitutes the We by creating the ideal moral agent and righteous person for the community of the end-time.

CONSTRUCTING THE OTHER: THE WOES AGAINST "SCRIBES AND PHARISEES, HYPOCRITES" IN MATTHEW 23

We might have examined passages relating to the chief priests or Roman officials as Other, but the chief priests lie in Matthew's past, and Rome is to Matthew as Assyria is to the Deuteronomistic Historian: too other to be Other.[22] Stated simply, in Matthew's symbolic world it is the Pharisees who define the mirrored edges of the community's identity, and this is most emphatically expressed in Matthew 23. The Sermon on the Mount, the first of Matthew's five discourses, and Matthew 23, part of the last, work together to construct the We and the Other.[23] Addressed to "crowds" and to disciples, they balance each other as bookends in that the beatitudes of the Sermon on the Mount can be contrasted with the woes in chapter twenty-three. In addition, the use of hypocrites as negative models in chapter six is matched by a denunciation of hypocrites in chapter twenty-three, while the statement that "your righteousness should exceed that of the scribes and Pharisees" in 5:20 foreshadows a condemnation of what is taken to be the self-righteous display of the scribes and Pharisees in Matthew 23. The relationship with God as Father is also emphasized in both. But more interesting, it is not coincidental that the Sermon on the Mount and Matthew 23 *contain most of the verses attributed to M*,[24] and they contain very little derived from Mark. As will become clear, M has perhaps contributed more to Matthew's particular conception of the Other than has Mark or Q.

Preamble of Matthew's Construction of the Other (Matthew 23:1–12)

Matthew 23 can be divided into three parts:

1) preamble: command to practice what the scribes and Pharisees preach, not what they do (verses 1–12)
2) seven woes against "scribes and Pharisees, hypocrites" (verses 13–31)
3) denunciation of Jerusalem (verses 32–39)

The beginning of Jesus' speech in Matthew 23 contains a striking, even shocking admission: "The scribes and Pharisees sit on Moses' seat; practice and observe whatever they tell you, but not what they do." What is the nature of the debate with the scribes and Pharisees that Matthew could acknowledge and even affirm their authority to teach, even if they fail to meet their own standards? This is especially odd since just a few chapters earlier Jesus had twice forbidden his followers to observe the traditions of the scribes and Pharisees (15:6–9, 16:5–12). It is likely that verses 2–3, along with verses 5 and 7b–10, are derived from M, which expresses a perspective slightly different from Matthew's own editing. M, not as far out the sectarian limb as Matthew, insists that one should practice all that the scribes and Pharisees teach, but also denounces them for matters that are not, strictly speaking, a debate over *principles*: "they do not practice what they teach." The respect that M shows for the authoritative teaching of the scribes and Pharisees has probably been retained by Matthew to increase the rhetorical impact of the denunciation that follows; the higher the perch, the greater is the fall of the hypocrite.[25]

Following this, Matthew 23:8–10 elaborates on the actions of the scribes and Pharisees. Part of this section is taken from Mark, and the rest is most likely from M:

Matthew 23:5–10	*Mark 12:38–39*
The scribes and Pharisees perform all of their deeds in order to be seen by others; for they make their *tefillin* wide and their *tzitzit* long, they love the places of honor at banquets, the best seats in the synagogues, receiving greetings in the marketplaces, and being addressed by people as "rabbi." But you are not to be called rabbi by people, for you have one teacher, and you are all brothers and sisters. And do not call anyone on earth your father, for you have one Father, who is in heaven. And also do not be called masters, for you have one master, the messiah.	Beware of the scribes, who like to walk about in long robes and receive greetings in the marketplaces, the best seats in the synagogues,[26] and the places of honor at banquets, who devour widows' homes and make a show of uttering long prayers. They will receive the greater condemnation.

The tone of Mark sounds very similar to Matthew, but on closer analysis we find that there are some significant differences. Mark's warning concerns the scribes alone, not scribes and Pharisees as in Matthew. Mark is very clear on the problem with the scribes: in a culture in which public honor and shame are very important, the scribes receive honor. This is similar to M, but Mark focuses on different external markers of honor. The opponents wear the robes of the wealthy and powerful, receive the greetings that their status would demand in a hierarchical society, and are seated at places of honor in the synagogues and feasts. From their privileged position the scribes can amass further wealth by exploiting the unprotected widows, all the while making a public show of piety with long prayers. Like the Q woes, this passage in Mark represents strong evidence that some New Testament texts protest the exploitation of the poor by the Jewish leaders. In taking over Mark's verses, however, Matthew has not kept the clear economic critique; "devouring widows' homes" has been removed, and Matthew has omitted the story of the poor widow which Mark recounts immediately afterward. Relative to Mark, Matthew here downplays the critique of economic exploitation.

What Matthew contains here that is lacking in Mark is probably from M: "The [scribes and Pharisees] perform all of their deeds in order to be seen by others. They make their *tefillin* [prayer boxes] broad and their *tzitzit* [fringes on prayer shawls] long." By incorporating M, Matthew modifies Mark's general statement condemning the public honor of the scribes and specifies religious observances that are hallmarks of the Pharisees' revitalization movement. Matthew's edited version marks the boundaries separating the good from the bad differently than does Mark. Matthew continues with the following lines from M:

> But you are not to be called rabbi by people, for you have one teacher, and you are all brothers and sisters. And do not call anyone on earth your father, for you have one Father, who is in heaven. And also do not be called masters, for you have one master, the messiah. (Matt 23:8–10)

These offenses are not as directly economic as they were in Mark, but relate more specifically to Jewish religious practices. According to M the scribes and Pharisees create a show of piety and take great pleasure in honorific titles: rabbi, father, master. It is likely that all three terms were interchangeable titles for Pharisaic leaders and teachers in the first century. M's rejection of earthly titles for religious superiors, roughly equivalent to the rejection of honorific titles by Quakers, is based on a belief in the equality of the community, with Jesus as the only teacher and master and God as the only father. Comparing the M sayings here with those in the Sermon on the Mount, we may add that hypocrisy consists in a showy piety that lacks heartfelt devotion.

Woes against "Scribes and Pharisees, Hypocrites"

Matthew proceeds next to a series of seven woes arranged in a formulaic way against "scribes and Pharisees, hypocrites."

Woe #1: Matthew 23:13/Q 11:52

Matthew 23:13	Q 11:52
Woe to you, scribes and Pharisees, hypocrites!	Woe to you, interpreters of the law!
For you shut people out of the kingdom of heaven. You neither enter yourselves, nor allow those who want to to go in.	You shut people out of the kingdom of God. You neither entered yourselves, nor did you allow those who wanted to to go in.

The woes in Q and in Matthew evoke the woes of the classical writing prophets of the Hebrew Bible. The "woe oracle" was a means of calling down God's judgment against the sins of Israel or the nations. The rhetorical pattern of this woe in Q presents a two-step cause for offense: (1) the opponents did not enter the kingdom of God themselves, (2) but what's more, they have also prevented others from entering. The two steps create an ironic or satirical tone, the second providing a punch-line that reveals the truth about the first.[27] The Q woes also include a direct attack on motives and integrity. In this passage Matthew retains the irony of Q, but we shall find that that is not the case in some of the other woes.

Woe #2: Matthew 23:15

Matthew's next woe is not borrowed from Mark or Q, but takes the same form as the Q woes, a two-step denunciation consisting of a description of a seemingly pious action and a punch line:

> Woe to you, scribes and Pharisees, hypocrites! For you travel over the sea and land in order to make a single convert, but when he becomes a convert, you make him twice the child of hell that you are!

The punch line, however, is hardly a clever revelation of the true nature of things. It is what may be called a "default to hell," a denunciation that is absolute, final, a judgment not meant to convert or even impress, as the Q woes are. It is often attributed to M,[28] but its blunt force is not similar to the other verses from M. It is similar, rather, to Matthew's own editing at 23:33, another default to hell ("You serpents, you brood of vipers! How will you escape being sentenced to hell?").

Woe #3: Matthew 23:16–22

The longest of Matthew's woes has no parallel in Mark or Q:

> Woe to you, blind guides, who say, "If anyone swears by the temple, it is not binding, but if anyone swears by the gold of the temple, it is binding." You blind fools! For which is greater, the gold or the temple which has made the gold sacred? You also say, "If anyone swears by the altar, it is not binding, but if anyone swears by the gift that is on it, it is binding." You blind people! For which is greater, the gift or the altar which has made the gift sacred? So the one who swears by the altar swears by it and by everything on it, and the one who swears by the temple swears by it and by the one who dwells in it; and the one who swears by heaven swears by the throne of God and by the one who sits on the throne.

It is often attributed to M, but probably incorrectly. Concerned about particulars of *halachah* rather than the more general issue of showy versus sincere, it is the section of chapter twenty-three that most clearly reflects Matthew's own point of view.[29] The condemnation of the opponents as blind corresponds to Matthew's own emphasis elsewhere (15:13–14 and below).

Woe #4: Matthew 23:23–24/Q 11:42

Matthew 23:23–24	*Q 11:42*
Woe to you, scribes and Pharisees, hypocrites!	Woe to you, Pharisees!
For you tithe mint and dill and cumin, but have neglected the weightier matters of the law, judgment and mercy and faithfulness.	You tithe mint and dill and cumin, but ignore judgment and mercy and faithfulness.
These you ought to have done without neglecting the others.	You should have done these without neglecting the others.
You blind guides! You are straining out a gnat but swallowing a camel!	

Tithing had always been required by Jewish law (Lev 27:30–33), but also became a central part of the Pharisees' revitalization movement (*Mishnah Maàserot* 1:1). Tithing was not just *a* practice of the Pharisees, but along with table purity (see below) was one of the banner practices associated with their movement, and as a result is emphasized by Q and Matthew. One might at first assume that Q would reject outright all such minute observance in favor of broader ethical concerns such as the covenant values of "judgment and mercy and faithfulness," but the following line assures us that *both* are important: "You should have done these without neglecting the others." Matthew retains the broad swipe at the Pharisees and adds in addition, "You blind guides! You strain out the gnat while swallowing a camel!" Both of the animals are nonkosher, but in Matthew's view, straining the gnat out of wine has prevented the scribes and Pharisees from seeing the camel on their plate. Because their zeal to be attentive to the minor impurities, their blindness has allowed them to become guilty of greater sins. Some of Matthew's special concerns can be seen here. Matthew adds the word "blind" to the condemnation, which occurs four times in this chapter. The blind motif that Matthew emphasizes so strongly pushes us to the conclusion that Matthew's definition of hypocrisy is self-deception rather than intentional deceit of others.

Woe #5: Matthew 23:25–26/Q 11:39

Matthew 23:25–26	*Q 11:39*
Woe to you, scribes and Pharisees, hypocrites!	You Pharisees
For you purify the outside of the cup and plate, but inside they are full of greed and depravity.	purify the outside of the cup and dish, but inside they are full of greed and depravity.
You blind Pharisee!	
First purify the inside of the cup and plate, so that the outside will also be pure.	First purify the inside of the cup and plate, so that the outside will also be pure.

The Pharisees' revitalization movement advocated table purity for all Jews that would be as exacting as the purity maintained in the temple, and as a result they ritually cleansed cups and dishes before eating. Q and Matthew both contrast this external purity with the hidden sin of their opponents, the inside of the cup, and Matthew adds the notion that the Pharisees are blind. Despite the fact that each woe in Matthew is addressed to scribes *and* Pharisees, here the emotional outburst is against the blind Pharisee only. It is probably the Pharisees more than the scribes whom Matthew would reckon as the Other, perhaps because Matthew *was* a scribe. Elsewhere Matthew can distinguish between good and bad scribes, but there are no good Pharisees, just as there were previously no good Canaanites (Theorem 5: Reduced to a single essence). The further question arises of why the Pharisees cannot be loved as enemies are to be loved (Matt 5:44), a difficult question that cannot be engaged here, except to suggest that for Matthew—more than for Mark, M, or Q (the source of "love your enemies")—the Pharisees arise as a special foe that is more than "enemy"; they are "Other." Since the Pharisees are subject to the default to hell, we may assume that there is an aspect of eschatological judgment that is specified in their case, and left unspoken in the case of other enemies.

Woe #6: Matthew 23:27–28/Q 11:44

Matthew 23:27–28	*Q 11:44*
Woe to you, scribes and Pharisees, hypocrites!	Woe to you, Pharisees!

For you are like whitewashed tombs, which outwardly appear beautiful, but inside are full of dead people's bones and all impurity. So also you outwardly appear righteous to people, but inside you are full of hypocrisy and lawlessness.	For you are like unmarked tombs which people walk over unawares.

Lying behind both texts is the Jewish belief that corpses and bones were ritually polluting. Graves were marked with whitewash during pilgrimage festivals so that pilgrims would not accidentally come in contact with graves and be unable to approach the temple. The application of the metaphor in each case is somewhat different. Q's metaphor seems to capture the real danger of unmarked tombs, but Matthew has pushed the metaphor in a new direction:

Q: You are like unmarked tombs, which people walk over unawares (and become polluted).

Matt: You are like tombs that are beautiful on the outside, but on the inside are full of bones (which are polluting).

The *invisible* graves of Q become the *showy* graves of Matthew; the danger of deception in Q becomes a contrast in Matthew between an ostentatious display of superiority and inner, hidden moral impurity. Matthew also reduces the full play of the metaphor. What in Q is a vivid, even satirical little parable of people walking over polluted graves becomes in Matthew a more static contrast of surface and underlying reality. Matthew, indeed, feels the need to follow up the already reduced metaphor with a full explanation of its meaning—lest anyone miss the point—while Q was apparently content to let the biting narrative speak for itself.

It may seem strange that Matthew condemns the lawlessness (*anomia*) of the scribes and Pharisees, since the latter were known for being observant. However, here, as elsewhere in Judaism, the charge of lawlessness may be a blanket condemnation of those who remain outside the sect. They are "lawless" in the sense that they are outside the covenant of God's law.[30]

Woe #7: Matthew 23:29–30/Q 11:47–48

Matthew 23:29–30	*Q 11:47–48*
Woe to you, scribes and Pharisees, hypocrites!	Woe to you!
For you build the tombs of the prophets and adorn the monuments of the righteous,	For you build the tombs of the prophets,

Matthew 23:29–30	*Q 11:47–48*
and say, "If we had lived in the days of our forefathers, we would not have joined with them in shedding the blood of the prophets."	but your forefathers killed them.
Thus you are witnessing against yourselves, testifying that you are descended from those who murdered the prophets.	Thus you are witnessing against yourselves, testifying that you are descended from those forefathers.

As above, so here also Q works with an ironic denunciation in two steps: the opponents build the tombs of the prophets even though, it is charged, their forefathers were the ones who killed them. They are creating a public show of piety even though by descent they are tainted with the guilt of killing the prophets. This discrepancy between the public show of the Pharisees and their actual guilt is emphasized in the few words of Q, but it is not stated whether the Pharisees are guilty of conscious deceit or are in denial. In Matthew, however, an intermediate point is added in which the scribes and Pharisees attempt to distance themselves from the sin of their forefathers. Their very disclaimer indicates that the scribes and Pharisees are in denial; Matthew repeats the motif from above that they are unconscious hypocrites, not conscious deceivers.[31]

It is possible at this point to draw some conclusions about the woes in Q and compare them with M and Matthew. Most of the seven Q woes have a two-step pattern in which the first step describes a typical, usually ostentatious practice, while the second is a punch line that uncovers the reality behind the practice. (Some of the woes also receive a third summary comment as well.) The two-step pattern, a description and satirical punch line, is the dominant rhetorical structure here in Q. The logic of the sayings, however, is not a strictly linear logic but a rhetorical pattern of vituperation. The Q woes depend on contrast and irony, metaphor and vividness, satire and broadside condemnation. They can be compared to ritual contests of verbal sparring in other cultures, and the concrete images may reflect oral composition. But this is not the case in Matthew. The two-step patterns are retained in some of the woes, but Matthew loses much of this artfulness, is less ironic, over-explains, and is more apocalyptic. In some cases Matthew drops this pattern altogether in favor of other patterns (seen most dramatically in Matthew 23:16–22).

Woes in the Hebrew Bible prophets condemn the false security of leaders who ignore covenant obligations to God and the people, and announce a day of judgment. The Q woes, which follow in this tradition, are what Richard Horsley calls an "indictment for violation of a covenant principle."[32] Matthew loses some of this focus. The woes in Matthew, except where they keep the wording of Q, do not invoke covenant traditions as clearly, and economic justice is not as discernible. What they do emphasize is halachic differences with the scribes and Pharisees and the sectarian boundaries that result. There may, in fact, be a general loss of the prophetic voice in Matthew in favor of a scribal voice. Michael Fishbane charts an analogous process in the rise of rabbinic Judaism, which he calls "a neutralization of the prophetic impulse—its scribalization, one might say, and its reemployment in the service of the Law."[33] It is not that Matthew exhibits an antipathy to prophecy, but more that a different voice is being cultivated. Lurking here is perhaps one more piece of evidence that Matthew condemns the scribes and Pharisees not because they are so different, but because they are very similar (Theorem 3).

We could proceed in this way through the whole of Matthew 23, but the nature of Matthew's sources and Matthew's own editing are now clear. As vitriolic and unrelenting as Matthew's final version seems in our own day, when intercultural and ecumenical understanding are highly valued, it is actually similar to the polemic against false philosophy found in other ancient authors. Luke T. Johnson provides abundant parallels to this sort of condemnation of opposing philosophers among the Greeks, Romans, and Jews that illuminate the argumentative world of Matthew. It is not just the mistaken beliefs and immoral actions of others that philosophers berate. They also attack the motives of their opponents, their dignity, their parentage, and so on, using very caustic language. Johnson concludes, "By the measure of Hellenistic conventions, and certainly by the measure of contemporary Jewish polemic, the New Testament's slander against fellow Jews is remarkably mild."[34] But here Johnson overstates the case. Matthew and John, in contrast to the ancient philosophers and rhetoricians, present an absolute condemnation that is born of an apocalyptic worldview and culminates in a default to hell. It is similar to the Dead Sea Scrolls, but not the Greek, Roman, or Jewish intellectuals. "It is only Essenes and Christians," says Elaine Pagels, "who actually escalate conflict with their opponents to the level of cosmic war."[35]

CONCLUSION

Matthew's gospel reflects an overall program of education or formation, a natural outgrowth of a scribal background. The Sermon on the Mount is the first of Matthew's five discourses, and embodies this transformative program to construct the We of the sectarian community at the end of time. Matthew 23, which begins Matthew's fifth and final discourse, constructs the Other by denouncing the negative example of piety, the scribes and Pharisees. Clearly, for Matthew it is the Pharisees who are the constant Other. The Sermon on the Mount and Matthew 23 are a matched set of bookends that use many of the same motifs and focus on the same issues:[36]

Sermon on the Mount	*Matthew 23*
Righteousness (5:6, 20)	Righteousness (23:35)
God as Father (5:16)	God as Father (23:9)
Jesus as teacher (7:28)	Jesus as teacher (23:8)
Scribes and Pharisees (5:20)	Scribes and Pharisees (23:2, etc.)
Hypocrites (6:2)	Hypocrites (23:13, etc.)
Entering kingdom of heaven (5:20)	Shutting kingdom of heaven (23:13)
Doing deeds to be seen (6:1)	Doing deeds to be seen (23:5)
In synagogues and streets (6:2)	In synagogues and marketplaces (23:6–7)
They love to pray in synagogues (6:5)	They love first seats in synagogues (23:6)
Mercy (5:7)	Mercy (23:23)
Pure ("clean") of heart (5:8)	Make "inside" (= heart) clean (23:25)
Children of God (5:9)	Children of hell (23:15)
Persecuting prophets (5:12)	Persecuting prophets and others (23:29–31, 37)
Swearing (5:33–34)	Swearing (23:16)
One master (*kurios*; 6:24)	One master (*kathēgētēs*; 23:10)
Speck and log in eye (7:3–5)	Gnat and camel in bowl (23:24)

We noted above that many of the similarities between these two discourses are derived from the hypothetical source M. As W. D. Davies and Dale Allison point out, there are many parallels between the M sections of the Sermon on the Mount and the M sections of chapter twenty-three, both in terms of motifs and in terms of structure. "Matthew," they suspect, "took up a pre-Matthean text on Christian piety, broke it in two, and deposited the first half in chapter 6, the other half in chapter 23."[37] Although Matthew took over sections of Mark and Q, often losing their prophetic edge, it is M which established themes that Matthew wanted to emphasize. M's criticism of public honor was used as a jumping-off point for a condemnation of Pharisaic *halachah* and a judgment that they were doomed to hell. Matthew invokes halachic differences to draw sharper sectarian boundaries with the Pharisees, and like other strongly sectarian groups, presumes a predestination of the righteous and damned. M perceived the Pharisees as the "public honor people," and for that they are condemned; Matthew perceived the Pharisees as that also, but in addition they were the "wrong *halachah* people"; for that they are to be damned to hell. Corresponding to this, the charge of hypocrisy in Q (6:42), Mark (7:6), and M (6:2) seems to carry the meaning of conscious deceit of others, while in Matthew it more likely refers to self-deception and unconscious denial, perhaps an inevitable development of sectarian predestination.

The gist of M is taken over and endorsed by Matthew, including the labeling of the opponents as hypocrites, the sincere worship of God as Father, and especially the continuing authority of Jewish law. But certain differences between M and Matthew can also be detected. M states unequivocally that the scribes and Pharisees retain authority in terms of their teaching, while Matthew insists that followers of Jesus should reject the special traditions of the scribes and Pharisees. And whereas M had forbidden swearing, Matthew passionately argues the proper means of swearing. This last example highlights what may have been the most important difference in approach between M and Matthew: M condemned the showiness of the scribes and Pharisees and their love of public honor and contrasts this with a sincere and even *secret* piety, but Matthew emphasizes instead the visible "fruits" of actions:

Matthew	M
Let your light shine before others so that they may see your good works and give glory to your Father in heaven. (5:16)	Do not practice your religious devotion in public in order to be seen by others, for then you will have no reward from your Father who is in heaven. (6:1) Scribes and Pharisees do all their deeds to be seen by others. (23:5)

It was M who introduced a strong emphasis on the proper inner disposition, and these quotations about visible fruits from Matthew might seem at first to be moving in a different direction. But Matthew may simply be pressing M's distinction more emphatically. It is not just that the action be carried out "in secret" as in M, but it must be "perfect." Matthew presumes, then, many of the beliefs of the sources, but has made significant alterations and additions that reflect a rather classic sectarian position: Matthew identifies with the venerated traditions of the parent-body and they must be followed with an absolute perfection. Following from this is an urgent need to define the boundaries that will mark off salvation and damnation at the end of time. As L. Michael White says, "It is a case of 'marginal differentiation,' where minutiae—or marginal features of faith and practice—are used to preserve a sense of difference between organisms that are otherwise substantially similar."[38] Matthew may, in fact, be composing an antidote for the problem of attraction to the Pharisees.

Sectarian groups in general often focus on orthopraxy over orthodoxy in order to establish the boundaries of the sect, and this has been as true of Christian sects over the centuries as others. But given the nature of the Pharisees' program of external observance and ritual purity, Matthew must also look inward to inscribe boundaries. The clearest distinction that Matthew can impose is the *approach* to purity. Klawans' distinction between ritual impurity and moral impurity applies here: Matthew draws a line in the sand over which approach will make one righteous before God. And one can certainly imagine a popular philosophical influence in Matthew's intense analysis of "perfect" and "righteous" as the model of the unified mind, and unconscious hypocrisy as the model of a divided mind, positive and negative poles respectively of a coherent moral psychology. We might characterize the Sermon on the Mount as a presentation of the right mind-set, and Matthew 23 as a presentation of the wrong mind-set for Matthew's sectarian school.

NOTES

1. Throughout this study I use the Greek text of Q as reconstructed by the International Q Project, available in James M. Robinson, Paul Hoffmann, and John S. Kloppenborg, *The Critical Edition of Q* (Minneapolis, MN: Fortress; Leuven, Belgium: Peeters, 2000). The English translations are my own. Note that throughout this study, Q passages are numbered according to their appearance in Luke.

2. For purposes of this discussion, I assign the distinctive sayings found in three different blocks of material to M: 5:21–22, 27–28, 33–37; 6:1–8, 16–18; and 23:2–3, 5, 7b–10. This is in agreement with W. D. Davies and Dale Allison, *A Critical and Exegetical Commentary on the Gospel according to Matthew*, 3 vols. (Edinburgh, UK: Clark, 1988–97), 1:125–27.

3. Anthony J. Saldarini, *Matthew's Christian-Jewish Community* (Chicago: University of Chicago Press, 1994), 124–64; Daniel J. Harrington, *The Gospel of Matthew* (Collegeville, MN: Liturgical, 1991), 1. Amy-Jill Levine, "Matthew, Mark, and Luke: Good News or Bad?" in *Jesus, Judaism, and Christian Anti-Judaism: Reading the New Testament after the Holocaust*, ed. Paula Fredriksen and Adele Reinhartz (Louisville, KY/London: Westminster/John Knox, 2002), 77–98, has asked whether Matthew is in the *final* stages of an inner-Jewish debate or at an *early* stage of a post-Jewish Christianity, and believes that the latter is the case, but I think it more likely that Matthew is in the later stages of an inner-Jewish debate. However, on the political implications of reading Matthew *as if* it were still Jewish and not Christian see Amy-Jill Levine, "Matthew's Advice to a Divided Readership," in *The Gospel of Matthew in Current Study: Studies in Memory of William G. Thompson, S.J.*, ed. David E. Aune (Grand Rapids, MI: Eerdmans, 2001), 39–40.

4. M. Jack Suggs, *Wisdom, Christology and Law in Matthew's Gospel* (Cambridge, MA: Harvard University Press, 1970), 125–27, contra Warren Carter, *Matthew and Empire: Initial Explorations* (Harrisburg, PA: TPI, 2001), 108–10.

5. It is now quite common to identify Matthew's community as a sectarian community; see L. Michael White, "Crisis Management and Boundary Maintenance: The Social Location of the Matthean Community," in *Social History of the Matthean Community: Cross-Disciplinary Approaches*, ed. David L. Balch (Minneapolis, MN: Fortress, 1991), 211–47; Anthony J. Saldarini, "The Delegitimation of Leaders in Matthew 23," *Catholic Biblical Quarterly* 54 (1992): 659–80; Anthony J. Saldarini, *Pharisees, Scribes, and Sadducees in Palestinian Society: A Sociological Approach* (Wilmington, DE: M. Glazier, 1988); and J. Andrew Overman, *Matthew's Gospel and Formative Judaism: The Social World of the Matthean Community* (Minneapolis, MN: Fortress, 1990), 16–19. I would no longer characterize the Pharisees as a sect, as I did in "Scribal Methods in Matthew and Mishnah *Avot*," *Catholic Biblical Quarterly* 63 (2001): 241–57. Albert Baumgarten describes the Pharisees as a voluntary association ("Greco-Roman Voluntary Associations," in *Jews in a Graeco-Roman World*, ed. Martin Goodman [Oxford: Clarendon/New York: Oxford University Press, 1999], 93–111), and elsewhere (*The Flourishing of Jewish Sects in the Maccabean Era: An Interpretation* [Leiden, Netherlands: Brill, 1997], 12–14), using the terminology of Bryan Wilson, characterizes both Pharisees and Sadducees as reformist sects, which is much the same as a revitalization movement.

6. White, "Crisis Management," 240; Seth Schwartz, *Josephus and Judean Politics* (Leiden, Netherlands: Brill, 1990), 200–208; Jacob Neusner, *Judaism, The Evidence of the Mishnah* (Chicago: University of Chicago Press, 1981), 230–56; Saldarini, "Delegitimation," 663.

7. Jonathan Klawans, *Impurity and Sin in Ancient Judaism* (Oxford: Oxford University Press, 2000). The rabbis would also have a place for intention, *kavvanah*, in both prayer (*Avot* 2:13) and actions (*bBer.* 13a), but for Matthew—and M—it is absolutely central.

8. The class designations that I use here are from Gerhard Lenski, *Power and Privilege: A Theory of Social Stratification* (New York: McGraw-Hill, 1966), 214–96; see the more detailed argument in Lawrence M. Wills, "Methodological Reflections on the Tax Collectors in the Gospels," in *When Judaism and Christianity Began: Essays in Memory of Anthony J. Saldarini*, ed. Alan J. Avery-Peck, Daniel Harrington, and Jacob Neusner (Leiden, Netherlands, and Boston: Brill, 2004), 251–66. On the social status and dress of the Pharisees, see Shaye J. D. Cohen, "The Place of the Rabbi in Jewish Society of the Second Century," in *The Galilee in Late Antiquity*, ed. Lee Levine (New York: Jewish Theological Seminary of America, 1992), 168; and Seth Schwartz, "Historiography," in *Oxford Handbook of Jewish Studies*, ed. Martin Goodman (Oxford and New York: Oxford University Press, 2002), 98–102.

9. Wills, "Methodological Reflections."

10. Ancient references to the toll collectors often place them with others of the merchant class, in one case in a discussion as to why an aristocrat should never *choose* these professions. Presumably, it is an option that is only rejected after reflection: Dio Chrysostom, *Orations* 14.14; Cicero, *De officiis* 1.42.150–51; Julian, *Against the Galileans*, 238E; Philostratus, *Life of Apollonius* 8.7.11.

11. On forgiveness of sins, see Richard Horsley, *Jesus and the Spiral of Violence: Popular Jewish Resistance in Roman Palestine* (San Francisco: Harper & Row, 1987), 222, and E. P. Sanders, *Jesus and Judaism* (Philadelphia: Fortress, 1985), 207–8, but note also Bruce Chilton, "Jesus and the Repentance of E. P. Sanders," *Tyndale Bulletin* 39 (1988): 1–18.

12. Jack T. Sanders, *Schismatics, Sectarians, Dissidents, Deviants: The First One Hundred Years of Jewish-Christian Relations* (Valley Forge, PA: TPI, 1993), 129–51; Anthony J. Saldarini, "The Gospel of Matthew and Jewish-Christian Conflict," in Balch, *Social History*, 38–61. Cf. also the narrative of special election by some groups to explain their deviant status: Peter Berger and Thomas Luckmann, *The Social Construction of Reality: An Essay in the Sociology of Knowledge* (Garden City, NY: Doubleday, 1967), 166–67.

13. K. C. Hanson, "Transformed on the Mountain: Ritual Analysis and the Gospel of Matthew," *Semeia* 67 (1994): 147–70. See also Jonathan Draper, "The Genesis and Narrative Thrust of the Paraenesis in the Sermon on the Mount," *JSNT* 75 (1999): 29–30; and James G. Williams, "Irony and Lament: Clues to Prophetic Consciousness," *Semeia* 8 (1977): 51–74.

14. This structure is an adaptation of that offered by Graham Stanton, *A Gospel for a New People: Studies in Matthew* (Louisville, KY: Westminster/John Knox, 1993), 297–98.

15. John S. Kloppenborg, "Didache 16:6–8 and Special Matthaean Tradition," *Zeitschrift für die neutestamentliche Wissenschaft* 70 (1979): 54–67.

16. Some liberation theologians have argued that Matthew's terms have not been spiritualized in relation to Q and that they do depict the marginalized; see Elsa Tamez, *Bible of the Oppressed* (Maryknoll, NY: Orbis, 1982), 72–74; Gustavo Gutiérrez, *The God of Life* (Maryknoll, NY: Orbis, 1991), 103–5. Some of these same categories exist at Qumran (such as poor in spirit, *anavei ruach*, 1QM 14:7) where they express a self-understanding of being God's chosen, not literally poor. Cf. also Ps 34:18 and see Draper, "Genesis and Narrative Thrust," 35–36. The economic meaning cannot be ruled out, but throughout the gospel Matthew is focusing on a series of binary oppositions between outward show and inner dispositions.

17. Draper, "Genesis and Narrative Thrust," 35.

18. Harrington, *Gospel of Matthew*, 86–92; Draper, "Genesis and Narrative Thrust," 39; and Jonathan Draper, "Christian Self-Definition against the 'Hypocrites' in *Did.* 8," *Society of Biblical Literature Seminar Papers*, ed. Eugene H. Lovering (Atlanta, GA: Scholars, 1992), 362–77.

19. Keith A. Roberts, *Religion in Sociological Perspective* (Chicago: Dorsey, 1984), 304.

20. Robert Banks, *Jesus and the Law in the Synoptic Tradition* (Cambridge, UK: Cambridge University Press, 1975), 180–81.

21. Lawrence M. Wills, "Ascetic Theology before Asceticism? Jewish Narratives and the Decentering of the Self," *Journal of the American Academy of Religion* 74 (2006): 902–25. The turn to the interior aspect of the ethical control can be compared with that of the Roman emperor Marcus Aurelius nearly a hundred years later. James Francis, *Subversive Virtue: Asceticism and Authority in the Second-Century Pagan World* (University Park: Pennsylvania State University Press, 1995), 28, calls this emphasis in Marcus Aurelius "asceticism of reason."

22. Matthew's gospel, according to Carter, *Matthew and Empire*, is an extended critique of Roman domination and economic exploitation, and Matthew perceives every instance of the dominance of Jewish leaders as an extension of the Roman overlords. Carter is surely right in his analysis of Roman social relations in general, and in the urgent quest of Matthew and other New Testament authors to establish alternative communities and social welfare networks. *In Matthew's telling,* however, economic exploitation was not the one grave sin that lay behind the general sinfulness of the age, and Rome was not singled out for censure.

23. Joachim Gnilka, *Matthäusevangelium*, 2 vols. (Freiburg, Germany: Herder, 1986), 1:115, 2:292; K. C. Hanson, "How Honorable! How Shameful! A Cultural Analysis of Matthew's Makarisms and Reproaches," *Semeia* 68 (1994): 81–111. The last discourse continues through chapter twenty-five, but I focus here on chapter twenty-three. Davies and Allison (*Matthew*, 3:309) resist seeing the Sermon on the Mount and Matthew 23 as a coordinated pair because they do not want to count Matthew 23 as instruction to the faithful, but rather as invective. Indeed it is invective that establishes boundaries, but its relation to the Sermon on the Mount is one of matched contrast, and instruction for the audience.

24. Harrington, *Gospel of Matthew*, 7.

25. Reinhart Hummel, *Die Auseinandersetzung zwischen Kirche und Judentum im Matthäusevangelium* (Munich: Kaiser, 1966), 31; David Garland, *The Intention of Matthew 23* (Leiden, Netherlands: Brill, 1979), 55; Steve Mason, "Pharisaic Dominance before 70 CE and the Gospels' Hypocrisy Charge (Matt 23:2–3)," *Harvard Theological Review* 83 (1990): 376.

26. Because of overlaps between Mark 12:38–39 and Q 11:43 at this point, it is not always clear precisely how Matthew was combining the two sources, but this does not affect our present discussion.

27. Richard Horsley, *Whoever Hears You Hears Me: Prophets, Performance, and Tradition in Q* (Harrisburg, PA: Trinity Press International, 1999), 287, notes well the biting satire of the Q woes as prophetic denunciations. See also Williams, "Irony and Lament." Garland, *Intention*, 89, observes the loss of irony in Matthew's editing of the woes.

28. Some scholars wrongly lump this woe and the next in M without comment. Stephenson H. Brooks, *Matthew's Community: The Evidence of His Special Sayings Material* (Sheffield, UK: Sheffield Academic Press, 1987), 12–15, 66–70, 159, 186–87, at least offers weak arguments, but I am not convinced.

29. The strict parallelism of this section is quite typical of Matthew's own editing style; see Wills, "Scribal Methods."

30. Overman, *Matthew's Gospel*, 16–19, 98–99.

31. Banks, *Jesus and the Law*, 180–81.

32. Horsley, *Whoever Hears You*, 285; see also Williams, "Irony and Lament."

33. Michael Fishbane, *The Garments of Torah: Essays in Biblical Hermeneutics* (Bloomington: Indiana University Press, 1989), 75; Ernst Käsemann, "Sentences of Holy Law in the New Testament," in *New Testament Questions of Today* (Philadelphia: Fortress, 1969), 66–81; Wills, "Scribal Methods."

34. Luke T. Johnson, "The New Testament's Anti-Jewish Slander and the Conventions of Ancient Polemic," *Journal of Biblical Literature* 108 (1989): 441. On polemic in Matthew and John, see also Jennifer Wright Knust, *Abandoned to*

Lust: Sexual Slander and Ancient Christianity (New York: Columbia University Press, 2006).

35. Elaine Pagels, *The Origin of Satan* (New York: Random House, 1995), 84.

36. I have expanded here on lists suggested by Hanson, "How Honorable," 100–101; Saldarini, "Delegitimation of Leaders," 672–73 n. 39; Bruce J. Malina and Richard L. Rohrbaugh, *A Social Science Commentary on the Synoptic Gospels* (Minneapolis, MN: Fortress, 1992), 47; and Davies and Allison, *Matthew*, 1:125–27.

37. Davies and Allison, *Matthew*, 3:266.

38. L. Michael White, "Crisis Management," 241. This relationship is also clearly described by Saldarini, "Delegitimation of Rulers," and Overman, *Matthew's Gospel*.

6

⚜️

The Jews in the
Gospel of John

To investigate the construction of the Other in the Gospel of John, one
must first understand how this author presents Jesus. More than the
other gospels, John emphasizes a "high christology," the aspects of Jesus
that reflect his divine nature: the eternal and cosmic origin and destiny of
Jesus, the close identity of Jesus with God, and the revelation of God
through Jesus. Although a high christology does not necessarily create divisions of We and Other, the fact that this high christology is *revealed* to a
small group does. In both the Jewish and Christian texts of this period, direct revelation is always associated with the sectarian division between
those who receive the revelation and those who do not.[1] What we will
find is that the language of revelation in John constructs a very powerful
picture of the human race divided into two groups.

The high christology in John can be seen from the very beginning, in
the opening clauses of the prologue: "In the beginning was the Word; the
Word was with God and the Word was God." Unlike the other gospels, the
close identification of Jesus with God is stated from the beginning, where
Jesus, Word, and God are closely connected. Although Word (*logos*) was a
Stoic philosophical term that denoted the reason that is shared between
the divine and human realms, in John Word is not strictly a Stoic concept,
but typical of the Stoic-Platonic synthesis that occurred in this period. It is
interesting to compare John's Word not with later Christian theology but
with the similar concepts of non-Christian authors: Word in Philo, Wisdom as sent from God in Wisdom of Solomon, the Cosmic Soul in Plato,
Hekate as she came to be identified with the Platonic "Cosmic Soul," and
Hermes in the Hermetic literature. But Jesus is not just a heavenly figure

in John; he is the Word in human form: "the Word became flesh and dwelled among us." The eternal Word that was identified with God was also incarnated as a human being, although "incarnated" in John is ambiguous. These first lines of the gospel later became the basis of the Christian theology of the trinity, but at the time they were written, toward the end of the first century, different conceptions of Jesus' essence and role in salvation were current. Given the variety of christological options expressed in first-century Christian texts, the distinctive nature of John's depiction of Jesus becomes even more remarkable. There is a drama in John, but it is not, as in Matthew, the drama of a righteous messenger who struggles to be vindicated on earth. It is instead the drama of a heavenly Son who is away from his Father and who will return to his Father.[2] And although Jesus' relation as Son to the Father is emphasized strongly in John, he only becomes a Son to the Father *during his incarnation*.[3] The Word *is* God in the pre- and post-incarnational periods. Thus the power of the Son/Father relationship in John partly results from its liminal character, that is, its special and unique nature in this in-between time when the Word is incarnated as a human being. It is a temporary and charged relationship until the Son returns home, analogous to the liminal or in-between period in rites of initiation. Despite this temporary separation, the virtual identity of Son and Father means that during the earthly phase Jesus, and Jesus alone, can provide access to God (14:6). In John, the disagreement between Jesus and his opponents always comes down to their diametrically opposed interpretations of this relationship. To deny the Son's close identity with the Father during this phase is understood as denying God. This bears repeating for the discussion that follows: for John, *to deny the Son's identity with the Father is to deny the Father.*

A range of literary techniques can be discerned in John that work together to give expression to the high christology. First, Wayne Meeks emphasizes the *vertical* nature of John's images.[4] The heavenly figure comes down in the incarnation, reveals truths about the heavenly as opposed to the earthly realm, and reascends. This vertical understanding and sharply dualistic distinction between heavenly and earthly are repeated often, in passage after passage, producing a consistent thematic "message" of the text. Second, a dizzying series of titles are used for Jesus. In the first chapter alone we encounter lord, messiah (Christ), prophet, rabbi, king, son of God. Third, although all the titles for Jesus found in chapter one could be taken as human titles (even lord, messiah, and son of God), other options are soon introduced that could only be titles for divine figures: Jesus' sonship is taken to mean that he is "equal to God" (5:18), and ultimately he is simply "God" (20:28). Third, Norman Petersen argues that John also employs a special way of using symbols to communicate this high christology. John's use of symbols, which so dominates the text, defies rational logic, and this is intentional: "The Word was *with* God and the Word *was* God"; "Before Abraham was, I am."[5] We may respond that these are examples of a divine paradox, and the familiarity of these verses may make the paradox seem natural, yet the language is not strictly logical. The same challenge to everyday language is encountered time and time again, and words which are very common and simple are imbued with a searching significance: "bread," "water," "door," "vine," and so on. In the prologue of John alone, we find a string of unexpected synonyms that presumably refer to the same thing: "Word," "God," "light," "life," "grace," and also a series of contrasts between the community that understands ("we have all received from his fullness grace upon grace") and the world that does not ("the world did not know him"). Likewise, the string of quite different titles for Jesus mentioned above also suggests that the *meanings* of the synonyms or titles are not crucial, but rather what is important is that they all point upward to the heavenly realm, which the world does not understand—consider again Meeks's emphasis on the vertical nature of John's message. John's gospel uses these simple words in a way different from their everyday use precisely to communicate this distinction: outsiders do not get it and will *inevitably* misunderstand. It is *above* their understanding, or *from beyond* their understanding. Petersen refers to the special use of symbols in John as the creation of an anti-language, because it intentionally takes simple words from everyday language and invests them with a wholly new meaning. The ambiguities in John's gospel in regard to time and narrative sequence mirror this intentionally ambiguous use of symbols.

Adele Reinhartz approaches this problem in a different way, but offers a solution that gives strong support to Petersen's conclusions.[6] At the same time that the gospel recounts the historical narrative of Jesus' ministry and death, it also tells a parallel story on the cosmological level, beginning with the first verse. The hero of this cosmological narrative "is the pre-existent Word who becomes flesh, having been sent by God his Father into the world to bring salvation." Throughout the gospel there are elements of this narrated struggle between the heavenly redeemer and the "ruler of this world" or Satan (13:27, 14:30). The historical narrative is set in Judea and Galilee and describes historical personages, while "the cosmological tale is universal in location and has eternity as its time frame." The cosmological narrative parallels the historical narrative, but more precisely, it provides the narrative framework for the historical narrative. One cannot understand the significance of the events in the historical narrative without understanding the cosmological narrative. If one stays within the historical narrative alone, one is limited to the category of those who did not know him. According to Reinhartz, the hymnic prologue of John is an overture to the cosmological narrative as a

whole: the Word descends, comes to his own, and reascends, empower-
ing followers to become children of God.

The historical and cosmological narratives can be traced as separate
tracks throughout the gospel. In the historical narrative of events in Jesus'
life, conflicts can go badly, he can be rejected and even crucified, but in the
cosmological narrative this is not the case. There the Son destroys Satan
(12:31). On the historical level, Jesus either rejects earthly kingship (6:15,
18:36) or is rejected as king (19:21), but on the cosmological level he rules
as king. In fact, the cosmological narrative is similar to hero legends cross-
culturally, where the prince or hero must leave his kingdom and venture
forth into a chaotic realm, slay a monster, and return to claim his throne.[7]
The first-century audience of the gospel recognizes both levels and perceives the cosmological origin and destiny of Jesus, but the characters in
the historical narrative of the gospel do not. This gives rise to comical and
ironic misunderstandings by marginal characters such as Nicodemus
("How can anyone be born after he has grown old?" 3:4), or the woman
at the well ("You have no bucket and the well is deep. How will you get
living water?" 4:11). Jerome Neyrey lumps the misunderstandings together and treats them negatively as markers of alienation from Jesus,[8]
but some characters seem less negative than others, and some misunderstandings arise in what we might call searching characters, even Pilate.
Still, some misunderstandings *do* indicate a profound alienation from Jesus. To put it simply, *when the characters who misunderstand are labeled "the
Jews" (7:27–42, 8:22, 9:26–29), they are almost always in conflict and do not understand at all; when they are not labeled "the Jews," they are neutral or even
sympathetic and understand partially, whether they are in fact Jews (Nicodemus
or the disciples), Samaritans (the woman at the well), or neither (Pilate)* (Theorem 7: Ambiguous groups reassigned).

We may wonder whether Jewish institutions as represented in John are
capable of pointing to the cosmological level or can only exist on the historical level. Apparently, it is the latter. In nearly every scene in the gospel
it is demonstrated that in the cosmological narrative Jesus supplants Jewish festivals and patriarchal figures that are referred to in the historical
narrative. It begins in John 2: water intended for Jewish purification rites
is transformed into a mysterious celebratory wine. Jesus next condemns
the practices of the temple, and it is learned that he has supplanted its position, since "he was referring to the temple of his body" (2:21). In John 4,
Jesus asserts that his living water is greater than Jacob's well (4:12–14),
and in the process he shows that he is also greater than Wisdom, which
will cause people to thirst for more (John 4:13–14; contrast Sir 24:21). In
chapter five Jesus challenges Sabbath laws by healing on the Sabbath. In
chapter six, Jesus offers bread from heaven that surpasses the bread that
Moses provided for the Israelites fleeing from Egypt (6:32–33). In chapters

seven and eight, at the festival of Sukkot (Booths), Jesus identifies himself with rivers of living water and the light of the world, two symbols associated with Sukkot. At the same time, Jesus also claims a priority over Abraham ("Before Abraham was, I am," 8:31–59). The vine in chapter fifteen probably arises out of the Jewish tradition of Israel as vine or vineyard (Isa 5:1–7, Ezek 15:1–8, 2 Esdr 5:23), but it is significant that in John Jesus is now the *true* vine.

Of Jewish institutions, only the Scriptures remain authoritative; ironically, Moses does not. The Jews tell a man healed by Jesus, "You are Jesus' disciple, but we are disciples of Moses" (9:28). The law that in Judaism was revealed in the Holy Scriptures has been abrogated, and is now "your law" (8:17, 10:34, 15:25). Jewish law has been replaced by Jesus' new commandment (13:34; 14:15, 21), just as access to God through the temple has been supplanted by access to God through Jesus. The authority of the Scriptures in John in no way implies a continuing rootedness in Judaism. Even later Gnostics, who declared their separation from Jewish institutions, revered the Jewish Scriptures as authoritative scripture. And the ignorance of John's audience regarding Jewish practices can be seen in the fact that many Jewish feasts and customs have to be explained. The *background* of this gospel lies in Jewish traditions, but John advocates a replacement theology; a new belief system will require a fundamental separation from Jewish institutions.[9] What we find in place of these Jewish institutions is a way of speaking that is new to Judaism. Even though they are not "Christians"—this term and self-understanding were probably still a few decades off—Jesus and his disciples have slipped the bonds of Judaism, and are almost never referred to as Jews.[10] *In the cosmological narrative, Jesus and his followers are not Jews.* Jesus presents himself as something new: living water, bread of life, light of the world, gate, good shepherd, true vine, way, truth, life. These symbols in some cases could be said to originate in Jewish tradition, but their moorings in that tradition have been cut, and they are all allowed to float upward, now unattached to the ground. The new use of these symbols simply rises above the landscape; they have been severed from the historical narrative and become part of the cosmological narrative.

What kind of group would do such a thing? This kind of group has been called an introversionist sect, a sect that withdraws from the world to create its own world of meaning, but in other sociological parlance it may be considered a cult-type group.[11] Regardless of the terminology, the key factor is that John's group, in distinction from Matthew's community, does not appear to focus on boundary definitions but on transcendence. While the synoptic gospels' distinctive words connote mission and change, appropriate to a missionary sect, John's connote stability and permanence. The community embraces an anti-language and an alternative view of the destiny of its members. Sects also claim to be the true heirs of the tradition, while cults claim either to be creating something new or introducing something foreign, in John's case the former. But similar to Matthew's group, there is an element of the sociology of deviance in John's language as well. Daniel Boyarin argues that since Judaism and Christianity were never really distinguished clearly until well into the second century or later, John could not be thinking of a true separation from Judaism.[12] However, here he may have a correct premise but a wrong conclusion. He seems to assume that if John's community is not yet "Christian," it must still be a part of Judaism. But John knows of an alienation and deviance from Judaism that existed before "Christianity" was an option. A clear boundary between Judaism and Christianity was indeed slow to form, but the newness of the symbols in John is typical of cult-type religious groups as opposed to sect-type. John envisioned a conclave of equal friends (John 15:12–17) who were uniquely connected to a redeemer sent from God, who was God. This gospel advocates a special sort of cosmic connection ("neither on this mountain nor in Jerusalem") that the community would think of as *no longer belonging to the larger Jewish community*. All symbols were now untethered from Judaism and allowed to float upward. The Jewish roots had not been severed, but transcended. John did not need a theologically defined Judaism from which to separate, and in reality may have also been separating from other followers of Jesus who maintained Jewish traditions.

THE MEANING OF "THE JEWS" IN JOHN

In Matthew, Mark, and Luke, Jesus' opponents consist of named groups within Jewish society: chief priests, scribes, elders, Pharisees, Sadducees, and others. John, however, often drops these specific terms, and the opponents become merely "the Jews." It is used seventy-one times in John as opposed to five or six times in the other three gospels. This is all the more surprising, since Jesus, all his disciples, and John the Baptist and all his disciples are Jews. How did the author of the fourth gospel at the end of the first century understand the opponents and apply to them the blanket term "the Jews"? The five most influential trends in modern scholarship to explain this anomaly are the expulsion theory, the geographical theory, the class theory, the polemics theory, and the symbolic theory.

The Expulsion Theory

The expulsion theory holds that in about the year 90 CE, a dramatic shift took place in the Palestinian synagogues which resulted in the exclusion of followers of Jesus from participation in worship. At three places in the gospel it is said that Jews who believed in Jesus were in danger of being "put out of the synagogue" (*aposynagōgos*; 9:22, 12:42, 16:2). This can be compared to statements in the other gospels and in Paul that followers of Jesus were beaten in synagogues (Mark 13:9, 2 Cor 11:24). J. Louis Martyn draws attention to the synagogue prayer that is called the *Birkat ha-minim*, "benediction concerning the heretics," which was recited in the context of the Eighteen Benedictions in the synagogue liturgy.[13] Martyn assumed that the cursing of the heretics was added intentionally at the end of the first century as a litmus test to exclude followers of Jesus from worship. The polemical attack in John against the Jews, then, would have been a reaction by the newly expelled community of believers in Jesus against the Jewish parent-body. John read the exclusion-from-synagogue motif back into the life of Jesus, but it really reflects events that had only recently taken place in John's day.

However, a number of reservations were soon raised about this comparison to the *Birkat ha-minim*. First, the heretics censured in the Jewish prayer might have been any number of Jewish sectarian groups, not just followers of Jesus. The careful analysis of this evidence indicates that there was friction between followers of Jesus and the larger community of Jews, but it was not formalized in the first century into a ban or exclusion from the synagogue, nor was there at this time any official Jewish sanction. One may wonder whether an effective Jewish ban would be possible only twenty years after the destruction of the Jewish temple, or whether synagogues were yet constituted in the first century to be authoritative institutions. Other scholars, including Martyn, have responded to this by saying that, despite the nebulousness of the Jewish evidence for the *Birkat ha-minim* in the first century, some such expulsion becomes a necessary postulate to explain the sharp polemic in the Gospel of John. The references in Paul and the other gospels to punishments in synagogues would also seem to give credence to the possibility of an expulsion of Jesus' followers. However, the beatings in synagogues mentioned in the other sources are a means of punishment of members, and not a means of expulsion.[14] Among sects there is often a myth of persecution that in the social memory becomes as real as persecution which actually occurred. Are the exclusion-from-synagogue passages in John to be explained as an accurate depiction of Jewish expulsion (whether in the year 30 or the year 90), or the myth-making that resulted from an evolving sectarian alienation? More to the point, Jewish discussions from the period in question define proper membership in the covenant community in terms of *halachah*—legal observance—and not doctrine, but the particular issue that in John becomes the dividing line between Jews and followers of Jesus concerns *doctrine*, whether Jesus is to be identified with God. In other words, in John Jews are depicted as excommunicating people for reasons which arose in the Jesus movement, not in broader Judaism.[15] The Jewish punishment of those in their midst who believed in Jesus as the messiah probably did occur, but we have no way of knowing when it occurred in each location or to what extent. The exclusion-from-synagogue motif thus becomes a myth of origins for John's community, perhaps even taking its point of departure from the beatings-in-synagogue motif found also in Paul and Mark.[16]

We should also raise at this point the question—which applies to all of the theories—of whether the real opponents of John's own community, the front on which the author is actually engaged, are not the wider body of Jews but followers of Jesus who retain Jewish law and more of a rootedness in Jewish tradition. Just as the Deuteronomistic Historian likely constructed Canaanites as a means to oppose internal opponents, so John may have wanted to discredit observant followers of Jesus by identifying them with "the Jews," redefining the internal opponents as external Others, and attacking the roots out of which they grew (Theorem 6: Internal Other linked to external Other).

The Geographical Theory

The geographical theory requires some historical introduction. As noted in chapters three and four, the English word "Jew" is derived from Hebrew *Yehudi*, Greek *Ioudaios*, meaning one from the region of Judah or Judea, where Jerusalem was located. As was typical in the ancient world, all religious observances were considered to have originated in a particular locale, no matter how many members migrated to other places or for how long. Even if, as many scholars argue, Jews living in the Diaspora were converting others to their faith, the converts were understood to have taken up a faith *from Judea*. Thus it is sometimes argued that John singled out "the Judeans" not because they were members of the Jewish religion, but because they were representatives of the temple authorities from the Judean region (Jerusalem), who were now imposing their control over other "children of Israel" in regions to the north (Samaria and Galilee). The situation would in that case be similar to the opposition between the returnees in Ezra-Nehemiah ("Judeans") and other children of Israel who were not centered in Judea, rendering Ezra-Nehemiah and John diametrically opposing voices on this issue. This originally geographical distinction could also have become somewhat symbolic. Jouette Bassler observes that there is a tendency in John for those who accept Jesus to become identified as Galileans, and those who reject Jesus to become identified as Judeans: ". . . once people reject Jesus, regardless of their geographical location, they become classified as *Ioudaioi*." And ". . .

the epithet 'Galileans' appears as a consistent but flexible positive counterpart to the negatively charged term *Ioudaioi.*"[17]

Certainly, we need not assume that the word "Judean" could only sustain a geographical meaning, "a member of the group from Judea." As noted in chapter four, the word "Judean" had already developed a cultural-religious meaning—what I called Judean-2—in addition to an ethnical-geographical meaning—Judean-1.[18] And although Bassler is correct that there is at least a layer of John that reflects a charged distinction between Galileans and Judeans, this is not a likely explanation for John's usage throughout. We may begin by questioning whether Judeans, after the destruction of the temple, could wield control over Galilee, but even granting that, the text reflects geographical confusion; it does not give voice to a clear geographical dualism, symbolic or real. David Rensberger points out that there are key passages in which the geographical theory will not work, for instance, the "purification rites of the Judeans" in Cana *of Galilee* (John 2:6).[19]

Boyarin, however, solves the apparent inconsistencies of the geographical use of "Judean" by positing two meanings of the term, a restricted, inner group of "Judeans"—descended from that self-consciously inner group of Judeans defined by Ezra-Nehemiah, and the more broadly recognized Judeans, coextensive with "greater Israel."[20] John 3:25, he notes, recounts a dispute between "John the Baptist and a Judean." Since John the Baptist is what would normally be called a Judean, surely this text is differentiating John and other peoples of the land from that inner group centered in Jerusalem. However, here and elsewhere Boyarin reads John as a snapshot of life in one time frame, and ignores the constant temporal slippage of this gospel. A comparison may help: American schoolchildren learn that Paul Revere rode through the countryside to warn the colonists, "The British are coming!" In fact, Paul Revere and the colonists were all British. What he would have said is: "The Regulars are coming!"—that is, soldiers from the regular army. The fact that Paul Revere was born in the colonies would not have changed that fact until later, when the Revolutionary War *redefined* him. In retelling the story, Americans have pushed a later distinction back into an earlier time frame in order to create a myth of origins. John has likewise taken a later distinction and read it back into the period of origins, the life of Jesus. In the shimmering reality of this gospel, it is possible for characters to be Jewish by birth but not Jewish in essence, just as Paul Revere is considered by Americans to have been British by birth but not in essence. In both cases, the social memory of the community is unconcerned by the telescoping of separate realities.

The real problem with interpreting John's usage is not just a historical and linguistic one, but also a question of the rhetorical function of this much-used term within the gospel. The tendency of John to use the term so comprehensively indicates the breadth and depth that the term is intended to cover. John's typical practice is to employ repetition with slight variation, and as Meeks has argued, the constant repetition of motifs serves to communicate a clear cosmological message within the changing conditions of the historical narrative.[21] Reinhartz adds:

> The fact that the same word (Jews) occurs numerous times and in a variety of contexts tends to blur the fine distinctions and nuances . . . and to generalize the meaning to its broadest possible referent, that is, the Jews as a nation defined by a set of religious beliefs, cultic and liturgical practices, and a sense of peoplehood.[22]

John creates a symbol world, and "the Jews" become a symbol within it. The opponents are identified as a group with a specific theology (9:28), not a geographical location. One might argue that it is specifically the Jerusalem-centered Israelites who are intended, but the opponents are identified by the combination of allegiance to Mosaic law and rejection of Jesus as God-on-earth. Indeed the most important symbolic transformation in John may be the dissolving of Jesus' and his disciples' rootedness in Judaism, at the same time that "the Jews" are reconstituted as enemies of God. The fact that John should be more negative about "the Jews" than about more distant gentiles should not surprise us. Matthew also vilified Pharisees but not more distant groups, as did the Deuteronomistic History and Ezra-Nehemiah. Throughout we have seen that one close group serves as the ideal, constructed Other (Theorem 3).

The Class Theory

It is also often argued that John depicts a class distinction between followers of Jesus and their Jewish opponents. The pyramid of power and economic relations in the Greco-Roman world would have consisted of a large base of peasants, slaves, and urban poor, and a tiny cap of rulers, aristocrats, landowners, and priestly temple administrators, with almost no band of a middle class in between. The Jewish authorities would have by necessity been servants of the Roman government, no matter how piously they may have affirmed their Judaism. It is argued that Jesus is associated with people who are from the large base, while the opponents are depicted as wielding the power of the Jewish temple hierarchy. According to this theory, there is thus a great distance in power and class between John's community and the social world of the Jerusalem authorities, and the latter become known simply as "the Judeans."[23] However, the destruction of the temple would make this unlikely, but further, in many cases "the Judeans" is used in John for people outside the power structure who react negatively (6:41, 52), and at 12:42 we are told that "many, even of the authorities, believed in him, but they did not confess it on account of the Pharisees." Thus, common people among the Jews can be depicted as negative, while authorities can be depicted as sympathetic, and even intimidated by those, such as the Pharisees, who were elsewhere identified with "the Jews."

A clear depiction of Jesus in opposition to the Jerusalem authorities as "Judeans," therefore, does not emerge in John. To be sure, *behind* the gospel of John, as behind Matthew, lies a social reality in which followers of Jesus may be further down the ladder of power than are many of the opponents. These unequal power relations may be partly responsible for the animosity on the part of John's community. Although it is necessary to keep in mind the social distinctions *behind* the gospel, even *reflected in* the gospel, John's own depiction of these relations does not define "the Jews" along class lines. The distinction between emic (insider's) perspective and etic (outsider's) must be kept in mind.

The Polemic Theory

The vilification of the Jews in John may in part be explained by ancient conventions of polemics. The gospel genre itself may contribute to the polemical tone by *requiring* an enemy and a moment of extreme conflict. John is similar not only to the other Christian gospels, but to non-Christian texts as well, such as the *Life of Aesop*. These texts typically contain a central scene of strong conflict that leads to the execution of the protagonist.[24] The *Life of Aesop*, dated by scholars to the first or second century CE, is a Greek "gospel" of the life and death of the famous sage Aesop. He runs afoul of the citizens of Delphi and tells a fable that describes the Delphians as descended from slaves. This has a function in the narrative similar to Jesus' denunciation of the Jews as offspring of the devil in John 8, and Mark's parable of the wicked tenants who represent the Jerusalem authorities (Mark 12). The opponents in each case who have been insulted by the protagonist get their revenge by executing him on the trumped-up charge of "blasphemy" (John 10:33, Mark 14:64, *Aesop* 132). The invective scene, then, is a typical element of these biographies of the righteous sage.

As noted in the previous chapter, Luke T. Johnson has also compared the polemical passages in the New Testament to those of the philosophers and intellectuals of the period and shown that they are often quite similar.[25] Yet John's invective goes beyond the Greek and Roman authors whom Johnson adduces, and beyond *Aesop* as well. Most polemics in the ancient world attack the motives and integrity of the opponent, but they do not consign the opponent to the category of the devil and a lost world—except in the case of dualistic movements such as the followers of Jesus and the community of the Dead Sea Scrolls. Thus the polemic in John is analogous to that of many Greek and Roman authors, but its depth and intensity is only matched by other apocalyptic sects.

As a subset of the polemic theory, many scholars also emphasize the role of John's language in creating a community identity. In order to bolster a sense of group solidarity within a small and embattled community, John *needed* an enemy (Theorem 1: From Other to We). The alienation of John's community from Judaism gave rise to a psychological necessity of identity formation through polemics. Johnson suggests this in his article, and Meeks also focuses on this explanation:

> One of the primary functions of the book . . . must have been to provide a reinforcement for the community's social identity, which appears to have been largely negative. It provided a symbolic universe which gave religious legitimacy . . . to the group's actual isolation from the larger society.[26]

The shortest route to group identity, then, is through a doctrine of the irredeemable wickedness of the Other.

The Symbolic Theory

An influential theory of the existentialist theologian and New Testament scholar Rudolf Bultmann is that the Jews are symbolic of "the world."[27] Whatever opposition John saw in the historical Jews, argued Bultmann, has really become incidental if we understand the more important message of the gospel, that is, that the Word is revealed to the world, but the world does not receive it. William Countryman has recently restated a similar position on John, and suggested that the text is more of a spiritual handbook on transcendence of the world.[28] But for both authors, we would have to ask whether this is more a modern recasting of a difficult text than an assessment of how the language functioned in the first century. The Jews may stand for the world in John, but they also stand for the Jews—and indeed, "the world" also stands for the Jews. Whereas in John 13–17 there is a transfer of the opposition from "the Jews" to "the world," this is only temporary. There is not a hint after that that the author wanted to make this transfer permanent. Further, as Werner Kelber rightly insists concerning the identification of Jews and the world, "far from moderating Johannine anti-Judaism, it magnifies it to cosmic proportions."[29]

After considering these various possibilities, my own conclusion is that the best explanation of the function of the repeated reference to the Jews is the subset of the polemics theory noted above: the strong construction of the Jews as Other reinforces a separatist identity. In every text we have analyzed, the use of sharp polemics gives rise to a sense of identity-in-opposition. This will be borne out in the discussion of the construction of the Other in John 8 and the construction of the We in the Farewell Discourses in John 13–17.

JOHN 8 AND THE CONSTRUCTION OF THE OTHER

I begin with the construction of the Other in John 8. This chapter contains many bold statements by Jesus, but the relation between the sayings and the narrative is not clear, nor is the flow of the chapter as a whole at every point. Helmut Koester proposes that the disjointedness of John 8 arises because sayings of a dualistic nature and a courtroom debate narrative concerning Jesus' testifying about himself are juxtaposed and only partially integrated.[30] The dualistic sayings in this chapter are also found in other early Christian texts that are either Gnostic or congenial to Gnosticism, while the debate material is similar to the courtroom debate motif in John 5 and 7. John may have utilized in three different places a single story about a courtroom-style debate that results in a near-arrest.

Here I divide the first half of John 8 into a number of sections and arrange them in such a way as to highlight the two kinds of material found in the chapter, the courtroom debate placed on the left, the dualistic sayings on the right. In both cases, John's own interpretation can also be found. The left-hand column in general relates issues of the historical narrative, and the right-hand column issues of the cosmological narrative. The dramatic tension of John 8 derives from the inability of the characters in the historical narrative to understand the issues of the cosmological narrative, a common theme in John.

Section 1

(12) Jesus said, "I am the light of the world. The one who follows me will never walk in darkness but will have the light of life."

(13) Then the Pharisees said to him, "You are testifying on your own behalf; your testimony is not valid." (14) Jesus answered, "Even if I testify on my own behalf, my testimony is valid.

I know where I have come from and where I am going, but you do not know where I come from and where I am going.

This section begins on the right with a saying that sharply contrasts light and darkness. Light and darkness are images used in the Hebrew Bible, but never contrasted as here. They are, however, placed in sharp contrast to each other in the Dead Sea Scrolls; members of this separatist Jewish sect called themselves children of light, and their opponents children of darkness. Still, the emphasis in John is much more clearly on the redeemer who can bestow the quality of light, and there is another important distinction as well. The dualism between good and evil, light and dark in the Dead Sea Scrolls is an example of ethical dualism, that is, a division of the world into mutually exclusive categories of good and evil people based upon their *actions*, as opposed to metaphysical dualism, in which the universe is divided into spirit and matter and people are associated by their *nature* with one or the other.[31] We may compare John's dualism with the metaphysical dualism found in *Gospel of Thomas* 24:

> There is light within a person of light, and he lights up the whole world. If he does not shine, he is darkness.

To be sure, ethical dualism is probably never without a metaphysical aspect, nor is metaphysical dualism ever without an ethical aspect. But in ethical-dualism texts such as the Dead Sea Scrolls, people are more likely to be judged to be good or evil based on their actions, even if they are predetermined, while in the metaphysical-dualism texts such as *Gospel of Thomas*, they are more likely to be seen as saved or lost based upon their "true origins" in the spiritual or material realm and their corresponding perception. John's dualism, however, lies *between* ethical dualism and metaphysical dualism. Many people are evil because of sins, as in ethical dualism, but the deeds that distinguish the good and evil people are reduced to only one sin: the acceptance or rejection of Jesus as the Son of God (16:9; Theorem 5: Other distorted and reduced to one identity). Failure to perceive Jesus as the true revealer of God is the only sin in the Gospel of John, and the opponents seem incapable *by their nature* of being able to perceive that Jesus was sent by God. As Jeffrey Siker says, "they were *never* God's children."[32]

The saying on light and darkness in the right-hand column becomes in the left-hand column—the historical narrative—the provocation for a polemical debate about Jesus' witnessing about himself. The second saying in the right-hand column communicates dramatically the notion of Jesus as the descending and ascending redeemer, which Meeks refers to as the Man from Heaven motif. A saying at *Gospel of Thomas* 49–50 is similar:

> You are from the kingdom, and you will return there again. If they ask you, "Where did you come from?" say to them, "We have come from the light."

According to Koester, the character of John's saying here is "patently gnostic," and George MacRae stated further that sayings such as this "resemble nothing in the ancient world so much as the Gnostic revealer myth."[33] Both Koester and MacRae, however, rightly insist that John stops short of a fully Gnostic theology. In fact, a consistent Gnostic theology probably only arose much later, even though John does share with *Gospel of Thomas* a dualism that can be seen on a trajectory to Gnosticism.

Section 2

The narrative continues with the testifying/judging theme of the court-room motif begun in the previous section, shown again on the left. John's version of this story here reflects a closer interweaving of the courtroom debate and the echo of a saying of Jesus, displayed on the right, concerning the close relation of the Son to the Father who sent him.

(15) You judge according to the flesh; I judge no one. (16) Yet even if I do judge, my judgment is valid. It is not I alone who judge, but I and

the Father who sent me.

(17) In your law it is written that the testimony of two witnesses is valid. (18) I testify for myself,

and the Father who sent me

testifies for me also." (19) Then they said, "Where is your father?"

Jesus answered, "You know neither me nor my Father. If you knew me, you would know my Father also."

The saying reflected on the right is known also from Q (note italicized words):

Whoever takes you in takes me in, and *whoever takes me in takes in the one who sent me.* Everything has been handed over to me by my Father, and no one knows the Son except the Father, and no one knows the Father except the Son, *and anyone to whom the Son chooses to reveal him.* (Cf. Lk 10:16, 22; Matt 10:40, 11:27)

This passage in Q is sometimes referred to as the "thunderbolt from the Johannine sky," although John, as the later text, has not influenced Q at this point, nor was Q likely read by John.[34] It is more likely the case that both texts have taken up a similar saying of Jesus, and John saw in this saying the potential for a major theological development (6:29–46, 12:44–45, 13:20, 17:8). The motif of God sending his son becomes the springboard both for John's descending/ascending redeemer theme and for the close relationship of the Son to the Father. This may even be said to be *the* central affirmation of John's gospel. Whether Jesus is God or is less than God is variable (compare 5:18 and 14:28), susceptible to John's typical theological drift, but that Jesus was sent by God is not variable, and this is what, according to John, the Jews fail to perceive.

John returns in verses seventeen through nineteen above to the courtroom-defense motif. Testimony in Jewish law for major trials required two witnesses (Deut 17:6, 19:15), and although Jesus concedes that he appears to be alone, he and the Father who sent him are of one voice. This response does not really satisfy Jewish law, since two witnesses *other than the accused* are required (*Mishnah Ketubbot* 2:9), but his words are not meant to satisfy Jewish law. If anything, they are intended to distinguish God's workings from Jewish law on this point. For John, Jesus bases his authority on his close identification with the Father, and this is to be contrasted with the opponents' argumentation. The phrase "your law" further distances John's community from Jewish law, and even stronger is the use of "their law" at 15:25.[35] The discussion in this section prepares us for the sharpest possible condemnation of the "offspring of Abraham" below.

Section 3

(20) He spoke these words while he was teaching in the temple treasury, but no one arrested him, because his hour had not yet come.

(21) Again he said to them, "I am going away, and you will search for me, but you will die in your sin. Where I am going you cannot come."

(22) Then the Jews said, "Is he going to kill himself? For he said, 'Where I am going you cannot come.'"

John may know a tradition of near-arrest (John 7:30, 44; 10:39), but its repeated use in this section is John's editing, and John here adds another saying (on the right) to the effect that the Jews cannot follow where Jesus is going. Compare *Gospel of Thomas* 38:

There will be days when you will seek me and not find me.

And *Apocryphon of James* 1, 2:2, 22–27:

> "Have you departed and removed yourself from us?" "No," said Jesus, "but I shall go to the place whence I came. If you wish to come with me, come."

There are slight differences among these three texts. John says that the *opponents* cannot follow, *Gospel of Thomas* says there will be a period in the future when the *followers* cannot find him, and *Apocryphon of James* says that the *followers* can come *now*—three different situations, three different responses, but what is similar is a focus on departure as salvation—indeed, salvation from the world.[36]

Earlier it was the Pharisees who objected to Jesus' statement, but now this has changed to "the Jews" (compare 9:13, 18). The otherworldly perspective in verse twenty-one is met with their worldly misunderstanding in verse twenty-two. This is a common literary technique by which John emphasizes the gap between Jesus' statements and people's ability to understand.

Section 4

From this section on, the chapter is organized in a different way. Still, there is a mix of material. The left-hand column is no longer a forensic dialogue and is not limited to a historical-narrative perspective, but is a saying based loosely on the tradition of the Son of Man (or better, Son of Humanity) as judge at the end of time.[37] The right-hand column is John's own composition, a mixture of historical and cosmological narrative issues.

(23) He said to them, "You are from below, I am from above. You are of this world, I am not of this world. (24) I told you that you would die in your sins, for you will die in your sins unless you believe that I am he [*egō eimi*]." (25) They said to him, "Who are you?" Jesus said to them, "Why do I speak to you at all? (26) I have much to say about you and much to judge, but the one who sent me is true, and I say to the world what I have heard from him." (27) They did not understand that he was speaking to them about the Father.

(28) And Jesus said, "When you
lift up the Son of Humanity,
then you will know that I am
he [*egō eimi*],

and that I do nothing on my own,
but I say these things as the
Father instructed me. (29) The
one who sent me is with me.
He has not abandoned me, for
I always do what pleases him."
(30) As he was saying these
things, many believed in him.

The right-hand column here expresses John's own dualism, reduced to its starkest form. The definition of Other has never been stated so simply: "You are from below." The vertical dualism of above and below that Meeks describes is applied here to the two main parties of the text, setting the standard for what is to follow. In verse twenty-four the opponents will die in their sins, and this seems at first to make the dualism of the parties *ethical*, that is, based on sins as in the Dead Sea Scrolls, rather than metaphysical, based on one's supposed *nature*, as in Gnosticism. But the verse continues: "you will die in your sins unless you believe that I am he." As elsewhere in John, the only sin is the inability to recognize Jesus as the true revealer of God; it is a combination of ethical and metaphysical dualism. A play on words occurs here in the Greek that reverberates through the entire gospel. "I am he," *egō eimi*, also means simply "I am," and was likely understood in John as a hidden reference to the name of God as given to Moses on Mount Sinai (Exod 3:14). When Moses asks God what he should say to the Israelites, God says, "Tell them 'I am' has sent me to you."[38]

Second Half of John 8

The second half of chapter eight betrays yet another difference in structure, and it cannot be divided into narrative and sayings as Koester has done for most of the first half. The rough materials of the first half of chapter eight have been absorbed by John and reworked into a more integrated text. Although the second half is ultimately even more negative, it begins on a positive note: "Jesus then said to the Jews who had believed in him, 'If you abide in my word, you are truly my disciples. You will know the truth and the truth will set you free." Although it is surprising and seemingly positive that John refers to "the Jews who had believed in him," the belief is short lived. The chapter will turn even more negative just below, and it is probably intentionally ironic that the appearance of openness on the part of the Jews is followed by an unequivocal parting of the ways in the next verses.

Verse thirty-two, "the truth shall set you free," is somewhat different from the sayings above. Although there are actually closer parallels in Stoicism than in Gnosticism, in John it seems to have been adapted to a dualistic application.[39] The provocations of the previous sayings now shift into a much higher register, as the Jews persist in interpreting this lofty, otherworldly theological statement in terms of worldly categories: "We are descendants of Abraham and have never been slaves to anyone." The Jews are not wrong in reading Jesus' statement as a reference to slavery; to be set free in first-century society would have naturally been understood in terms of slavery. Where they are wrong is in seeing it on a worldly and not a heavenly level. It is also ironic in that it implies that Jesus' opponents *are now* enslaved to the world but cannot perceive it.

John then continues the debate with a concession: "I know that you are descendants [*sperma*, seed] of Abraham" (8:37). In early Christianity there are many polemical debates on the true children of Abraham. Siker has analyzed these debates closely, and rightly describes John 8 as the most polemical of them.[40] Here Jesus does not deny that Jews descended from Abraham, nor does he detract from Abraham's status, but by their rejection of Jesus the Jews prove that they cannot be children (*tekna*) of Abraham (8:39–40). John imposes a distinction between descendants according to the flesh (*sperma*) and true children (*tekna*) of Abraham, and creates a somewhat paradoxical double-view of the world, seen through the lens of both the historical narrative and the cosmological narrative. Thus when Jesus refers to "your father Abraham" (8:56), it seems odd at first; Jesus has denied the Jews this relation. But, as Siker notes, it must mean "Abraham, whom you *claim* as a father," or "your father according to the flesh." This distinction can also be seen in the following section as well. John, at any rate, has little use for consistency. Siker notes that the use of Abraham in John's argument changes. In 8:31–47, John had argued that the Jews are not true children of Abraham; in 8:48–59, however, John argues that Jesus is greater than and paradoxically *prior* to Abraham: "Before Abraham was, I am" (8:58). John's ungrammatical statement places in Jesus' mouth the same elliptical phrase for the name of God that he used above, "I am." A debate about the true children of Abraham has been transformed into an assertion of superiority to Abraham and an identity of Jesus with God. The roots in Jewish tradition have once again been transcended, and Jesus is said to have cosmological origins prior to Abraham.

But while this contrast is being played out, John introduces another contrast as well. The Jews claim to be children of God (8:41), but Jesus replies that he was sent from God; if they were truly children of God, they would recognize the common origin. Their cosmological identity is different;

they are "children of the devil," says John, and cannot receive his words. This reflects the combination of metaphysical and ethical dualism: the Jews' deeds separate them from those who receive Jesus, but whether they hear or not depends upon which realm they are from. This is the most strident point of opposition to the Jews in John, and provided a dramatic motivation for later Christians' view of the process by which Jews rejected the Christian message. Even Pilate in John's gospel seems to weigh an acceptance or rejection of Jesus, while the Jews are not capable of that reflection; they are "from below." The groundwork for the persecution of Jews is established in John as an explanation of Otherness. As Gedaliahu Guy Stroumsa argues, marginal groups often present for themselves a scenario of divine compensation, of God's reckoning of final justice, but they use violent language that is unreal and compensatory: "violence remains only verbal."[41] It was when John was taken out of the context of a marginal cult and placed in the hands of elite theologians who could appeal to the Roman powers—who in fact became the Roman powers—that the language of demonization and eschatological threat could become realized. By then John's words had become an enduring justification for perceiving Jews as an eternal Other that should be destroyed. Indeed, *this is the point at which Jews become an eternal Other* (Theorem 9).

THE FAREWELL DISCOURSES (JOHN 13–17) AND THE CONSTRUCTION OF THE WE

The discussion of the negative construction of the Jews as Other in John 8 can be compared with the positive construction of the We in John 13–17. Most of the second half of John's gospel, chapters thirteen through seventeen, is taken up with Jesus' Farewell Discourses. Jesus' final scene with his disciples in John is five chapters long, the longest single episode in the gospels. The other gospels place Jesus' last discourse with the disciples in a precise time-line that divides events into stages: the last supper, Jesus' prayer in Gethsemane, the trial, crucifixion, appearances of the risen Jesus, and so on. In John, however, the division into episodes and the time designations in general have become ambiguous. John has taken parts of the gospel story that appear in different places and joined them in one long discourse of Jesus to his disciples. In the liminal period of religious rituals, normal time ceases to apply and everyday social distinctions are reversed or dissolved; in the same way the Farewell Discourses depict a charged interlude in which normal social relations are either reversed or dissolved, and normal time is disrupted (13:5, 15:15). Jesus' words are thus spoken as though from a timeless perspective, and temporal confusions abound. The Farewell Discourses create a space apart and a time apart for Jesus to present teachings that only the disciples will hear. Just as the period of Jesus' incarnation can be seen as a liminal period with a special charged relationship between the Son and the Father, so also the Farewell Discourses read as a liminal period within this liminal period, a unique period of transparent revelation between Jesus and his disciples. The liminal aspect of the Farewell Discourses is reflected in the special things that Jesus reveals. He delivers important messages to his disciples, but they are also understood as addressed to the gospel audience, John's own community in about 90 CE.

During this liminal period of the Farewell Discourses, one may say that the historical narrative becomes *less real* than it had been (though it is still referred to), and the cosmological narrative becomes *more real*. In the Farewell Discourses the Jews are referred to only once (13:33), and the opponents are now known as "the world," used thirty-eight times in the Farewell Discourses.[42] The Jews are the opponents in the historical narrative, but the world opposes Jesus and the disciples in the cosmological narrative. In the cosmological narrative, the world also now has a leader, the "ruler of this world" or Satan. The Farewell Discourses are so long and so important as the central focus of the last part of John because the disciples, set apart, are *now being instructed in the cosmological narrative*. This is what Jesus is revealing.

The overall theme of Jesus' words is that it is time for his departure—crucifixion is not emphasized, but departure—and he acknowledges that the disciples are filled with sorrow as a result. He reassures them that although the world will persecute them, there is also consolation and hope: the Father will send a *paraklētos* or Paraclete to teach and nurture them. Similar to the holy spirit in the other gospels and Paul, the Paraclete is identified as the spirit that will descend upon the community after resurrection (14:17). *Paraklētos* in Greek means helper or comforter, but the term is also used for advocate or intercessor. Is the meaning "comforter" being emphasized here, or the meaning "advocate," as one who will defend the disciples from the judgment that is to come? Probably both. Reinhartz notes that at 16:8–11 the Paraclete will "cross-examine" or "convict" (*elenchein*) the world of its sin, just as the Jews had sought to convict Jesus in 8:46.[43] The conflict on the cosmological level is now resolved in favor of Jesus and against his accusers—ironically, just as the *historical* narrative is preparing to move to the worldly trial, conviction, and execution of Jesus.

Sources and Development of the Farewell Discourses

There are some fundamental problems with the narrative order in the Farewell Discourses. In the middle Jesus says, "Rise, let us be going" (14:31), yet the discourse continues for three chapters, and only then do

Jesus and his disciples proceed on their way. Further, at 16:5 Jesus rebukes his disciples by saying, "Why have you never asked me where I am going?" while at 13:36 Peter had in fact posed exactly this question. Some scholars try to make sense of these inconsistencies within the Farewell Discourses as they are, while others argue that the order of some of the sections has been transposed, and still others suggest that several discourses composed at different times have been placed together with little effort to harmonize them.[44] Here I follow this last group of scholars, and argue that what was once a shorter Farewell Discourse has been enlarged by the addition of alternative discourses to attain the present configuration. Not only are the problems above accounted for, but the fact that chapters fourteen and sixteen contain so many similar terms and motifs is explained. Once combined, however, the variant discourses function together to create a large tapestry that constructs the We.

There are five discrete sections of the Farewell Discourses. Fernando Segovia rightly separates off the last section, 17:1–26, as being significantly different from the others and perhaps added last. A pattern then emerges among the first four sections, a parallel between the outer two on the one hand and the inner two on the other:[45]

13:31–14:31	departure of Jesus and its immediate consequences
15:1–17	extended consequences: testing and proving
15:18–16:4a	extended consequences: testing and proving
16:4b–33	departure of Jesus and its immediate consequences

The first and fourth are more reassuring, the second and third more pessimistic.[46] In the first and fourth we find reference to Jesus' departure after a "little while," along with the question of where he is going, the sorrow at his departure, the coming of the Spirit-Paraclete, the resultant access to God, the power of the disciples to make petitions to God on their own behalf, and the problems with unbelief. As noted above, the two passages are so similar in their use of motifs that it is often suggested that they are alternative versions of a single tradition. But these sections are not only similar to each other, they are also similar to the account in Luke 24 and Acts 1 about the teachings of Jesus *after* he has been resurrected from the dead. It seems probable that John utilized an older tradition of the words of the *resurrected* Jesus to his disciples, and placed them back in the life of Jesus.[47] John has also introduced some significant changes: while Luke is emphatic that Jesus will *return*, John is just as emphatic that the disciples will *join Jesus*. Rather than the world being redeemed by Jesus' return, the disciples will be redeemed by being removed (despite 17:15, on which see below).

This describes the two outer sections; the two inner sections, John 15:1–17 and 15:18–16:4a, are both more negative. The former opens with a typical Johannine "I am" statement, "I am the true vine." The disciples are connected to this true vine as branches. But branches that do not abide in Jesus do not bear fruit; they are cut off and thrown into the fire:

> God removes every branch in me that bears no fruit. . . . Just as the branch cannot bear fruit by itself unless it abides in the vine, neither can you unless you abide in me. I am the vine, you are the branches. Those who abide in me and I in them bear much fruit. (15:2–5)

This appears to be a development of two sayings found independently in Q:

> Every tree that does not bear good fruit will be cut down and thrown into the fire. (Lk 3:9)

> No good tree bears bad fruit, nor does a bad tree bear good fruit. (Lk 6:43)

But John points toward a predestined salvation: "You did not choose me but I chose you" (15:16). One might argue that in John there is a decision process, but it is not in producing good works as in Q. It is in remaining (*meno*) in Jesus (John 15:4–5).

The other inner section, John 15:18–16:4a, is similar to Mark's account of Jesus' predictions of coming persecutions (Mark 13):

John 15:18–16:4a	*Mark 13*
They will persecute you (15:18–20)	They will persecute you (13:9)
You will be put out of synagogues (16:2)	You will be beaten in synagogues (13:9)
Paraclete will testify, and you also are to testify (15:26–27)	You are to testify, but it is not you who are to testify but the Holy Spirit (13:11)
The world will hate you on account of my name (15:18–21)	You will be hated on account of my name (13:13)

It is likely that John knew the same account of Jesus' prediction about sufferings that appears in Mark 13.[48] As noted above, the strong emphasis on followers of Jesus being *put out* of the synagogue—which occurs only in John—was perhaps developed out of the motif of being *beaten* in synagogues that is found here in Mark.

Whatever conclusions one draws about the origins of the first four sections, the final chapter of the Farewell Discourses, John 17, stands out as an even more dualistic text. On the basis of this chapter Ernst Käsemann argued for a strongly dualistic interpretation of the gospel as a whole.[49] In his analysis John developed a view of Jesus as fully divine but not fully human, as "God striding over the earth." Other scholars have disagreed with his conclusions, and although there is much in this chapter that Käsemann could call on for his argument (17:9, 14, 21), there are other statements about the world that could be interpreted in a more positive way, and that look ahead to the possibility of a mission in which at least some of the world would come to believe in Jesus. The world would somehow be redeemed in the post-resurrection period.[50] Jesus has sent the disciples into the world, and one may assume that it was to find other believers: "I ask not only on behalf of these, but also on behalf of those who will believe in me through their word" (17:20). Although it is a slim basis for a mission theology, it does reflect the awareness that part of the world did respond to the disciples' message, and that this gave rise to John's community. In this case, however, the world is only treated positively in the context of a reference to John's own community, and this group may not have perceived continued mission as an urgent requirement. That is, John's community was likely a cult rather than a missionary sect, and this verse merely recognizes the conversions that brought John's community into existence.

The various sections of John's Farewell Discourses, then, are probably derived from sources that arose from different settings in the earlier gospel tradition. Now, however, they have been joined together as Jesus' last testament before his death. More than anything else they serve to bolster community identity; they construct the We. The Farewell Discourses operate with a number of powerful images of the new bonds that exist between God, Jesus, and members of the community. At the core of the Farewell Discourses is the new commandment to love one another: "I have loved you, so also should you love one another" (13:34). The commandments to love one another is interesting both for being similar to Jewish tradition and for being different from other New Testament statements on Christian love. It is similar to the commandment to love one's neighbor in Leviticus 19:18, 34, but is surprisingly narrower in scope than either this love of neighbor or the love of enemy in the Sermon on the Mount; it extends only to the circle of believers. This is the basis of the unity of the new community.

The love the disciples are to have for each other is parallel to the love Jesus has for them, and the disciples will also have another experience parallel to Jesus': they will be hated by the world just as Jesus was hated. Love and hate define the difference between the disciples and the world: "The Father himself loves you, because you have loved me" (16:27), and "Whoever hates me hates my Father also" (15:23). The world's hatred is depicted as extreme, and the sharpest possible contrast between love and hate defines this community. As Segovia describes it:[51]

> This series of contrasts between the disciples and the world also has a repetitive and cumulative effect . . . , showing thereby an ever-widening gulf between the disciples and the world. Although the disciples may have "peace" in Jesus, they also find themselves in the midst of an unloving and unbelieving world.

The tightness of the bond between God, Jesus, and the community is directly proportional to the power of the hatred that the world has for them (Theorem 1). John is aware of the account of persecution and develops it into a division of the human race into two groups: the world is composed of the kind of people who hate, and the disciples are the kind of people who love each other.

Thus the Farewell Discourses constitute the We by setting up a series of parallels: Jesus and the disciples will love each other in the same way, suffer the same persecution, be hated in the same way, perform the same works. The parallel experiences erase the superiority of teacher to student typical in the ancient world. Equal now to their teacher, the disciples are no longer slaves but friends (15:15); the foot-washing scene has ritually enacted this change (13:1–11).[52] This parallel relationship between Jesus and the disciples is also broadened in the Farewell Discourses to include God in a triangular relationship: as God loves Jesus, so Jesus loves the disciples, and the disciples love God. No longer dependent upon Jesus' intervention, the disciples will now be able to ask anything of the Father directly. Only in the Farewell Discourse does God become fully present and available to the disciples. It is here that Jesus also bestows upon the disciples the name of God: "I have made your [that is, God's] name known to those you gave to me" (17:6, 11). The name of God is likely the phrase "I am," which figured so prominently and suggestively above.[53]

Nowhere else in the gospels are the benefits of salvation painted so richly. Within their tight-knit communities, members of sects often experience the reversal of shame; the feeling of being marginalized in the larger society is reversed within the community as the members feel accepted and affirmed. In John's community we find such a self-image of radical belonging. At first, the disciples do not know what Jesus means when he says he will be gone for a little while; their lack of understanding is very similar to that attributed earlier to the Jews (7:32–36). But Jesus instructs them in the cosmological narrative: just as God sent his son, so also God (or the risen Christ, who is now one with God) will send the Spirit-Paraclete. The special status of being sent by God is now extended to the disciples: "As you have sent me into the world, so I have sent them into the world" (17:18). There will be eternal life for the members of the community, but more specifically, they will be called to God and Christ; that is, Jesus will not return to them so much as they will come to the risen Christ.[54]

But it should also be kept in mind that, from the point of view of John's audience sixty years after Jesus' death, some of these events have already taken place. The crucifixion of Jesus is in the past, the promised Spirit-Paraclete has already come and instructed the community, and the audience now understands things that the disciples in the story did not know (2:22, 12:16). John's community now has absolute conviction about the truth of the past and that those who rejected Jesus have been judged:

> When he comes, he will convict [or cross-examine, *elenchein*] the world concerning sin, concerning righteousness, and concerning judgment: concerning sin, because they do not believe in me; concerning righteousness, because I am going to the Father and you will not see me any longer; concerning judgment, because the ruler of this world has been condemned. (16:8–11)

Their experience of joining the risen Christ is expressed in the future, but for the audience it is a present experience of the role of the Paraclete in their lives. That which is expressed elsewhere as a final reward at the end of time is already present for these believers; it is realized eschatology, found elsewhere in John (5:24–25), but more specifically we may wonder whether John advocates realized *resurrection*, the doctrine that the community already experiences a resurrection into eternal life. This doctrine is referred to, positively or negatively, in such New Testament texts as 1 Corinthians 15:12–29, Ephesians 2:6, Colossians 2:12, and 2 Timothy 2:18, and is defended in the later *Treatise on Resurrection*. The experience of oneness with God and Christ and the alienation from the world may have led John's community to the belief that they had indeed already been resurrected.

CONCLUSION

The high christology of the Gospel of John is communicated through a drama played out on two levels, that of the historical events depicted, and a parallel reality on the cosmological level. Jesus, alone of the characters in the gospel, can perceive both levels clearly, but misunderstandings of the other characters are many. Still, there is a spectrum of reactions and misunderstandings, and only some are fundamentally opposed to Jesus. The opponents on the historical level may be named using various terms, but the terms are almost always assimilated to "the Jews"; it is by far the most common designation. Whether it also evoked class distinctions or geographical distinctions may be debated, but in the narrative world of the text it gels as a cipher for the Other, and it is probably the case that John's community experienced alienation and deviance from the parent-body of Jews, whether as "cult" or "introversionist sect." The most strident language of this opposition comes in John 8, a chapter that interweaves references to both the historical and cosmological narratives. It is here that the Jews are called "children of the devil," and it is implied that their level of understanding is restricted to their historical-narrative zone.

This is confirmed when we turn to the section that defines the We, the Farewell Discourses. The two zones of the gospel are here more clearly defined. The disciples are called into close community with Jesus and God, and the simple words of the Gospel of John become, if this is possible, even simpler in the Farewell Discourses. A number of words are used significantly more here than in the rest of John—love, joy, peace, friends, glorify, know, name, truth, ask—and they are indicative of the special relationship to Jesus and God and the special experience that the disciples share. Certain negative words also appear more in the Farewell Discourses, for instance, "world." The world is the opponent in the cosmological narrative, the Jews the opponent in the historical narrative, and the Farewell Discourses provide the zone in which the cosmological narrative can now be perceived. The audience see themselves as escaping from the historical narrative and merging with the cosmological narrative and eternal life. Upon leaving the Farewell Discourses, the historical narrative returns with a vengeance in the trial and crucifixion, where Jesus is condemned. The Jews return as opponents, but are now seen as relegated to the historical narrative, where they will remain. As John says, they are already judged. But the audience of John's gospel has been changed by the Farewell Discourses. Their community identity is forged as a We that understands itself as being united with God and Christ, separated from the world, an uncomprehending opponent.

NOTES

1. George W. E. Nickelsburg, "Revealed Wisdom as a Criterion for Inclusion and Exclusion: From Jewish Sectarianism to Early Christianity," in *"To See Ourselves as Others See Us": Christians, Jews, "Others" in Late Antiquity*, ed. Jacob Neusner and Ernst S. Frerichs (Chico, CA: Scholars Press, 1985), 73–91.

2. See Gail O'Day, "John," in *Women's Bible Commentary*, ed. Carol A. Newsom and Sharon H. Ringe (Louisville, KY: Westminster/John Knox, 1998), 303–4.

3. Norman R. Petersen, *The Gospel of John and the Sociology of Light: Language and Characterization in the Fourth Gospel* (Valley Forge, PA: Trinity Press International, 1993), 61–66.

4. Wayne Meeks, "The Man from Heaven in Johannine Sectarianism," *Journal of Biblical Literature* 91 (1972): 44–72. See also Godfrey Nicholson, *Death as Departure: The Johannine Descent-Ascent Schema* (Chico, CA: Scholars Press, 1983).

5. Petersen, *Gospel of John*, esp. 57–62; Werner H. Kelber, "Metaphysics and Marginality in John," in *What Is John? Readers and Readings of the Fourth Gospel*, ed. Fernando F. Segovia (Atlanta, GA: Scholars, 1996), 129–54.

6. Adele Reinhartz, *The Word in the World: The Cosmological Tale in the Fourth Gospel* (Atlanta, GA: Scholars Press, 1992); the quotations are from pp. 4, 36. She actually distinguishes three levels and not two as noted here; I omit her ecclesiastical narrative for the present. John's distinction can also be seen as a more dualistic version of what Philo says in *On the Creation of the World*, 146: "Every person, in respect to mind is allied with the divine Word, . . . but in respect to body to the whole world."

7. Lawrence M. Wills, "Judith," in *New Interpreter's Bible*, 12 vols. (Nashville, TN: Abingdon, 1998–2003), 3:1084–87; Judith L. Kovacs, "'Now Shall the Ruler of This World Be Driven Out': Jesus' Death as Cosmic Battle in John 12:20–36," *Journal of Biblical Literature* 114 (1995): 227–47, contra Nicholson, *Death as Departure*, 128, 163.

8. Jerome Neyrey, *An Ideology of Revolt: John's Christology in Social-Science Perspective* (Philadelphia: Fortress, 1988), 42. David Rensberger rightly distinguishes the different levels of misunderstandings (*Johannine Faith and Liberating Community* [Philadelphia: Westminster, 1988], 37–54, 92–95).

9. Jeffrey Siker, *Disinheriting the Jews: Abraham in Early Christian Controversy* (Louisville, KY: Westminster/John Knox, 1991), 128–41; Fernando F. Segovia, *The Farewell of the Word: The Johannine Call to Abide* (Minneapolis, MN: Fortress, 1991), 194 n. 42.

10. See only John 4:9, 18:35. Jesus is identified as a Jew in chapter four, but what he *says* is "neither on this mountain nor in Jerusalem will you worship the Father"; see Adele Reinhartz, *Befriending the Beloved Disciple: A Jewish Reading of the Gospel of John* (New York and London: Continuum, 2001), 63.

11. David Rensberger, *Johannine Faith*, 28–29, applying the categories of sociologist Bryan R. Wilson, refers to John's community as an introversionist sect. For the terminology of cult versus sect, see Rodney Stark, *The Rise of Christianity: A Sociologist Reconsiders History* (Princeton, NJ: Princeton University Press, 1996), 33, 44–45. The lists of words distinctive to each gospel are found in C. K. Barrett, *The Gospel According to St. John: An Introduction with Commentary and Notes on the Greek Text*, 2nd ed. (Philadelphia: Westminster, 1978), 5–6. I am indebted to a former student, Brad Brockman, for this comparison of the terms.

12. Daniel Boyarin, *Border Lines: The Partition of Judaeo-Christianity* (Philadelphia: University of Pennsylvania Press, 2004); Daniel Boyarin, *Dying for God: Martyrdom and the Making of Christianity and Judaism* (Stanford, CA: Stanford University Press, 1999); Daniel Boyarin, "The *Ioudaioi* in John and the Prehistory of 'Judaism,'" in *Pauline Conversations in Context: Essays in Honor of Calvin J. Roetzel*, ed. Janice Capel Anderson, Philip Sellew, and Claudia Setzer (London: Sheffield Academic Press, 2002), 216–39. Also cf. J. Albert Harrill, "The Cannibalistic Language in the Fourth Gospel and the Greco-Roman Polemics of Factionalism (John 6:52–66)," *Journal of Biblical Literature* (forthcoming), who shows

that the language of eating the body of Christ is treated as self-stigmatization in regard to cannibalism.

13. There is now a vast scholarship on this issue, but see J. Louis Martyn, *History and Theology in the Fourth Gospel*, 2nd ed. (Nashville, TN: Abingdon, 1979); Reuven Kimelman, "*Birkat Ha-Minim* and the Lack of Evidence for an Anti-Christian Jewish Prayer in Late Antiquity," in *Jewish and Christian Self-Definition*, ed. E. P. Sanders et al., 3 vols. (Philadelphia: Fortress, 1981), 2:226–44; and Adele Reinhartz, "The Johannine Community and Its Jewish Neighbors: A Reappraisal," in *What is John? Volume 2: Literary and Sociological Readings of the Fourth Gospel*, ed. Fernando F. Segovia (Atlanta, GA: Scholars Press, 1998), 111–38.

14. Boyarin, "*Ioudaioi* in John," suggests that "put out of the synagogue" does not imply permanent expulsion but a temporary punishment, but the context of the sayings in John—especially 9:22—argues that it does mean permanent expulsion. See also Gören Forkman, *The Limits of the Religious Community: Expulsion from the Religious Community within the Qumran Sect, within Rabbinic Judaism, and within Primitive Christianity* (Lund, Sweden: Gleerup, 1972).

15. Wayne O. McCready, "Johannine Self-Understanding and the Synagogue Episode of John 9," in *Self-Definition and Self-Discovery in Early Christianity: A Study in Changing Horizons*, ed. David J. Hawkin and Tom Robinson (Lewiston, ME: Edwin Mellen, 1990), esp. 155, 159. On the creation of a myth of persecution, see Mu-chou Poo, *Enemies of Civilization: Attitudes toward Foreigners in Ancient Mesopotamia, Egypt, and China* (Albany: State University of New York Press, 2005), 21.

16. Lawrence M. Wills, *The Quest of the Historical Gospel: Mark, John and the Origins of the Gospel Genre* (London and New York: Routledge, 1997), 112–14.

17. Jouette Bassler, "The Galileans: A Neglected Factor in Johannine Community Research," *Catholic Biblical Quarterly* 43 (1981): 243–57; Malcolm Lowe, "Who Were the *Ioudaioi*?" *NT* 18 (1976): 101–30. Reinhartz, *Befriending*, 73–74, objects to Lowe's conclusions on the grounds that in the Diaspora, where John's community was likely situated, the distinctions between Galilean Jews and Judean Jews would be lost. However, although the origins of John's gospel are traditionally located in Ephesus in Asia Minor, it is possible to look instead to the borderlands between Judeans on one hand and Galileans and Samaritans on the other, precisely where this distinction between "provincial" worshipers of the God of Israel would apply; see, in addition to Bassler, Wayne Meeks, "Galilee and Judea in the Fourth Gospel," *Journal of Biblical Literature* 85 (1966): 159–69; and Wayne Meeks, "Breaking Away: Three New Testament Pictures of Christianity's Separation from the Jewish Communities," in Neusner and Frerichs, *To See Ourselves*, 93–115.

18. Shaye J. D. Cohen, *The Beginnings of Jewishness: Boundaries, Varieties, Uncertainties* (Berkeley: University of California Press, 1999), 14, 69–106. In addition to the examples that Cohen adduces, there are other passages that should be brought into the discussion. In *Migration of Abraham* 97–100 and *Antiquities* 20.17–96, Philo and Josephus describe Jews who hold propositional definitions of Judaism, even though the authors reject that.

19. David Rensberger, "Anti-Judaism and the Gospel of John," in *Anti-Judaism and the Gospels*, ed. William R. Farmer (Harrisburg, PA: Trinity Press International, 1999), 122–24. Note also that Mark, who works with a much stronger distinction between Galilee and Judea, does not refer to the opponents as "Judeans."

20. Boyarin, "*Ioudaioi* in John"; Boyarin, *Border Lines*, 263–64; Boyarin, *Dying for God*, 127–30. Unlike Cohen's suggestion of two meanings, for which there is ample evidence, Boyarin's is more of a postulate.

21. Meeks, "Man from Heaven."

22. Reinhartz, *Befriending*, 74–75.

23. Raymond E. Brown, *The Gospel according to John*, 2 vols. (Garden City, NY: Doubleday, 1966–1970), 1:428; Rensberger, *Johannine Faith*, 87–106; Urban C. von Wahlde, "The Gospel of John and the Presentation of Jews and Judaism," in *Within Context: Essays on Jews and Judaism in the New Testament*, ed. David P. Efroymson, Eugene J. Fisher, and Leon Klenicki (Collegeville, MN: Liturgical, 1993), 61–74; Urban C. von Wahlde, "The 'Johannine' Jews: A Critical Survey," *NTS* 28 (1982): 33–60.

24. See Wills, *Quest*, 23–50; a translation of *Aesop* appears on pp. 181–215. See also Lawrence M. Wills, "The Death of the Hero and the Violent Death of Jesus," in *Religion and Violence: The Biblical Heritage*, ed. Jonathan Klawans and David Bernat (Sheffield, UK: Sheffield Phoenix Press, 2008), 79–99, and Lawrence M. Wills, "The Aesop Tradition," in *The Historical Jesus in Context*, ed. John Dominic Crossan, Dale Allison, and Amy-Jill Levine (Princeton, NJ: Princeton University Press, 2006), 222–37.

25. Luke T. Johnson, "The New Testament's Anti-Jewish Slander and the Conventions of Ancient Polemic," *Journal of Biblical Literature* 108 (1989): 419–41.

26. Meeks, "Man from Heaven," 70; Seán Freyne, "Vilifying the Other and Defining the Self: Matthew's and John's Anti-Jewish Polemic in Focus," in Neusner and Frerichs, *To See Ourselves*, 117–43; and Segovia, *Farewell*, 120.

27. Rudolf Bultmann, *Theology of the New Testament*, 2 vols. (New York: Scribner's, 1951–1955), 2.3–69; Rudolf Bultmann, *The Gospel of John: A Commentary* (Philadelphia: Westminster, 1971), passim.

28. William Countryman, *The Mystical Way in the Fourth Gospel: Crossing Over into God*, rev. ed. (Valley Forge, PA: Trinity Press International, 1994).

29. Kelber, "Metaphysics," 132.

30. Helmut Koester, "Gnostic Sayings and Controversy Traditions in John 8:12–59," in *Nag Hammadi, Gnosticism, and Early Christianity*, ed. Charles W. Hedrick and Robert Hodgson, Jr. (Peabody, MA: Hendrickson, 1986), 97–110; cf. Neyrey, *Ideology of Revolt*, 34–42; Brown, *John*, 1:315, 343; and Harold Attridge, "Thematic Development and Source Elaboration in John 7:1–36," *Catholic Biblical Quarterly* 42 (1980): 160–70.

31. James H. Charlesworth's distinction of different kinds of dualism is excellent ("A Critical Comparison of the Dualism in 1QS 3:13–4:26 and the 'Dualism' Contained in the Gospel of John," in *John and Qumran*, ed. James H. Charlesworth [London: Geoffrey Chapman, 1972]), but for the sake of discussion I use here slightly different terminology and fewer categories. My category metaphysical dualism is called by Charlesworth physical dualism. Brown argues that John asserts an ethical dualism, not metaphysical dualism ("The Qumran Scrolls and the Johannine Gospel and Epistles," in *The Scrolls and the New Testament*, ed. Krister Stendahl [New York: Harper & Brothers, 1957], 183–207), and Charlesworth presses this even more strongly, but in my view Brown and Charlesworth advocate a rationalized version of John's thought that de-emphasizes the metaphysical elements.

32. Siker, *Disinheriting the Jews*, 134; see also Fernando F. Segovia, "The Love and Hatred of Jesus and Johannine Sectarianism," *Catholic Biblical Quarterly* 43 (1981): 258–72; and Adele Reinhartz, "Love, Hate, and Violence in the Gospel of John," in *Violence in the New Testament*, ed. E. Leigh Gibson and Shelly Matthews (Edinburgh, UK: T & T Clark, 2005), 109–23.

33. Koester, "Gnostic Sayings," 101–2; George MacRae, "Gnosticism and the Church of John's Gospel," in Hedrick and Hodgson, *Nag Hammadi*, 93. See also Helmut Koester, "The Story of the Johannine Tradition," *Sewanee Theological Review* 39 (1992): 17–32. In essential agreement are James M. Robinson, "Jesus from Easter to Valentinus (or to the Apostles' Creed)," *Journal of Biblical Literature* 101 (1982): 25, and Meeks, "Man from Heaven." Jeffrey A. Trumbower, *Born from Above: The Anthropology of the Gospel of John* (Tübingen, Germany: Mohr, 1992), goes further than I do and specifies what John does not: not only does Jesus have a heavenly origin, so do the followers.

34. Although some scholars would argue that John knows these sayings from Matthew or Luke, it is more likely that John is not familiar with Matthew, Mark, or Luke, nor with Q, but taps into the orally circulating sayings of Jesus; see Wills, *Quest*. Since, however, there is no consensus on whether John knew the other gospels, I would simply note that that would make no substantial difference for the discussion here.

35. "Your synagogues" in Matthew and "your law" in John function differently in the two texts. It is an anachronism to assume that "synagogue" stood for Judaism in the first century, but "your law" is associated with "the Jews" in John.

36. This despite John 17:15, which appears to be a corrective gloss to the anti-world saying at 17:14. Ambiguity about the time frame—that is, before or after resurrection—is inherent in these texts, and is addressed instructively by Robinson, "Jesus from Easter to Valentinus," 22–25; see also Brown, *John*, 2:581–82; Segovia, *Farewell*, 298–99; and C. H. Dodd, *The Interpretation of the Fourth Gospel* (Cambridge, UK: Cambridge University Press, 1968), 390–411. On subtle but important differences between John and *Thomas*, see Elaine Pagels, *Beyond Belief: The Secret Gospel of Thomas* (New York: Random House, 2003), 40–41, and April D. DeConick, *Voices of the Mystics: Early Christian Discourse in the Gospels of John and Thomas and Other Ancient Christian Literature* (London: Clark, 2004). DeConnick is probably correct (131–32) that John advocates a faith mysticism rather than an ascent mysticism, but imagines that the union will be in the audience's future, rather than already realized.

37. Wills, *Quest*, 93–95, 174–76; Adela Yarbro Collins, "The Influence of Daniel on the New Testament," in John J. Collins, *Daniel* (Minneapolis, MN: Fortress, 1993), 90–112.

38. See Brown, *John*, 1:533–38.

39. C. H. Dodd, *Historical Tradition in the Fourth Gospel* (Cambridge, UK: Cambridge University Press, 1963), 380. In Stoicism, the meaning is this: the philosophical ideal of understanding the true nature of things (*physis*) can free one from mere social convention (*nomos*).

40. Siker, *Disinheriting the Jews*, 128–41. See the discussion of the contributions of Caroline Johnson Hodge and Denise Kimber Buell on the children of Abraham motif in chapter seven.

41. Gedaliahu Guy Stroumsa, "Early Christianity as Radical Religion," in *Barbarian Philosophy: The Religious Revolution of Early Christianity* (Tübingen, Germany: Mohr Siebeck, 1999), 8–26; David Frankfurter, "The Legacy of Sectarian Rage: Vengeance Fantasies in the New Testament," in Klawans and Bernat, *Religion and Violence*.

Rensberger, "Anti-Judaism," 150–51, provides a compelling plea to understand John's ironic destabilizing of the Judeans as a strategy of the marginalized. Johannine irony, he says,

> is a tool not of cruelty but of resistance. Irony from below is not an instrument of marginalization but a defense against marginalization. . . . I would insist, then, that John cannot be said to marginalize "the Jews," since it speaks *from* the margin against the authorities whom it calls "the Jews."

But it is not clear exactly how John is "below" Jews if the temple has been destroyed. In addition, a warning comes from a different perspective in Fernando F. Segovia, "Inclusion and Exclusion in John 17: An Intercultural Reading," in *What Is John? Vol. 2: Literary and Social Readings of the Fourth Gospel*, ed. Fernando F. Segovia (Atlanta, GA: Scholars, 1998), 208:

> Strategies of inversion I also find ultimately counterproductive: they continue in their own way the very discourse of center and margins. In so doing, they may quite easily slip into similar situations of outright disdain and oppression of the "other" and become enormously destructive.

42. Raymond Edward Brown, *The Community of the Beloved Disciple* (New York: Paulist, 1979), 63, suggests a chronological development at this point: in chapters one through twelve the Jews are the opponents, and that shifts in chapter thirteen to the world. But the Jews return as opponents after the Farewell Discourses; it is only in the liminal state of the Farewell Discourses that the world is highlighted as the opponent. Brown is also incorrect in associating the world with *gentile* rejection of the Jesus movement.

43. Brown, *John*, 2:1136, points out that the Paraclete here acts more like an accuser in condemning the world, but that is the double nature of judgment: the Paraclete saves the good and condemns the bad. Another parallel for the comforter aspect is the returning presence of the dead hero at the hero's tomb; see Jennifer Berenson Maclean, "Jesus as Cult Hero in the Fourth Gospel," in *Philostratus's Heroikos: Religion and Cultural Identity in the Third Century C.E.*, ed. Jennifer Berenson Maclean and Ellen Bradshaw Aitken (Atlanta, GA: SBL, 2004), 195–218.

44. Brown, *John*, 2:582–601, and Segovia, *Farewell*.

45. Segovia, *Farewell*, 288–91, 297.

46. Brown, *John*, 2:586–97.

47. See W. Boyd, "The Ascension according to St John," *Theology* 70 (1967): 207–11.

48. Wills, *Quest*, 112–14.

49. Ernst Käsemann, *The Testament of Jesus: A Study of the Gospel of John in the Light of Chapter 17* (Philadelphia: Fortress, 1968).

50. Brown, *John*, 2:778.

51. Segovia, *Farewell*, 107–8, 75–77; see also Reinhartz, "Love, Hate."

52. At Wis 7:27, Wisdom is also capable of making sages into friends of God, but this is more symbolic. Sharon H. Ringe, *Wisdom's Friends: Community and Christology in the Fourth Gospel* (Louisville, KY: Westminster John Knox, 1999), focuses on the positive definition of We, but may obscure the negative side of community formation. Barbara Bowe notes some of these problems in her review, *Catholic Biblical Quarterly* 63 (2001): 560.

53. Brown, *John*, 1:533–38. See also 18:6.

54. Dodd, *Interpretation*, 405.

7

⌒

Jew and Gentile
as Other in Paul

It is often stated that Paul more than any other figure—even Jesus—defined Christianity as a religion that was divorced from Judaism and Jewish law. This interpretation of Paul's theology as a movement from Jewish legalism to Christian faith, and from ethnic Judaism to Christian universalism, has dominated almost all streams of western Christian theology for two thousand years. At the turn of the twentieth century, the eminent church historian Adolf Harnack could say, "It was Paul who delivered the Christian religion from Judaism. . . . It was he who confidently regarded the Gospel as a new force abolishing the religion of the law."[1] But Jewish observance of law was distorted and caricatured by Christian scholars such as Harnack. A multifaceted form of worship came to be described in a one-dimensional way (Theorem 5: Other distorted and reduced to one essence): Jews thought, so it was assumed, that by performing the things that were required in the law they could render themselves righteous before God. The doctrine of Jewish legalism came to be described by Christian theologians as works-righteousness, or the view that righteousness before God can be achieved by human effort. Early on this distinction became a fulcrum in Christian theology: Jewish legalism was rejected in favor of Christian faith without the law.

It is easy to see where Christian readers would have perceived the basis of this in Paul's work. Consider, for instance, Romans 9:30–31, 10:3:

Gentiles, who did not strive for righteousness, have attained it, that is, righteousness through faith. But Israel, who did strive for righteousness based on the law, did not succeed in fulfilling that law. . . . They have not submitted to

God's righteousness, because they are ignorant of the righteousness that comes from God and seek to establish their own.

Paul seemed not only to provide a theoretical justification for the Christian rejection of Jewish law, he lost restraint at times and opened up a sharp attack on those followers of Jesus who continued to observe Jewish law. In 2 Corinthians 3, Paul refers to the Ten Commandments as the "ministry of death," and at Galatians 5:12 he exclaims, "I wish that those who unsettle you (by requiring Jewish law) would castrate themselves!"

Post-Pauline Christian theology certainly institutionalized the construction of Jewish legalism as Other, down to and including liberal theologians of the present. *Even after the Holocaust*, prominent Christian theologians could describe Jewish law as an institution of the fallen state of humanity, a foil for true salvation in Christ. Ernst Käsemann, author of one of the most influential commentaries on Romans, summarizes the relation of Christianity to Jewish legalism in this way: "Failing to understand the law, [Israel] falls into illusion and is overthrown. Christ exposes the illusion."[2] Such prejudicial language issued forth unchecked, and at times—again, after the Holocaust—took on a peculiar animus, as in this reference book entry on Pharisees by the leading New Testament scholar Matthew Black:

> Pharisaism is the immediate ancestor of rabbinical Judaism, the largely arid religion of the Jews after the fall of Jerusalem. . . . It is a sterile religion of codified tradition, regulating every part of life by a halachah, observing strict separation, and already as entrenched in its own conservatism as that of the Sadducees.[3]

One can find in the pages of even the liberal Christian theologians of the twentieth century the notion that Christian salvation in faith is a response to the hubris of the Jewish quest for works-righteousness. Investigation into what real Jews thought and did was unnecessary for scholars if the mythical Jews who opposed Jesus and Paul had already been constructed. And it was not just the conservative, moderate, or liberal theologians who assumed a development from Jewish legalism to Christian faith. Some feminist and liberation theologians could not construct a liberating Jesus without contrasting him to an unhistorical picture of Jewish legalism and purity codes, a view of Jesus that owes more to the Christian tradition about Paul than to the gospel texts themselves (Theorem 5: Other distorted).[4]

For two thousand years Paul has been seen as the theoretician of how Christianity first rejected and then replaced Jewish law, and by that, Judaism as well. The rejection-replacement of Judaism has come to occupy a central place in Christianity's myth of its own origins. Both Christian and Jewish commentators often see Paul in this way, although for Jews it is obviously a reason for criticizing him; he has until recently been seen as a turncoat who abandoned his religion and became its fiercest critic, distorting it in the process. As a result, it is assumed by both Christian and Jewish scholars that if Paul turned on his observant, Pharisaic, Jewish upbringing, became a Christian, and developed *the* theory of why Christianity has supplanted Judaism in God's plan of salvation, then Jews are the Other in Paul's thought. But is it possible that the rejection-replacement theory of Judaism, and thus the basis of the Jew-as-Other interpretation of Paul, is a misreading of Paul that is only possible because of church developments that occurred after his death?

PROBLEMS IN THE INTERPRETATION OF PAUL

One of the reasons that Paul's theology as a whole is difficult to understand is that his letters were urgent and argumentative communications with living communities, not systematic reflections on theology. They were addressed to different congregations and covered the issues that happened to arise in each community. Only Romans is written for a community that Paul did not found, and it is the only one that orders the theological issues in a more systematic way. (Paul probably did not write all of the letters in the New Testament that are ascribed to him. Here I follow the scholarly consensus that limits the undisputed letters of Paul to Romans, 1 and 2 Corinthians, Galatians, Philippians, 1 Thessalonians, and Philemon.) And just as each of the letters was addressed to a different community situation, they were also written over a period of almost ten years, and may reflect a development in Paul's thinking. It is thus possible to reconstruct "Paul's theology," but always with the caveat that the conditions under which they were written must be taken into consideration.

It may first be helpful to summarize the traditional version of Paul's theology. It is divided here into "human plight" and "divine solution":[5]

Traditional View of Paul's Theology

Human Plight

- Humans are imprisoned in sin through the fall of Adam, and sin is a barrier, even a chasm between humans and God.
- God's nature is revealed through scripture, but is also known to gentiles through creation.
- The invisible nature of the one true God is willfully obscured by all, who replace God with objects of their own making (idolatry).

- The immorality of gentiles is a result, but that of Jews is also.
- The law of Moses, instituted by God and reflecting the will of God, does not protect Jews, but provides a false goal of self-justification before God (works-righteousness), and as a result the law only condemns Jews all the more clearly.
- The judgment against humanity is absolute: "There is none that is righteous, not even one" (Rom 3:10, quoting Eccl 7:20).

Divine Solution

- God brought about a new dispensation in the death and resurrection of Jesus Christ.
- The preexistent Christ was humbled, crucified by the "rulers of this age" so that the wisdom of this age, Greek and Jewish, would be made foolish by the paradoxical but true wisdom of God.
- Those in Christ were acquitted of their sin, and justified before God where condemnation of the law no longer applies.
- Justification before God now comes about for Jew and gentile alike through faith, and not through works of law.
- Sin as a barrier was thus removed for those in Christ, as was death as the end for humans.
- Paul's mission to the gentiles thus does not require observance of the law; this arrangement was agreed to by the "pillars" in the Jerusalem church, Peter, James, and John.
- In terms of justification before God, the old social distinctions are dissolved: "In Christ there is no longer Jew or Greek, slave or free, male or female" (Gal 3:28).
- Continuation of observance of the law is permissible for Jews, but for gentiles who were never under the law, observance denies the new dispensation through faith and is thus opposed to God's plan.
- As a result, the law is now often described as negative: "babysitter" (Gal 3:24), "ministry of death" (2 Cor 3:7).
- Most Jews deny the new dispensation, but the gathering of gentiles in Christ will make Jews jealous, and both Jews and gentiles will be saved in Christ (Rom 9–11).

This traditional reading of Paul would clearly construct as the Other those Jews who persist in denying Jesus, even though Paul had begun his life as a pious Jew. It prevailed in Christian tradition until the last half of the twentieth century, but has been questioned in recent decades in many of its parts. The upsetting of the applecart has come in three challenges over the last forty years, which betray some important differences, among them:

- feminist and liberationist critiques of Paul
- analyses of Paul's response to the Roman imperial situation
- the so-called new perspective of scholars who question Paul's rejection of Judaism

The first two will be set aside for the moment, and we will begin by discussing the challenges of the "new perspective."[6] By the end of the twentieth century a number of scholars had challenged not just one plank or another of the traditional interpretation of Paul listed above, but the whole structure. This development has been very influential in that most liberal and many moderate scholars of Paul have been brought into this "new perspective" to one degree or another, despite some important differences. Here I will summarize a few of the key figures, focusing on points that figure directly into the question of Paul's construction of the We and Other.

It may be said that the new perspective was inaugurated along two tracks, a moderate track that has received wide support, and a more radical track that remains something of a minority position. The moderate track was compellingly stated by E. P. Sanders in 1977 with the publication of his book *Paul and Palestinian Judaism*. The groundwork for the radical track had actually been laid much earlier in 1960 by Krister Stendahl with the first publication of his article "The Apostle Paul and the Introspective Conscience of the West."[7] Both Sanders and Stendahl argued that Paul was at heart a *missionary* theologian, not a philosopher of the human condition. This starting point, indeed, is the central assumption of all new-perspective scholars. Sanders concluded that Paul developed a mission to gentiles without the law (the Divine Solution above) *and only then* was forced to justify the mission by describing the Human Plight, one might say, by *inventing* the Human Plight. Thus the solution, a celebration of the ingathering of the gentiles at the end of time predicted in scripture (Isa 2:2–4, 25:6–10, 56:6–8; Zech 14) came to Paul before he worked out the predicament. Paul only fitfully composed the theology of the plight section to defend a central tenet of his solution, which was that in his communities gentiles were not required to obey Jewish law.

According to Sanders, Paul did not intend a thorough critique of Judaism or Jewish law, but only wanted to demonstrate that the highest religious attainment to date, Judaism, had been surpassed at the end of time by God's culminating act in history, the advent of faith in Christ: "In short, *this is what Paul finds wrong in Judaism: it is not Christianity.*"[8] This may seem a mere adjustment to the framework of Paul's theology, but it is fundamental. The traditional interpretation of Paul is based on the assumption that the human condition is very negative; people are trapped in sin, and Jewish law (and Judaism) is not just *part* of a fallen world, but it is what would tempt us into a false sense of self-worth, a false sense of our ability to meet God's demands through our own efforts, in other words, works-righteousness. Sanders argues that not only did Jews not hold that view of the role of Jewish law, *Paul never accused them of holding that view*. As Sanders says, "The supposed objection to Jewish self-righteousness is as absent from Paul's letters as self-righteousness itself is from Jewish literature."[9] This construction of the Jew as Other came not from Paul, but from those who followed in his footsteps. What Jews believed, and what Paul recognized that Jews believed, was that God bestowed the covenant to the Jews as a gift, not based on their merit. To remain in the covenant, Jews were required to obey God's law as a form of worship and recognition of the covenant. After a thorough analysis of many ancient Jewish texts, Sanders concludes that most of the Jews of Paul's day espoused a doctrine of "covenantal nomism." Salvation for Jews entailed being a member in good standing of Israel, of being in a covenant relation with God. Thus getting in is by grace, staying in is by law-as-response, or one might say, law-as-worship.[10]

Sanders's challenge to Pauline scholars, both liberal and conservative, was quite successful. He argued that Paul was not as negative toward Judaism as the traditional view had held, but he still argued that for Paul Jewish law was no longer sufficient by itself as a means of remaining in covenant with God. It had been replaced at the end of time by a focus on faith in Christ. Sanders had thus rejected some of the main planks of the traditional conception of Paul's theology, but he had kept one, the rejection-replacement theory of Judaism. True, Sanders reminded the reader that the only problem with Judaism was that it was not Christianity, but in his view Paul still operated with a benign rejection-replacement model. A group of other scholars questioned whether Paul espoused a rejection-replacement view of Judaism at all. Stendahl, Stanley Stowers, John Gager, and Lloyd Gaston denied even this last plank of the traditional reading.[11] When Paul finally turned at long last to the actual situation of Jews in God's scheme (and not Jewish followers of Jesus), he did *not* conclude that the Jewish path to God was closed:

> I want you to understand this mystery: a hardening has come upon part of Israel until the full number of the gentiles has come in. And so all Israel will be saved. . . . Just as you [gentiles] were once disobedient to God but have now received mercy because of their [the Jews'] disobedience, so they have now been disobedient in order that, by the mercy shown to you, they too may now receive mercy. (Rom 11:25–26, 30–31)

But when the Jews are finally gathered to God at the end of time with the gentiles, will they enter as believers in Christ or simply as Jews confirmed in the covenant with God? Although it has been assumed for two thousand years that the language here of Israel's final acceptance referred to turning to Christ, it is stunning to note that this is never stated, especially where one might expect it:

> On the one hand, as regards the gospel they [Israel] are enemies for your sake, but on the other hand, as regards election they are beloved for the sake of the patriarchs. (11:28)

In the traditional reading, there was no question that what Paul meant was that Jews will come around at the end and enter as believers in Christ. Evangelical Christians to this day cultivate positive relations with Jews and the State of Israel in anticipation of this moment. And there are passages in Romans that seem to support this. Romans 10:9: "If you confess with your lips that Jesus is Lord and believe in your heart that God raised him from the dead, you will be saved." It appears at first that Jews will also have to confess Jesus as Lord, but the radical new perspective scholars urge a second look at these texts. This passage, they argue, is likely addressed to gentiles, not Jewish followers of Jesus. Paul has stated that, contrary to the prevailing belief among the followers of Jesus, there is a way to God for gentiles without the law: "If you (gentiles) confess that Jesus is Lord, you will be saved." This is true for the recipients of the letter, but does it say anything at all about Jews? Gentiles are included through the faith of Christ, but is this necessary for Jews as well? The same question applies to the verses that follow. Emphasized are the centrality of faith and the availability of Christ for both Jew and Greek, but Paul may have meant these lines as an assurance to gentiles, not a requirement for Jews. Further, these verses are still talking about the period *before* the end, not the end itself, which Romans 11 will describe. Paul can say that there is presently, in phase one, only a "remnant" of faithful Jews (11:5), but in phase two "all Israel" will be saved (11:26). In the first stage of the end, there is a drama of Jewish rejection of the message of Christ, the period of stumbling. Not all have heard about Jesus, nor have all responded. From there Paul will transition to the final phase of God's relation to Jews. And strikingly, from 10:18 through the end of chapter eleven, Christ is conspicuously and totally absent, at exactly that crescendo where one would have expected Christ to be central if he were necessary for the Jews' salvation. Paul describes the final phase of the end by focusing on the relation of *God* to Israel, not Christ.

The radical new perspective pushes back the boundaries of what most readers would think of as possible for Paul's theology. The concept of being "in Christ" is so dominant in Paul's writings that it is difficult to imagine that at the end of time Jews would not also have to believe and confess that Jesus is Lord. We may pause at this point to retrace some of the arguments that led the radical new-perspective scholars to this challenging conclusion. First I will outline what I will call "Stendahl's paradox" and then "Gager's paradox." (It is possible that they are not really paradoxes at all, but only seem to be paradoxes when compared to the traditional interpretation.) Stendahl's paradox is this: Paul speaks often in dichotomies, Jews and gentiles (or "Greeks"), but more often, observant Jewish followers of Jesus versus non-observant gentile followers of Jesus. But what is startling is that, except in Romans 9–11, Paul does *not* contrast Jews on the one hand and gentile followers of Jesus on the other.[12] He does not place these two together as a marked contrast in his writings, even though this dichotomy was listed above as a central part of the traditional interpretation of Paul, and is indeed what most people think of as *the* religious dichotomy for Paul. Paul does not address the ecumenical problem of the relation of two groups, Jews and gentile Christians, nor even two religions, Judaism and Christianity.

Now Gager's paradox. Despite the fact that Christian tradition, and most twentieth-century biblical scholars, saw Paul as a proponent of a rejection-replacement view of Judaism, the letters of Paul are actually filled with apparently contradictory statements on Israel, circumcision, and the law.[13] Gager arranges statements from Paul in an anti-Israel list and a pro-Israel list. The anti-Israel statements include:

- "For all who rely on works of the law are under a curse." (Gal 3:10)
- "No one is justified before God by the law." (Gal 3:11; cf. Rom 3:20)
- "Israel, who pursued righteousness which is based on the law, did not succeed in fulfilling that law." (Rom 9:31)
- "As regards the gospel, Jews are enemies of God for your sake." (Rom 11:28)
- The Ten Commandments are a "ministry of death": "The minds of Jews were hardened. For to this day, when they read the old covenant, the veil (over Moses' face) remains, because only through Christ is it taken away." (2 Cor 3:7, 14)

Yet there is also a pro-Israel set of statements which project a different attitude:

- "What is the advantage of the Jew? Or what is the value of circumcision? Much in every way." (Rom 3:1)
- "Do we overthrow the law through faith? By no means. On the contrary, we uphold the law." (Rom 3:31)
- "The law is holy, and the commandment is holy and just and good." (Rom 7:12)

- "To the Israelites belong the adoption, the glory, the covenants, the giving of the law, the worship, and the promises. To them belong the patriarchs, and from their people, according to the flesh, is Christ." (Rom 9:4)
- "Has God rejected his people? By no means. . . . All Israel will be saved." (Rom 11:1, 26)

Now, contradictions can arise in the works of any bold and original thinker, and indeed some scholars simply attribute this discrepancy to Paul's development or to the different situations of the letters.[14] Note especially that the anti-Israel statements occur more often in the early letters of Paul, Galatians and Second Corinthians, and pro-Israel statements in the late letter, Romans. Further, the Letter to the Romans was the only letter addressed to a community that Paul did not found and that he did not know well. But be that as it may, in the traditional view of Paul's attitude toward Judaism, the anti-Israel statements are considered the truer reflection of Paul's own beliefs, and the pro-Israel statements are attributed to a diplomatic need on Paul's part not to alienate Jewish followers of Jesus. By various means, then, many scholars have harmonized these contradictions by assuming that the anti-Israel statements presented Paul's true beliefs, and that the pro-Israel statements had to be subordinated to this image of an anti-Jewish Paul. But as Gager asks,

> Why is it . . . that subordinationist readers always place the ultimate weight on the anti-Israel passages, as if they give the final word, while treating the pro-Israel passages as inconsistent? What would happen, for example, if we began with the pro-Israel set and worked in the other direction?

If we begin from the perspective of the pro-Israel statements, almost all of the traditional interpretation is dramatically altered. As Stendahl noted, many of Paul's statements that were thought to be about law and Judaism actually concerned followers of Jesus who observed the law, not Jews outside the movement. When Paul argues in Galatians or in Romans, for instance, that the law cannot by itself make one righteous before God, he is speaking only about gentile followers of Jesus. As Stowers argues, the one hypothetical Jewish teacher that Paul addresses in Romans 2:17–29, far from representing all Jews, merely represents the Jewish follower of Jesus who would require gentile followers of Jesus to live their lives in accordance with Jewish law.[15] This hypothetical Jewish teacher is like the "false brothers secretly brought in" in Galatians 2:4 or the "super-apostles" of 2 Corinthians 11:5. Another way of stating this is that God's covenant with Jews is never really questioned by Paul. He expresses challenges to the ability of the Jewish covenant to reconcile *gentiles* to God, but after this buffeting the covenant is seen to be still constitutive for Jews at the final phase of the end. What is added is a new banner of faith and promise to the gentiles, who will enter in Christ, but the covenant with Jews is never subtracted.[16]

Although in the traditional reading of Romans it is generally assumed that the community was composed of both Jews and gentiles, the radical new-perspective scholars argue that the audience was more likely gentile. This is not an absolutely necessary assumption for a radical new-perspective reading—Paul may be writing to Jewish and gentile believers but talking about gentiles—but it does make the argument more plausible. Paul's own mission from God is to "bring about the obedience of faith among all the gentiles," the order of priority is still "the Jew first and also the Greek" (Rom 1:5, 16). If Paul is arguing so fervently for a revolution in which the gentiles are brought into God's salvation without the necessity of observing Jewish law, why do the Jews still maintain a priority in the scheme of salvation? What advantage has the Jew?

> The advantage of the Jew is not just in knowledge of sin through the law. To Israelites belong the adoption, the glory, the covenants, the giving of the law, the worship, and the promises; to them belong the patriarchs, and from them, according to the flesh, comes the messiah. (Rom 9:4–5)

Paul conceives the new dispensation in Christ as coming out of Judaism. It is not so much a "new dispensation" in Paul's mind—however much Christians have wanted to see it that way—as an old dispensation realized at the end of time, the fulfillment of promises given to Abraham. Jews are bearers of God's law, and although Paul is at pains to demonstrate that the law is not binding on gentiles who have faith in God's plan, he is equally at pains to show that Jewish law really is part of that plan.

The problem with the law in Paul's view is that it was not meant to make gentiles righteous before God, and indeed is a deterrent to gentiles, for whom it acts as a prosecuting attorney.[17] However, it has been a central plank of the traditional view that Paul is writing about the human condition, and that there is something fundamentally wrong with the whole of Jewish law. But this view comes face-to-face with a problem. If there were something fundamentally wrong with Jewish law, how could Paul affirm in Galatians 2:7–10 the mission of Peter, James, and John to Jews with the law? This is no minor quibble. In the fifth century, the Christian theologian Jerome was sure that a unitary view of Christian truth would not have allowed for the possibility of a continuation of Jewish law even for Jewish converts, but Augustine disagreed, drawing the obvious and accurate conclusion that Paul continued to honor the mission to Jews with the law.[18] The Jews will recognize the inclusion of gentiles, but the mission to Jews with the law is never canceled by Paul. How could Jewish law remain valid for Jewish followers of Jesus if there were something fundamentally wrong with it? Surely, argue the radical new-perspective scholars, there is only something wrong with the law *in regard to gentiles*. It impedes the gentile mission. Later followers of Paul did interpret him to mean that there was something fundamentally wrong with Judaism, but that shift could occur only when the mission to Jews had become a distant memory in the Pauline churches. The traditional view of Paul's theology is more likely a reconstruction that developed after Paul's death in order to explain how Christianity separated from Judaism, as Acts would indicate.

And yet perhaps it is not Jews who must be granted a "special way" to God at the end but gentiles in Christ. Perhaps Christ is a subset in God's plan. At 1 Corinthians 15:24–28, Paul goes so far as to insist that in phase two of the end, Christ will be subordinated to God. Rather than being *contrasted* to Jewish law, perhaps Christ is to be understood as *complementary* to Jewish law. In the radical new perspective, Christ is not the *end* of the law as the traditional reading held, but the *goal* of the law (the Greek word *telos* can mean either). And the most important distinction in Paul's letters, as in so much of early Christian literature, is the distinction between the mundane time that defined history up to the present and the special time of the end. In some sense, the law is appropriate for mundane time compared to Christ's "extraordinary." According to Veronica Koperski, for Paul the problem with the law is its lack of eschatological awareness; it is "characterized by ignorance that in Christ the messianic age has dawned."[19]

We may see this especially in Paul's distinctive, end-time use of the Greek term *katargeō*, which means "cause to wither" or "bring to naught." In early letters Paul says that the world as we know it is being brought to an end (1 Cor 1:28, 2:6, 6:13). In some of Paul's early negative statements about Jewish law, even Moses' glory is brought to an end (2 Cor 3:7, 11, 13, 14). But in Romans we are told that the law is *not* brought to an end (3:31), even though, says Paul, prophecy will be (1 Cor 13:8)! This comports with the fact that in Paul's letters the law is not always bad (Rom 2:14, 3:20), and not clearly opposed to faith. The law is an adequate response to God's covenant with Moses, but it was Christ's death that inaugurated God's universal promises made to Abraham. The promises came before the covenant with Moses, but are fulfilled only at the end of time. Those who are saved are the ones who recognize the new life—even Jews with the law must recognize the promise to the gentiles—while those who do not are mired in mundane time, the age that is being brought to naught. In the more typical Jewish conception of the end, Jews would come to God and gentiles would join them. Paul envisions a paradox of reversal: Christ will allow gentiles to arrive at the finish line first, but this act stirs up Israel to acknowledge God's promise to gentiles and arrive second. What Jews will recognize at the end is not Christ but God's plan, the promises to the gentiles, and the impartiality of God.[20] Alternatively, Paul may have imagined Christ as the Lord of the end, but worship would be worship of God. (Compare the subordination of Christ to God in the final phase of the end, 1 Corinthians 15 above.) But according to the radical new-perspective scholars, to be more specific on this question may be going beyond the text.

Other scholars, however, insist that this is willfully ignoring the entire thrust of Romans. The dean of the moderate new-perspective scholars, Sanders, cannot follow his radical counterparts to their conclusion:[21]

> It is incredible that (Paul) thought of "God apart from Christ," just as it is that he thought of "Christ apart from God." This is where the interpretation of Rom 11:25f. as offering two ways to salvation (one for gentiles with Christ and one for Jews without Christ) seems to me to go astray.

And there are certainly passages in Romans that appear to point to the necessity of confessing Christ for Jews as well as gentiles:

> Now we are discharged from the law, dead to that which held us captive, so that we are slaves not under the old written code but in the new life of the spirit. (Rom 7:6)

> Gentiles, who did not strive for righteousness, have attained it, that is, righteousness through faith. But Israel, who did strive for righteousness based on the law, did not succeed in fulfilling that law. . . . They have not submitted to God's righteousness, because they are ignorant of the righteousness that comes from God and seek to establish their own. (Rom 9:30–31, 10:3)

> Christ is the end [or goal?] of the law so that there may be righteousness for everyone who believes. (Rom 10:4)

> Even Jews, if they do not persist in unbelief, will be grafted in. (Rom 11:23)

However, the radical new-perspective scholars argue that in each case the *particular* situation of Paul must be taken into account: he is arguing for the addition of gentiles. Does the "we" in the first quotation refer to Jews and gentiles, or is Paul identifying with gentiles alone? In the second quotation, is the righteousness that comes from God an attitude toward the law, or the promise of impartiality at the end? In the third quotation, is Christ the end of the law, or the goal of the law in activating the advent of God's promises to gentiles? In the fourth, is unbelief the lack of faith in Christ or the lack of faith that pertains to God's promises?[22]

WHO, THEN, IS THE OTHER IN PAUL'S VISION?

Even if one is not convinced by the arguments of the radical new perspective, the moderate new-perspective authors still hold that Jews are not the Other. Then who is? The answer is obvious: gentiles.[23] Paul's assumption, shared by Jewish apologists before him, was that gentile religion was degraded:

> You turned to God from idols. (1 Thes 1:9–10)

> For though gentiles knew God, they did not honor him as God or give thanks to him, but they became futile in their thinking, and their senseless minds were darkened. (Rom 1:21)

> Formerly, when you did not know God, you were enslaved to beings that by nature are not gods. (Gal 4:8)

> You know that when you were gentiles [but not yet in Christ], you were enticed and led astray to idols that could not speak. (1 Cor 12:2)

This should sound familiar; it is merely an updated version of the Deuteronomistic History's condemnation of the Canaanites' predilection to sin. There the view was not extended to all gentiles, but as the Diaspora of the Jews brought them into intimate contact with many foreign cultures, the negative effect of idolatry among the Canaanites was extended to all other religions. Paul followed the Hellenistic Jewish intellectuals in seeing Judaism as a superior philosophy, just as Greek intellectuals affirmed their own philosophy as superior to that of barbarians. Although it may be argued that Paul can also distinguish between the few righteous gentiles and the mass of idolatrous gentiles (Rom 2:14), he clearly takes up a theme that was common in Judaism: idolatry—that is, polytheism—is an affront to God, just as it was in the Deuteronomistic History and in Ezra-Nehemiah. If there was any fundamental belief that Christians retained from Judaism, it was that their religion was superior to gentile religion.

Indeed, we may be lenient toward Paul for doing what nearly every western religious thinker has done, claim a superiority for his or her own religious worldview. But like early Christian views about Judaism, this superiority has an effect many centuries later for which Paul's followers are accountable. Modern observers are just as liable to replicate Paul's negative views of gentile religion as they are the negative views about Judaism. Because there are so few Isis or Asklepios worshipers alive today to object, the assumption of a negative "paganism" is not questioned, and too easily becomes the basis of a Christian superiority to other religions. N. T. Wright, for instance, though a Christian theologian in the moderate new-perspective fold, expresses negative statements about the gentile religion of Paul's day:

> The pagan world was, one might almost say, infested with gods of every sort and for every purpose. . . . Paul was telling the true story of the world in opposition to pagan mythology. . . . Against the essentially ahistorical worldview of paganism, and over against the "golden age" dreams of some philosophers of history, Paul articulated a linear view of history, from creation to new creation.[24]

One is reminded of the negative language of Matthew Black concerning Pharisaism quoted above. Wright continues a tendency of both Jewish and Christian scholars to affirm the value of their religions by contrasting them with the religions of the ancient near east or Greek and Roman worlds. One's religion is described as positive because it began as a divinely inspired revolution against something that was not enlightened. In such a case, both the background religion and the foreground religion become distorted (Theorem 5: Other distorted).

But how can gentiles be the Other if Paul wants to convert them? Paul's view of the impartiality of God and the promise to gentiles extends to their persons but not to their religion. The traditional Jewish hope of gentiles coming to worship at Jerusalem at the end was a compensation fantasy held by a group that *in reality* was ruled by greater empires. Paul discovered a loophole to make a reality of this fantasy of the colonized, a restatement of Judaism that would, he imagined, win over the entire empire without an ethnic distinction, what Daniel Boyarin calls a "new humanity of no difference."[25] Christ makes the domination of gentiles possible in a way that Jews could only have fantasized. Gentiles are transformed to children of God and are no longer gentiles (1 Cor 12:2). Just as Judaism had required that a convert become Jewish (and this is somehow seen by modern Christians as exclusive), belief in Christ requires that one become un-gentile. The historical effect of Paul's strong dichotomy of "in Christ" versus gentile has resulted in the demonizing and destruction of gentile religions. One could argue that the distortion of Jewish religion by the followers of Paul has been more tragic because of the history of anti-Semitism and the Holocaust, but there has been an enduring tragedy as well in the form of the conversion of masses of people to Christianity, often accompanied by war, colonialism, and cultural domination. In a world now concerned about the rising domination of the West, it is important to note how this domination first spilled out of the Mediterranean basin.[26]

It might be charged at this point that the new perspective in both its moderate and radical forms arose simply as a liberal attempt to surgically remove objectionable parts of Paul's letters, just as some of the passages that subordinate women (for instance, 1 Cor 14:34, "women should keep silent in church") are often considered later interpolations. But there are numerous aspects of Paul's letters that liberals have found objectionable in addition to the rejection-replacement theory of Judaism, for instance:

- Paul's authoritarian suppression of disagreements in the community
- Paul's subordination of women in 1 Corinthians 11 (even if 1 Cor 14:34 is a later insertion)
- Paul's use of slavery metaphors in a way that assumes the validity of slavery
- Paul's retention of the extreme condemnation of same-sex love

Only the rejection-replacement theory of Judaism is altered in the radical new perspective. If the latter were a liberal program of revisionism (and I think it is not), then it would be very limited; these other four objectionable aspects remain unchanged. And under the radical new perspective the removal of the rejection-replacement theory of Judaism also makes *even more pressing* a further objection. Paul himself never intended a rejection-replacement theory of Judaism, but he did intend a rejection-replacement theory of gentile religion. What was objectionable in regard to his view of Jews has simply been shifted from one religious Other to a different religious Other. In Paul's letters, the gentiles are Other, unless they choose to become a We (Theorem 7: Ambiguous groups reassigned). While it is true that Jewish texts which addressed this issue also subordinated gentiles at the end of time, Paul can envision a wholesale *transformation* of gentiles which will eventually give rise to the largest religion in history. For two thousand years, the conversion of gentiles by Christians has meant the wholesale destruction of Others, and it takes its origins in Paul. "In the Old Testament," notes Regina Schwartz, "vast numbers are obliterated, while in the New Testament vast numbers are . . . converted."[27] It is a great irony that under the traditional interpretation Paul caricatured Jews, while in the radical new perspective he actually caricatured gentiles *in a way that was typical of Jewish writers.*

Christians will not easily set aside the notion that gentile religion was idolatrous and primitive, nor that its replacement by Christianity was one of the great advances of civilization. And by the same token, Christians are not going to dispense easily with the notion that members of gentile religions today should be evangelized and converted to Christianity. This is a hope of many Christians that must be acknowledged before dialogue can begin. I can respect the beliefs of those, like Christopher Bryan, who say:

Certainly we must aver that Jesus is Lord and Messiah. We cannot back away from that and remain faithful. I have no time at all for that notion of "interfaith dialogue" which involves all religions abandoning their claims to uniqueness and universality.[28]

But Professor Bryan seems to envision here a roundtable discussion among trained clergy of major religious faiths, not colonialism, crusades, religious wars, and ethnic violence.

In the greatest of all possible ironies, Paul transformed Judaism-as-a-minority-religion into an empire-wide phenomenon that would do Augustus Caesar's view one better. Eventually Augustus' successor, Emperor Constantine, would make the Roman Empire Christian. But the seeds of this are already present in Paul himself. Paul blithely predicts that all gentiles—or at least most—would be saved. The colonized became the colonizer.

SIGNS OF THE INTERNAL OTHER

We may also wonder whether there are other Others—internal Others—and whether Paul's characteristic complexity carries over to this question as well. First Corinthians is almost totally devoted to settling disputes that have arisen within the church at Corinth, and Paul serves as a model of how to facilitate a dialogue among disagreeing parties. Concerning the question of whether gentiles in Christ are free to eat meat that has been sacrificed to idols, or whether, like the legally observant members of the community, they must abstain, Paul takes an especially conciliatory position. Although he implies that he himself would eat meat sacrificed to idols (1 Cor 10:25–30), he grants that this would cause offense to the more observant members of the community. Therefore, he says, members should abstain so as not to cause offense. This counsel must have seemed successful to him, because in his latest letter, he repeats it in a more succinct form (Rom 14:1–6). Paul even grants that there is a positive role for differences of opinion: "Indeed, there have to be factions among you, for only in that way will it become clear who among you is genuine" (1 Cor 11:19). But although eating meat sacrificed to idols does not seem to exercise Paul, other issues do. When Paul's authority is threatened, he lashes out strongly: "Some want to pervert the gospel of Christ!" (Gal 1:7). Further, his opponents among the followers of Jesus are "false brothers secretly brought in" (Gal 2:4). Paul's language is often scathing, although since we only have Paul's account of these disagreements, we do not know whether the motives of the opponents are as crass and worldly as Paul asserts: "Some proclaim Christ from envy and rivalry, . . . out of selfish ambition" (Phil 1:15, 17). As in Matthew and John, some of the polemic is typical of that in Greek and Roman authors, where an opponent's motives are questioned, but also as in Matthew and John, some of it is expressive of a cosmic battle of good and evil: "Many live as enemies of the cross of Christ" (Phil 3:18). And we should remember that Paul aims his polemic at *fellow followers of Jesus.* Just as polemical statements in the Deuteronomistic History, Ezra-Nehemiah, or John may have been intended for wayward fellow members of the community, so also Paul is thinking of insiders more than outsiders.

One might easily conclude that his angry denunciations were generally leveled at those who retained a reverence for Jewish law, and this is often true: "Beware of the dogs, the evil workers, who mutilate the flesh [that is, who practice circumcision]" (Phil 3:2). Yet surprisingly, Paul's angry words are also directed at those who assert their freedom from Jewish law (1 Cor 5). Paul can accuse both groups of being concerned with the flesh only, oriented toward their bellies or their appetites (Rom 8:7, 9, 9:8; Phil 3:18–19). We may even speculate that Paul thinks of them as mired in a pre-spiritual existence, mired in mundane time. (Compare the Gospel of John and those mired in the historical narrative.) In addition, many feminist scholars have argued that Paul with one hand seems to hold out equality for women (Gal 3:28; Rom 16:1, 3, 6, 7; 1 Cor 7), while taking it back with the other (1 Cor 11:2–16, 12:13).[29] Women and men who engage in same-sex love also represent the Other for Paul, but despite the modern obsession that places homosexuality at the center of social morality, Paul only mentions it once (Rom 1:18–32), and like other Jewish authors of this period, he is actually speaking of homosexual acts as a common error of gentiles.[30] Same-sex love is more a sign of gentile idolatry in Paul's writings than a recurring attribute of internal Others. Paul's more prevalent marking of internal Others, then, includes those who are either too oriented toward Jewish law or too lax in their recognition of any restraints, but especially women who are too lax as regards the law.[31] Paul's two-pronged strategy appears to be consistent in that he tries to eliminate the requirements of Jewish law for gentile followers of Jesus and eliminate the attractions of what he would perceive as a spiritual enthusiasm spun out of control. Both are defined by Paul as an orientation toward the flesh, toward mundane time and not spirit time. To side with mundane time is to deny the spirit time, a grievous sin for Paul.

PAUL'S MEANS OF CONSTITUTING THE WE

With the external and internal Other more clearly defined, we may now turn to the construction of the We. Paul describes the special experience of the We often. Followers of Jesus experience miracles and healings, prophetic utterances and speaking in tongues, insights into the heavens and God's plan for the end of time: "We speak God's wisdom, secret and hidden, which God decreed before the ages for our glory" (1 Cor 2:7). "We have peace with God" and "share the glory of God" through "our Lord Jesus Christ, through whom we have obtained access" (Rom 5:1–2; compare the Farewell Discourses in John). He contrasts two modes of being: a worldly mode caught in worldly time (flesh, sin), and a mode, inaugurated by the death of Christ, which includes possession of the spirit at the end of time as judgment nears. Paul's symbolic world is a struggle between the end-time reality of followers of Jesus and the mundane-time realities—flesh, sin, death—threatening to drag the saints back into mundane time.

How are the members of the We to treat each other? What is the community ethic for the We in Christ at the end of time? Paul exhorts his recipients to subordinate their own needs and wants to the needs of their fellow members:

> Do nothing from selfish ambition or conceit, but in humility regard others as better than yourselves. Let each of you look not to your own interests, but to the interests of others. (Phil 2:3–4)

Paul, in effect, defines the We as those who—in the spirit, in Christ—give up their own good for that of the other members. This may be called a community ethic of mutual self-abnegation, and although it may seem too utopian an arrangement to last, it was still in evidence to non-Christian authors over a hundred years later. It is important to note that the strong community ethic of mutual support among followers of Jesus was not Paul's invention, but Paul has his own way of advocating for this principle, and it reflects his self-denial and voluntary loss of status: "Through love enslave yourselves to each other" (Gal 5:13). Paul presents mutual self-abnegation as an individual choice, but it is—theoretically, at any rate—enjoined on all members of the community equally, a heroic, utopian, millenarian self-abnegation at the end of time. Thus, although Paul rarely uses the kingdom-of-God language that is found in the gospels, he nevertheless emphasizes the notion of shared identity and a mutual support network. Some scholars, such as Stowers and Troels Engberg-Pedersen, have rightly likened this to a utopian application of Greek and Roman philosophy.[32]

Following the practice of the previous chapters we may also consider the terms Paul uses for the We. There is no word for "Christianity" or even "Christians" in the first century (unless Acts is dated before 100 CE, which I consider unlikely). In order to cement the bonds of a new identity, Paul uses terms such as "saints," those "in Christ," and "assemblies" or "churches," and also terms of fictive kinship typical of religious associations and sectarian groups cross-culturally, "brothers" (for both "brothers" and "sisters"). Paul's most common identifier of the We is the term "in Christ." It is not just a way of naming those within the new religious association. It has been emphasized by scholars as a transference and a participation in Christ that is more than metaphorical. This *real* connection is maintained by another *real* thing, the Spirit, which makes possible a new spiritual and ethical existence. In addition to spiritual insights, prophecy, healings, and speaking in tongues, the possibility of a truly ethical life is now bestowed upon the members. Paul has ruled out a rote appeal to Jewish law, but in his mind a true community of the spirit—mutual self-abnegation—is now possible at the end of time. The term "saints" is used often and without any explanation in Paul, such that it must have been an accepted designation, at least in the communities Paul founded. Saints (*hagioi*, singular *hagios*) is a term from the temple sacrifice in Judaism, where it refers to priestly purity appropriate for offerings to God. The term *ekklēsia*, usually translated "church" but literally "the body of those called out," has two different possibilities among Jewish groups. In the Greek translation of the Hebrew Bible it was used to translate *qahal* or congregation in Ezra-Nehemiah. It was also used in Greek and Roman society to mean civic assembly or association, and since Paul often uses it in the plural, this city-by-city meaning is also in evidence. Paul's churches may appear roughly equivalent to the Greek and Roman civic and religious associations, but the sectarian consciousness in Paul's *ekklēsiai* is stronger. There could, for example, be a merging of the two meanings: the congregation of Israel at the end of time, now understood as being realized not in Jerusalem but in each city. Paul sees the plural churches as communities in Christ in each city of the Roman Empire, transformed by the spirit, but mixing in the marketplaces with Roman society. Paul's concept of *ekklēsia* is not weaker than that in Ezra-Nehemiah, but it is replicable rather than unitary. Despite the general use of the term in everyday Greek, for Paul it is a specially marked or divided-off group, those in Christ. The term thus names a We, those in Christ, the saints, the brothers and sisters, who were found in each city to which the mission had come.

Granting the importance of these various terms for the We in Paul's letters, we should also consider whether there is one overarching notion of how the members are constituted as a We. This is often found in Paul's concept of the new unity in Christ and the abolition of difference: "In Christ there is no longer Jew nor Greek, there is no longer slave nor free, there is no longer male nor female, for all of you are one in Christ Jesus" (Gal 3:28). The traditional interpretation of Paul would assert that his churches rejected the exclusivism of Judaism in favor of a universalism that was open to all ethnic groups without distinction. Even new-perspective interpreters such as Wright and Bruce Longenecker interpret Judaism's metaphor of belonging as national or racial, and Paul's as inclusive of all ethnic groups.[33] But in any period the dominant culture creates a myth of its own universalism, which functions to obscure the ethnic nature of its cultural markers. What was born as a new particularism among Jesus' followers came later to appear universalistic. One might, for instance, imagine a modern Unitarian Universalist asserting—correctly!—that baptism and the Lord's Supper are particularistic rituals that separate Christianity from other religions and thereby render Christianity exclusive. Trinitarian Christians might counter that baptism and the Lord's Supper are not ethnic markers, but it is simply the privilege of the dominant culture to identify its markers as generic or even "universal" and not "ethnic." Boyarin has also restated the distinction between Judaism and Paul's openness to outsiders, but sees the latter as typically Greek, a product of several centuries of Greek universalism. One might compare, for instance, the Stoic Zeno's notion that in the ideal commonwealth those who are good are kin and those who are evil are foreigners (Plutarch, *Fortunes of Alexander* 329b-c). Paul, influenced by the philosophical affirmation of unity over plurality, rejects the separateness of Jewish markers and presses instead for a "new humanity of no difference."[34] A utopian, Hellenistic ideal person at the end of time would look like an unmarked human being: neither Jew nor Greek, slave nor free, male nor female.

To be sure, there may have been a brief, quantitative, eschatological distinction between Paul and broader Judaism. Paul claimed for his group what all other sects and cults claim to offer: access to God that is unmediated through the institutions of the parent-body. It should be noted, however, that inclusion is an inevitable strategy of any religion that is based on conversion. Islam, for instance, is an equally inclusive religion, or, more contemporary to Paul, we could compare the spread of the Isis cult or Pythagoreans across ethnic boundaries. But some would also question whether Paul's churches were a community of *no* ethnicity or a community of a *new* ethnicity. First, Paul defines the gentiles in Christ as the new *descendants* of Abraham or of God. One is tempted to say "virtual descendants" or "metaphorical descendants," but the transformation is stronger than that, and uses adoption language that makes it more real than virtual. The research of Caroline Johnson Hodge and Pamela Eisenbaum has confirmed what was argued also by Stowers.[35] The We is triumphantly constituted by inclusion in a *new family*:

> The promise rests on grace and is guaranteed to all Abraham's descendants, not only to the adherents of the law but also to those who share the faith of Abraham—for he is the father of all of us. (Rom 4:16)

> All who are led by the spirit of God are children of God. (Rom 8:14)

Immediately before and after Paul's formula of "neither Jew nor Greek" (Gal 3:28) it is emphasized that those who have been baptized into Christ are now children of God and children of Abraham. Paul, and other writers of the early church, quickly developed new language of being children of God, an extended kinship group. All ethnicity in the ancient world was understood as genealogy, and Paul bestows a new family tree on the converted gentiles. As Denise Kimber Buell also argues, this quickly evolved into notions of a new people (*ethnos*), a third race (*genos*).[36] Thus, far from rejecting kinship for gentile followers of Jesus, Paul includes them in the lineage of God through adoption. Paul begins with an oppositional notion of gentiles as Other, but sees in the death of Christ a revolution that allows gentiles to become an aggregate of Jews: true Israel by faith, adopted in baptism to become fellow children of Abraham or children of God: you and we share a common ancestor.[37] Thus the transformation in Paul's mind is not from an ethnic group to the universal body of all humanity, but from one extended family to a larger extended family. Jewish eschatology often envisioned the inclusion of gentiles at the end of time, but Paul differed in this respect: gentiles would enter as adopted children of Abraham—ahead of Jews!—and not as a separate and secondary people. Ironically, his sect was so much smaller than Judaism, but it was understood as a newly enlarged family by adoption. And the new family definition is not just theoretical; it is practical as well. After only a few years, Pauline Christians would have been as marked by ritual practices (baptism, Eucharist) and purity restrictions (no offerings to the emperor, no meat sacrificed to other gods) as Jews. Pauline Christianity is not the triumph of open religion over ethnocentrism, but the triumph of the end-time family of Abraham, consisting of Jews and gentiles, over the mundane-time family of Abraham consisting of Jews alone. Paul may have been merging Greek notions of unity with kinship, and was bolder and more emphatic on the inclusion principle than was Judaism or the Isis cult, but the difference was more quantitative than qualitative, and apocalyptically driven.

It is true that the Christian tradition as early as the second century developed a social memory of its founding as "universal" in a way that was different from the mundane time of Judaism. Christianity understood itself as "religion" or "true doctrine" abstracted from ethnicity, and understood Judaism as ethnicity stripped of its warrant from God[38]—how better to see true doctrine abstracted from ethnicity than to see Judaism, the Other, as ethnicity itself! (Theorem 5: Other distorted, reduced to one essence.) Boyarin also points out that Paul's formula looks *to Christians* like tolerance, but *to Jews* it is the eradication of a minority cultural identity in favor of "coercive sameness." Averil Cameron credits Michel Foucault for clarifying the role of Christian universalism as "the provider of a totalizing and therefore repressive discourse,"[39] a discourse that says, "We will make universalists of all of you."

CONCLUSION

Despite Paul's use of a complex and provocative style, we can now summarize how he defines the We and the Other. While the new perspective in both its moderate and radical forms emphasizes that Paul's theology was developed in response to his needs as a *missionary* theologian at the end of time, the radical wing emphasized in addition that the letters were addressed almost entirely to gentile followers of Jesus, and not to the situation of Jews. For these scholars, Paul's final discussion, the letter to the Romans, retains a live option for Jews as a body, *whether in Christ or not,* and for gentiles as well through faith in Christ. Paul does not develop in Romans a rejection-replacement view of Judaism. I refer to this scholarly challenge as the "radical new perspective" because it questions such a central assumption of all the interpretations of Paul's theology to date, whether conservative, moderate, liberal, or liberationist. And although these scholars themselves are liberal scholars, they were not simply trying to update Paul for a new age, avoiding in a post-Holocaust era the negative depiction of a "moribund" Judaism. Certainly, one of the results of their study has been an emphasis on the validity and integrity of first-century Judaism, but their goal was to show that Paul was not thinking in the same anti-Jewish dichotomies that the church only institutionalized after his death.

Paul provides an idealized description of the community of those in Christ. As a result of Christ's death, those who are in Christ through baptism become through adoption children of God or children of Abraham. Corresponding to this is a view of the present fallen state of humanity, the humanity of mundane time, which is in need of such a transformation: "While we were still weak, at the right time Christ died for the ungodly" (Rom 5:6). Paul's ideal view of the We is no longer Israel, but potentially, the whole world: "Just as one man's trespass [Adam's sin] led to condemnation for all, so one man's act of righteousness [Jesus' death] leads to justification and life for all" (5:18). It is not clear how many Jews and how many gentiles he thought would be found in that number, but that does not dampen his sense of the dramatic resolution of a cosmic drama. Elsewhere Paul may concede that not every individual will be saved, but here he speaks in universal terms. Ideally, the We is everyone, but only if they recognize the promises of God to Abraham at the end of time. The Other is the gentiles, who can now, at the end of time, be adopted as We. As a compensation fantasy of a tiny sectarian group this seems quaint, but when the group was no longer tiny and began to provide the theological justification for world empires, the rejection of gentile religion took on more tragic powers, as it does today.

NOTES

1. Adolf Harnack, *What Is Christianity?* (New York: Williams and Norgate, 1901), 190.

2. Ernst Käsemann, *Commentary on Romans* (Grand Rapids, MI: Eerdmans, 1980), 283.

3. Matthew Black, "Pharisees," in *Interpreter's Dictionary of the Bible*, ed. George Arthur Buttrick, 4 vols. (Nashville, TN: Abingdon, 1962), 3:781.

4. Judith Plaskow, "Anti-Judaism in Feminist Christian Interpretation," in *Searching the Scriptures*, vol. 1, *A Feminist Introduction*, ed. Elisabeth Schüssler Fiorenza (New York: Crossroad, 1993), 117–29; Susannah Heschel, "Anti-Judaism in Christian Feminist Theology," *Tikkun* 5 (1990): 25–28, 95–97; Schüssler Fiorenza, *Jesus and the Politics of Interpretation* (New York: Crossroad, 2000), 116–44; the roundtable discussions in *Journal of Feminist Studies in Religion* 7 (1991): 95–133, 20, no. 1 (2004): 91–132, and 20, no. 2 (2004): 189–92.

5. Adapted, with changes, from Howard Clark Kee, *Who Are the People of God? Early Christian Models of Community* (New Haven, CT: Yale University Press, 1995), 74–75.

6. The term "new perspective" was introduced by James D. G. Dunn, "The New Perspective on Paul," *BJRL* 65 (1983): 94–122, reprinted in his *Jesus, Paul and the Law* (Louisville, KY: Westminster/John Knox, 1990), 183–214.

7. E. P. Sanders, *Paul and Palestinian Judaism: A Comparison of Patterns in Religion* (Philadelphia: Fortress, 1977); Krister Stendahl, "Paulus och Samvetet," *Svensk Exegetisk Årsbok* 25 (1960), 62–77, later translated as "The Apostle Paul and the Introspective Conscience of the West" and now available with other essays related to the radical new perspective in *Paul among Jews and Gentiles, and Other Essays* (Philadelphia: Fortress, 1976).

8. Sanders, *Paul and Palestinian Judaism*, 552; also 17, 75.

9. E. P. Sanders, *Paul, the Law, and the Jewish People* (Philadelphia: Fortress, 1983), 156.

10. But Stephen Westerholm raises an interesting question (*Perspectives Old and New on Paul: The "Lutheran" Paul and His Critics* [Grand Rapids, MI: Eerdmans, 2004], 341–51): If the grace/works distinction is actually a Christian invention, how can we say that Jews believed the covenant was given by grace and not merited by works? That is, why would they make a distinction between grace and works, such that one could say that they placed them in the "right" order, grace and then works? Westerholm goes further: Jews did not distinguish these two clearly, and therefore Sanders' "Protestant" Jews who believed in grace is an invention on his part, just as surely as legalistic Jews were an invention of previous Christian scholars. While it is true that Sanders may have been caught in an overstatement to counter the prevailing anti-Judaism of Christian theology, the Jewish

texts generally do express a theology of grace preceding works. Rigorously *distinguishing* grace and works is a later obsession, not theirs, but *if we press the question* of the relation of free grace and human works, many of the Jewish texts express a relationship in which the grace of God is emphasized as the first act, e.g., *Mishnah Makkot* 3:16 (about 200 CE): "Rabbi Hananiah ben Akashya says, 'The holy one, blessed be he, was pleased to confer favor upon Israel; therefore, he increased the Law and commandments for them.'" Grace and works are brought together and are in some sense inseparable, but if the question of order is pressed, it is definitely grace-works. Still, according to Michael Satlow, Jewish inscriptions of the period often express a works-then-grace theology ("Giving for a Return: Jewish Votive Offerings in Late Antiquity," in *Religion and the Self in Antiquity*, ed. Michael Satlow, David Brakke, and Steven Weitzman [Bloomington: Indiana University Press, 2005], 94–95). But so does the New Testament: "Your alms should be done in secret, and your father who sees in secret will reward you" (Matt 6:6; see also 6:1, 6, 18). *And even in Paul*: "God will repay according to each one's deeds: to those who by patiently doing good seek for glory and honor and immortality, he will give eternal life; to those who are self-seeking and who obey not the truth but wickedness, there will be wrath and fury" (Rom 2:6–10). It appears that both Jewish and New Testament texts *balance* grace and works. Oh, the horror!

11. Stanley Stowers, *A Rereading of Romans: Justice, Jews, and Gentiles* (New Haven, CT: Yale University Press, 1994); John Gager, *Reinventing Paul* (Oxford: Oxford University Press, 2000); Lloyd Gaston, *Paul and the Torah* (Vancouver: University of British Columbia Press, 1987).

12. Stendahl, *Paul among Jews*, 1–7, 84.

13. Gager, *Reinventing Paul*, 5–7.

14. Heikki Räisänen, *Paul and the Law* (Tübingen, Germany: Mohr, 1987), 201–2; Hans Hübner, *Law in Paul's Thought* (Edinburgh, UK: Clark, 1984); J. C. O'Neill, *Paul's Letter to the Romans* (London: Harmondsworth, 1975), 16; J. C. O'Neill, *The Recovery of Paul's Letter to the Galatians* (London: SPCK, 1972).

15. Stowers, *Rereading*, 144–58.

16. On the separate routes to God for Jews and gentiles, see especially Stendahl, *Paul among Jews*, 40, and *Final Account: Paul's Letter to the Romans* (Minneapolis: Fortress, 1995), 33–44; Stowers, *Rereading*, 206.

17. Neil Forsyth, *The Old Enemy: Satan and the Combat Myth* (Princeton, NJ: Princeton University Press, 1987), 258–62.

18. For the debate between Jerome and Augustine, see Carolinne White, *The Correspondence (394–419) between Jerome and Augustine of Hippo* (Lewiston, ME: Mellen, 1990), 120–32 (112.7–17); Daniel Boyarin, *Border Lines: The Partition of Judaeo-Christianity* (Philadelphia: University of Pennsylvania Press, 2004), 205–6, 209. According to Jerome, Peter and Paul only went along with Jewish observances out of fear of the Jews. Further, Jerome claims that he can prove Augustine wrong because Acts 10 states that Peter had already left Jewish observances behind before he had even met Paul. Thus the later, simpler, post-Jewish text of Acts is used by Jerome to interpret the complex inner-Jewish argument of Galatians 2. Clearly, however, Augustine has captured Paul's intention, and Jerome has adopted the post-Jewish perspective of Acts.

19. Veronica Koperski, *What Are They Saying about Paul and the Law?* (New York: Paulist, 2001), 74. See also Stowers, *Rereading*, 235–36.

20. Jouette Bassler, *Divine Impartiality: Paul and a Theological Axiom* (Chico, CA: Scholars Press, 1981); Stowers, *Rereading*, 303–4.

21. Sanders, *Paul, the Law*, 194. See the discussion in Christopher Bryan, *A Preface to Romans: Notes on the Epistle in Its Literary and Cultural Setting* (Oxford: Oxford University Press, 2000), 189–93; and Joseph Fitzmyer, *Romans* (New York: Doubleday, 1993), 619–20.

22. Other examples are more complex and subtle; on Rom 10:5–8, for example, see Stowers, *Rereading*, 307–10.

23. Stowers, *Rereading*, 90–92, 107, 227, 239, 248, 273–74; Caroline Johnson Hodge, *"If Sons, Then Heirs": A Study of Kinship and Ethnicity in the Letters of Paul* (Oxford: Oxford University Press, 2007).

24. N. T. Wright, *What Saint Paul Really Said: Was Paul of Tarsus the Real Founder of Christianity?* (Grand Rapids, MI: Eerdmans, 1997), 87–90.

25. Daniel Boyarin, *A Radical Jew: Paul and the Politics of Identity* (Berkeley: University of California Press, 1994), 4–6.

26. Paul rethought the salvation of Israel on the model of the universal salvation of Augustus Caesar. The postcolonial criticism of Homi Bhabha, *The Location of Culture* (London: Routledge, 1994), 84–95, 112–20, 129–38, is critical here. Did Paul adopt the symbols of Roman religion or critique them? Is his colonial mimicry a challenge to Caesar's view of the cosmos, or simply a way of expressing the drama of the end of time using Caesar's power symbols? Does Paul appropriate the symbols of Caesar not because of his political critique, but because Caesar is the *pontifex maximus* of gentile religion? Colonized people are caught between their own traditional culture and the culture of the colonial powers. To succeed in this brave new world, the person who has the intellectual means may mimic the colonial power in terms of education, dress, language, and mental habits, and try to find a role within colonial institutions. Yet this can also be a technique of resistance: the individual acquires the appearance of being transformed while remaining "native." The problem with mimicry, however, whether it occurs in nature or in colonial society, is that it is difficult to discern precisely how it is to be interpreted. Mimicry *by definition and intention* is deceptive. (Similarly on Mark: Tat-siong Benny Liew, "Tyranny, Boundary and Might: Colonial Mimicry in Mark's Gospel," *Journal for the Study of the New Testament* 73 [1999]: 7–31.) My own view is that Paul retains the mutual support networks that were the common innovation of the early Jesus movement, but it is not clear whether he increases the critique of Roman social relations or domesticates that critique. But see also Richard A. Horsley, ed., *Paul and the Roman Imperial Order* (Harrisburg, PA: Trinity Press International, 2004); Richard A. Horsley, ed., *Paul and Politics: Ekklesia, Israel, Imperium, Interpretation: Essays in Honor of Krister Stendahl* (Harrisburg, PA: Trinity Press International, 2000); and John Dominic Crossan and Jonathan L. Reed, *In Search of Paul: How Jesus' Apostle Opposed Rome's Empire with God's Kingdom: A New Vision of Paul's Words and World* (New York: HarperSanFrancisco, 2004).

27. Regina Schwartz, *The Curse of Cain: The Violent Legacy of Monotheism* (Chicago: University of Chicago Press, 1997), 19.

28. Bryan, *Preface to Romans*, 235.

29. See esp. Elisabeth Schüssler Fiorenza, *In Memory of Her: A Feminist Theological Reconstruction of Christian Origins*, 2nd ed. (London: SCM, 1995); Elizabeth A. Castelli, *Imitating Paul: A Discourse of Power* (Louisville, KY: Westminster/John Knox, 1991); and Antoinette Clark Wire, *Corinthian Women Prophets: A Reconstruction through Paul's Rhetoric* (Minneapolis, MN: Fortress, 1990). Do the differences between pro-feminist and anti-feminist statements in Paul result from the fact that the egalitarian impulse was already asserted by the followers of Jesus and Paul is less committed, or from the fact that the perceived excesses of women leaders in Corinth convinced him to rein in their activities? The first implies that a gap existed between Paul and the egalitarian impulse of the community from the beginning, the second that a gap arose over time as Paul responded to the active women in Corinth.

30. John J. Collins, *Between Athens and Jerusalem: Jewish Identity in the Hellenistic Diaspora* (New York: Crossroad, 1982), 141–43; Stowers, *Rereading*, 273–74.

31. Bernadette Brooten, in fact, argues that Paul is always ready to set aside Jewish law unless it pertains to sex, in which case he follows Jewish law in an orthodox and legalistic manner ("Paul's Views on the Nature of Women and Female Homoeroticism," in *Immaculate and Powerful: The Feminine in Sacred Image and Social Reality*, ed. Clarissa W. Atkinson, Constance H. Buchanan, and Margaret R. Miles [Boston: Beacon, 1985], 61–87; also see her *Love between Women: Early Christian Responses to Female Homoeroticism* [Chicago: University of Chicago Press, 1996]). One might also say, with Stowers (*Rereading*, 117, 157, 235–36) and Alan F. Segal (*Paul the Convert: The Apostolate and the Apostasy of Saul the Pharisee* [New Haven, CT: Yale University Press, 1990], 124), that Paul's vision affirms that part of the law that was binding upon all peoples, and not the ritual law that applied to Jews only, but the clear lines of demarcation are difficult to establish, and Paul never really delineates it for us.

32. Stowers, *Rereading*, 42–82; Troels Engberg-Pedersen, *Paul and the Stoics* (Edinburgh, UK: Clark, 2000).

33. Wright, *What Saint Paul Really Said*, 84; N. T. Wright, *The Climax of the Covenant: Christ and the Law in Pauline Theology* (Minneapolis, MN: Fortress, 1992), 240, cf. 261; Bruce Longenecker, *The Triumph of Abraham's God: The Transformation of Identity in Galatians* (Nashville, TN: Abingdon, 1998), 140. A question not treated here is, if Paul advocated a new inclusivity in contrast to the old exclusivity of Judaism, was Jesus not with the old guard (as Gal 1–2 would indicate)?

34. Boyarin, *Radical Jew*, 4–6; see also Boyarin, *Border Lines*, esp. 324–25 n. 19.

35. Johnson Hodge, *If Sons, Then Heirs*, 56–58, 210; Pamela Eisenbaum, "A Remedy for Having Been Born of Woman: Jesus, the Gentiles, and Genealogy in Romans," *Journal of Biblical Literature* 123 (2004): 671–702; Stowers, *Rereading*, 227–30; and cf. a slightly more muted position by Philip F. Esler, "Group Boundaries and Intergroup Conflict in Galatians: A New Reading of Gal. 5:13–6:10," in *Ethnicity and the Bible*, ed. Mark G. Brett (Leiden, Netherlands: Brill, 1996), 215–40. Carol Delaney, *Abraham on Trial: The Social Legacy of Biblical Myth* (Princeton, NJ: Princeton University Press, 1998), anticipated some of the theoretical issues.

36. Denise Kimber Buell, *Why This New Race? Ethnic Reasoning in Early Christianity* (New York: Columbia University Press, 2005).

37. Jonathan Hall, *Ethnic Identity in Greek Antiquity* (Cambridge, UK: Cambridge University Press, 1997), 47, divides approaches to ethnic identity into oppositional models ("We are not like you") and aggregative models ("You and we share a common ancestor"). As Johnson Hodge also notes (*If Sons, Then Heirs*, 210, 220), just as the Greek/Roman aggregate was hierarchical—Greek is the superior partner—so also Jewish/gentile is hierarchical for Paul. Paul's constitution of the We of his communities is also accomplished by a parallelism between God's activity and Paul's own. One cannot help but notice that for gentiles to become children of God they must also become children of Paul. As founder of new communities and the one who called people to be in Christ, Paul is the "father" of many children; so Pamela Eisenbaum, "Paul as the New Abraham," in *Paul and Empire: Religion and Power in Roman Imperial Society*, ed. Richard A. Horsley (Harrisburg, PA: Trinity Press International, 1997), 130–45; and see also Carol Lowery Delaney, *The Seed and Soil: Gender and Cosmology in Turkish Village Society* (Berkeley: University of California Press, 1991), 8.

38. Boyarin, *Border Lines*.

39. Averil Cameron, "Redrawing the Map: Early Christian Territory after Foucault," *Journal of Roman Studies* 76 (1986): 266–71. See further Boyarin, *Radical Jew*, 32, 346; G. Gedaliahu Stroumsa, "Early Christianity as Radical Religion," in *Concepts of the Other in Near Eastern Religions*, ed. Ilai Alon et al. (Leiden, Netherlands: Brill, 1994), 191; and Schwartz, *Curse of Cain*, 88.

8

⚜

The Other in the
Acts of the Apostles

Our last text is Acts of the Apostles. This history of the earliest disciples and their missions was composed by the same author who
wrote the Gospel of Luke. Although Luke-Acts is attributed to Luke, the
companion of Paul, this ascription was assigned later by the church, and
as was the case with Matthew and John, we do not know who wrote these
texts or exactly when. Luke and Acts are often dated as early as the year
80 CE or as late as the middle of the second century, but because of the at-
tenuation of apocalyptic expectations in Luke-Acts, the accommodation
to Roman authority, and other reasons which will be given below, a dating in the second century seems more likely. Although the author reveres
the Jewish scriptures and claims that Christians have inherited the mantle of "Israel," we no longer see before us a sect within Judaism. Jewish
apostles of Jesus' mission are depicted, and yet a distinction is developed
that reflects a period when believers in the author's community are no
longer Jewish.[1] Granted, many believers in Jesus remained ambiguous in
their separation from Judaism for decades or even centuries after the crucifixion, but Acts reflects a cleaner and surer distinction from Judaism
than is found in the other texts we have analyzed. The term "Christian"
(*Christianos*) is first used here (11:26), and the author looks back on the arguments with Judaism as completed in the past. Acts constructs a post-
Jewish Paul who, oriented toward Roman authorities, bests Jewish opponents and founds a missionary movement for gentiles. For these reasons,
I will use the term "Christian" to refer to this text, a term that I have intentionally not used with Matthew, John, and Paul.

Acts, like the Greek romances of the period, reads like a series of repeatable episodes. Yet there is also a quality of deceptive simplicity, with the result that it is not always clear what the episodes are pointing toward. How they are to be interpreted remains controversial, especially in regard to the attitude toward Jews and Judaism. Apparently inconsistent passages can be found in Luke and Acts that have challenged scholars to force broad contradictions into one schema. At the beginning of Luke, for instance, we find a note sounded in the canticle of Simeon that seems hopeful for both gentiles and Jews: "My eyes have seen your salvation, . . . a light for revelation to the gentiles, and for glory to your people Israel" (2:30, 32). Luke-Acts also portrays Jesus and Paul as being extremely pious in regard to Jewish customs. However, Luke lays an increased blame on the Jews for the crucifixion of Jesus,[2] and Paul meets constant opposition from Jews in his mission journeys. He is also, like Jesus, brought to trial at Jewish instigation in what we may call the "Pauline Passion" (Acts 20–28). Jewish reactions to the preaching of the first generation of Jesus-believers are often negative, and the speeches in Acts on one hand seem thoroughly condemning of the Jews' obstinacy, while on the other hand at times they mollify this vehemence by conceding that the Jews acted in ignorance (3:17, 13:27).

Although many scholars assert that there is a single perspective on Luke-Acts that will make sense of all the passages, the same verses are often adduced as evidence for opposite interpretations. Consider the following debate. First, Jack Sanders:

> Beginning with the Thessalonian mission (Acts 17) the Lukan Paul *always* goes first to a synagogue when he arrives in town, and he is *always*, except in Athens, opposed by Jews.[3]

Second, in a response article in the same volume, and referring to the same passages, Marilyn Salmon:

> I am not convinced that after Acts 9:22 the Jews are uniformly enemies of Christianity. . . . Some [Jews] are persuaded in Thessalonica (17:4), and in Beroea noble Jews receive the word with eagerness, and many believed (17:11–12). Paul persuades Jews at Corinth (18:4), and Jews at Ephesus urge him to stay (18:20).

For one scholar, the Jews uniformly oppose Paul; for the other they offer much hope for a Jewish mission. The key to the different interpretations lies in what they omit. To complete Sanders' account, it must be said that Jews often do respond positively to Paul in the second half of Acts, but to complete Salmon's, it must also be noted that following the positive responses by Jews there is in most of these passages a dramatic turn in which the Jews react negatively (17:5, 13; 18:6).

A number of alternative interpretations of the depiction of the Jews in Luke-Acts have been propounded and can be summarized briefly. A common position is that the Jews in Acts, as a result of having themselves crucified Jesus and rejected the gospel as preached by Paul and the apostles, have been rejected as the chosen people of God. The mission to the gentiles is thus inaugurated, and this is the real point of interest to the author.[4] Others have noted that a division is set up within Israel between those Jews who convert and those who do not, or in some cases, between the Jewish leaders and the people.[5] In either scenario, so the argument goes, we must be careful not to see a blanket condemnation of all Jews. It is still the failure of the Jewish mission, however, which shifts the entire weight in Acts over to the hope for gentiles. Yet a third possibility begins with the assertion that it is not the *failure* of Jews to convert that is emphasized, but rather the *successes* among Jews. Jews are often mentioned as converting to Christianity, sometimes in large numbers, and this in both halves of Acts. These are viewed as positive because they constitute the basis for a triumphal opening of the mission to the gentiles.[6] The conversion of Jews primes the pump for the conversion of everyone. (In all of these discussions it should be noted that "positive" or "negative" in regard to Jews is understood in terms of whether Jews convert to Christianity. The question of whether Luke should recognize Jews who did not convert is rarely raised.)

To return to the position of Sanders, his view is that the apparent inconsistencies of the text of Acts can be explained as a literary plan of the author that seeks to move from one, somewhat mixed, perspective to a final, clarified, negative view of the role of Jews in salvation history. Sanders points out that there is a discrepancy between the speeches in Acts and the narrative. The speeches are uniformly negative toward the Jews (even if we take into consideration the occasional concession that Jews acted in ignorance), but the narrative up until chapter seven gives some positive hope about the Jews' reaction to Christianity. One finds a "Jerusalem springtime"—Gerhard Lohfink's term[7]—in which the Christian message is well received, and even the negative reaction is more civil. Nevertheless, the narrative after chapter seven depicts the Jews as *becoming*, as Sanders puts it, "what they from the first *were*," that is, the resistant body which the speeches describe.[8] The Jews are fundamentally in opposition to God's plan in Jesus. Sanders is thus aligned most closely with the first group of scholars mentioned above, but perceives an even stronger anti-Jewish strain in Luke-Acts: a first hidden, then revealed, anti-Jewish theme.

THE DEPICTION OF CROWD SCENES

We may enter into this debate by paying closer attention to the stylized way in which Jews are often represented in the crowd scenes in Acts. In Acts 17:1–9, for instance, Luke paints a vivid portrait of the Jewish community of Thessalonica responding to the success of Christian preaching: "But the Jews were jealous, and taking some wicked fellows of the rabble [*agoraiōn andras . . . ponērous*], they gathered a crowd, set the city in an uproar, and attacked the house of Jason" (17:5). Luke does not simply present views of theology and salvation history in an abstract way; the typical method is to take a few simple theological doctrines and develop them repeatedly and persistently, and it is in this process that the author's considerable ability lies. In this passage, for instance, the author in just a few lines has created an intense, dramatic situation, filled with danger and violent confrontation. Luke, of course, would not have known *how* the Jews engineered a protest, but there is introduced into the story at this point an exciting political intrigue that has far-reaching theological significance. In other scenes in Acts as well a worldwide mission to Jews is met with the Jews' rejection, and this passage would seem to be just one more incident of this sort.

The mob is portrayed here as a chaotic and explosive force that is so prone to disorder that the mere suggestion of a riot by others could incite them to action. In one verse we see the disturbance gather storm as it moves around the marketplace and erupts into violence. This passage has not been composed in a vacuum, but reflects the common Roman assumptions about the nature of the masses and insurrection, especially as it is found in Roman historical writing. In his classic study of the representation of social classes in western literature, Erich Auerbach showed that Roman historians were quick to portray lower-class members of society as scurrilous and incendiary rebels.[9] He takes first as an example a passage from Tacitus' *Annals* (1.16):

> In the camp was one Percennius, formerly a busy leader of theatrical factions, . . . of a petulant tongue, and from his experience in theatrical party zeal, well qualified to stir up the bad passions of a crowd.

Even more telling in Auerbach's view is this quotation from Sallust's *Catiline* 38.1:

> Various young men, whose age and disposition made them aggressive, . . . began to excite the commons by attacks upon the senate and then to inflame their passions still more by doles and promises.

That this view of the troublemakers is class-based is readily apparent (see also Tacitus, *Histories* 1.4), and has also influenced Jewish historians such as Josephus (*Jewish War* 2.258–59):

> There arose another group of scoundrels, . . . cheats and deceivers, who schemed to bring about revolutionary changes by inducing the mob to act as if possessed.

In each of these examples there are two crucial elements: a volatile crowd and one or a few firebrands. There is no allowance by any of these writers that there could possibly be any justification for the potential rebellion, nor is there any hesitation about attributing the basest of motives to their actions. The Roman ruling class stood in perpetual fear of rebellion, *seditio* in Latin or *stasis* in Greek. An entire theory of society lies behind this—we may call it "imperial sociology"—in which the good order of the empire is taken as an ideal, and the lower classes are perceived as continually on the verge of rebellion. This view of the masses evidently rose to the fore as a stock element of history writing in the Roman imperial period. Taking Thucydides' description of *stasis* on the island of Corcyra (3.82–84) as a model, the Roman historians generalize it to more common local uprisings, applying the typical rhetorical art of blame to scurrilous masses everywhere.[10] The role of the Jews in the crowd scene in Acts above must be seen as corresponding to this incendiary role, in contrast to the group of newly converted followers of Jesus who are peaceful and respectable, consisting as it does of "God-fearing Greeks and many of the leading women." Elsewhere Luke constructs this same basic scenario of a crowd stirred up by Jewish instigators and expresses a point of view very similar to "imperial sociology." The *class* distinction is less in evidence in Acts than in the Roman historians, but the typically Roman elite distrust of the lower classes is applied by Luke to all those who would allow themselves to be influenced by the Jews' accusations. The *mob* is still dangerous, even if those who disturb them are elite. Luke manipulates the stigma of *stasis* or *seditio* in a way that is profoundly Roman. Important similarities between Josephus and Acts have been demonstrated by scholars,[11] and especially noteworthy is the same attempt to favor one group in Roman eyes—Pharisees in Josephus and Christians in Acts—while at the same time placing the onus of guilt onto another—Zealots in Josephus and Jews in Acts. Both of these last groups are characterized by a threat to the Roman order.

We may now move from one dramatic scene above (17:1–9) to a consideration of the large number of opposition scenes in the second half of Acts in which the opponents are Jews (13:13–49, 13:50–52, 14:1–7, 14:8–23, 14:24–15:35, 17:1–9, 17:10–15, 18:1–8, 18:9–18, 19:8–10, 19:11–20, chapters twenty to twenty-eight ["Pauline Passion"], and 28:17–31). As Wayne Meeks noted in regard to the Gospel of John, myth often operates in narrative through repetitions of key themes and oppositions, retold in different ways.[12] By this process of repetition, the variations and extraneous actions of a narrative fade into the background as "static," and the core repeated actions come to the fore as stable mythological realities. So it is with this fundamental narrative pattern in the last half of Acts. To be sure, in two passages opposition arises from gentiles (16:16–40, 19:23–41), but there are thirteen scenes in which Jews oppose the mission. Further, in the two opposition scenes involving non-Jews—the owners of a slave girl cured by Paul, and the silversmiths at Ephesus— the parties responsible for inciting the crowds are motivated by greed, an intolerable sin to Luke. The fact that these two scenes are similar to the ones about Jewish opposition indicates that this mercenary motive and the Jews' motives were seen as equally scurrilous.

An important organizing principle of the Jewish opposition scenes— perhaps the most important organizing principle of the Book of Acts—is the repeating cycle of three dramatic phases: (1) missionary activity meets with some success, often among Jews; (2) the limited success triggers strong Jewish opposition and danger; and (3) release and expansion results in even more dramatic missionary success. This creates a recurrent pattern of threat and release, the pattern that pervades the ancient Greek romances as well.[13] Ezra-Nehemiah was also characterized by a dynamic of opposition-and-identity, and Acts, in the style of romance, repeats this often, with enough variation to avoid the danger of tediousness or cliché. For example, the first recipients of the missionary message may be Jews, Jews and gentiles, gentiles alone, or an unspecified group. The dramatic new successes in phase three also sometimes vary: movements to new areas, turning to the gentiles, or experiences of the holy spirit. In all of these cases, however, the result is meant to communicate the superabundance and grace of God's guidance of the mission. The tone is often one of hyperbole: "all of Asia heard" (19:10), or "the word of the Lord spread throughout all the region" (13:49). And indeed, in the third phase Jews are sometimes said to be part of the dramatic expansions (18:6–8; 19:9–10, 15–20). It is in the middle phase, however, where we see more regularity: the *agents* of the threat and opposition are in almost every case Jews, or in some cases, followers of Jesus who were observant of Jewish law. The repeating message of the narrative, which can be perceived through the variations and static, is that Jews or observant followers of Jesus oppose the mission to the gentiles without the law, while the mission overcomes this opposition and expands miraculously and abundantly in every direction, guided by God's hand, all the way to Rome. Thus those scholars are correct who point out that some successes do occur among Jews, but it is not these that inaugurate the blessings of God's mission; it is rather the *opposition* of the Jews that consistently inaugurates the successes of the worldwide gentile mission. The occasional presence of Jews as recipients in phase three is not an inconsistency in the pattern. In Luke's eyes the worldwide mission may have included some Jews, at least *in the past*, in the time of the narrative. But the regularity in phase two indicates that the larger body of Jews opposed Christianity, and by this dynamic gave rise to a triumphal expansion.

And this is just what Acts says. At 13:46–49 Paul and Barnabas respond to Jewish opposition by declaring, "It was necessary that the word of God should be spoken first to you. Since you reject it and judge yourselves to be unworthy of eternal life, we are now turning to the gentiles." This statement becomes such an influential paradigm for the spread of the mission that most Christians today would offer it as a one-sentence summary of the history of the early church: Paul preached to Jews, they rejected his message, and therefore he turned to the gentiles. The programmatic statement is repeated at 18:1–8, where Paul is even more blunt: "Your blood be on your own heads! I am innocent. From now on I will go to the gentiles." When we look to the ending of Acts, the judgment is sealed: "Let it be known to you Jews that this salvation of God has been sent to the gentiles; they will listen." Although the Jewish opposition here is not unanimous, that hardly matters. It is the disbelief of a significant portion that prompts the final, culminating, programmatic statement that God's plan of salvation will turn to the gentiles, and from the perspective of the audience of Acts, that had already occurred decades earlier. The prophecy had been fulfilled. Luke also chose to end Acts on the positive note that Paul was allowed by Roman authorities to speak freely, even though Luke and the audience would have been aware that Paul was executed by those same authorities. Combined with this, the harshness of the final prophetic denunciation of unbelieving Jews and the announcement that the message of salvation had been sent to the gentiles indicates a directionality to the conclusion. Paul's preaching causes one last great divide, with unreceptive Jews falling on one side and receptive gentiles and Roman authorities on the other. Although some scholars, such as Loveday Alexander, would argue that Acts "is a plea for a fair hearing at the bar of the wider Jewish community in the Diaspora,"[14] this does not register the full import of the increasingly negative verdict on the Jews who refuse to join the movement.

We have noted in previous chapters the constitutional language in the definition of Judaism, present in the covenant tradition, in the redefinition of returning Judeans as the true citizens of Judah by Ezra and Nehemiah, in the Mosaic constitution language in 1 Maccabees and the Greek constitutional terminology in 2 Maccabees. David Balch suggests that constitutional language is played upon in Acts as well. Specifically, the Greek tradition of founding colonies and reconstituting cities with a new form of government lies behind the structure of Luke-Acts. In Luke's hands, the scriptures and traditions of Israel are transferred from Jews to this new *politeia*, Christians.[15] Balch grants that there is one impediment to likening Luke-Acts to the reconstitution of a city: in Luke's view there is no new *city* for Christians, not even Jerusalem. But the influence of the tradition may still be felt. Jonathan Z. Smith distinguishes between the locative religious sensibility tied to a holy place and the diasporic sensibility that roamed the Greek and Roman cities.[16] Later Christian authors such as Diognetus certainly spoke of the universal *politeia* of Christians, and Philo and Josephus had prepared for this development by describing the Jewish *politeia* in similar terms. If Balch is correct, then in the case of Acts Christians operate under a new constitution, analogous to but different from the Jewish *politeia* under the Mosaic constitution.

SCHOLARLY INTERPRETATIONS
OF NEGATIVE PORTRAYALS OF JEWS

Every scholar grants that negative things are said about Jews in Acts, but a consensus is lacking as to the proper interpretation to place upon it. A large number of scholars, following Hans Conzelmann and Ernst Haenchen, see consistency in the overall plan of Luke-Acts to blame the Jews for killing Jesus and rejecting God's gospel.[17] But other scholars have suggested interpretations that would soften the charge of anti-Judaism. It would be quite simple, for example, to distinguish the Jewish leaders from the people.[18] It is the leaders who are condemned in many scenes, not the people of Israel as a whole. Some passages, such as Luke 19:47–48, support such a view, but most interpreters note that in the last half of Acts Jewish opposition is not limited to the leaders. Some have also argued that there is an early pro-Jewish layer of Acts, and a later anti-Jewish layer, and Dixon Slingerland would even specify that the first half of Acts is the older layer and the second later and more anti-Jewish.[19] However, while there may be early traditions contained within Acts, the negative portrayal of Jews is likely part of the vision of the author of the whole. This vision guides both halves of Acts and the Gospel of Luke as well, and it is more likely that Sanders' notion of a first hidden, then revealed character of the Jewish people is what is presented.

Others would argue that Luke is not *negative* toward Jews, but views the Jews' failure to respond as a *tragic* development; there is a gulf between the positive expectations held out for the Jews and the negative reality that obtains in the last half of Acts. Luke in this reading is actually sympathetic with the Jewish nation and pities the Jews their separation from the benefits of God's plan. David Tiede agrees with this assessment, but adds that, in a way parallel to Romans 9–11, the author looks beyond this temporary intransigence on Israel's part to a time of general conversion.[20] However, many of the scholars who try to find some way of ameliorating Luke's negative view toward the Jews fail to note the tone of the passages. The depiction of Jews in several of the important scenes in the last half of Acts does not reflect a tragic sense of pity, but a derision that borders on contemptuousness. Despite a romanticized depiction of traditional Judaism—the religion of Israel that Luke believed Christians had inherited—actual Jews in the narrative are presented in an increasingly negative way, as scurrilous and seditious citizens. And seditious here is not considered "good" as part of a subversive critique of Roman rule; Christians, it should be noted, are depicted as orderly and are even protected under the wing of the Roman authorities. In the perspective of Luke, some Jews in the early days of the movement may have converted, but the general body of Jews later in the story attacked the apostles at every turn. Their opposition only gives rise to greater successes as a sign of God's favor, but Jews contemporary to the writing of the work are discredited, as are legally observant followers of Jesus as well. For the earliest readers of Acts the story does not end as a tragedy. The ending of Acts is triumphant—without the Jews joining Paul's community. Paul's program in the past of moving from Jews to gentiles is affirmed.

Despite Luke's interest in the Jewish *origins* of Christianity, then, there is a negative portrayal of the relations with the body of Jews encountered in the apostles' mission. The depiction of Jews in Acts is part of a larger apologetic program, especially in respect to the Roman state. Conzelmann and Eckhard Plümacher, for instance, argued that Luke developed a positive portrayal of the relationship of the church with Rome.[21] First, the movement is said not to be isolated to a corner of the world but is "open" and part of world history. Second, Roman officials comment on Christianity favorably and hand down decisions in its favor. Third, a spirit of reason and orderly citizenship pervades the Christians' activities. Fourth, at 25:11 Paul expresses loyalty to Roman law: "If I have committed any capital offense, I will not avoid the death penalty!" Robert Maddox attempts to nuance this conclusion by arguing that not all Roman officials are depicted in a positive light. Felix and Festus, for example, are eager to take bribes in their exercise of authority, which indicates a variegated view of Roman authorities.[22] Yet even here, Luke appears to advocate a pro-Roman perspective: these two officials were remembered *negatively by Romans*. In fact, Roman officials who were likely remembered negatively by Romans are depicted negatively in Acts, while those who enjoyed a positive Roman reputation are depicted positively.[23] The provincial officials who come to Paul's defense (Acts 19:31) held a well-respected position. Jewish leaders as well who were well regarded in Rome are depicted positively in Acts—King Herod Agrippa II (viewed positively by Romans according to Josephus, *Jewish War* 2.345–404), while King Herod Agrippa I, who would have been despised in Roman tradition as a rebel, is described as persecuting the church, and having extended the persecution even further "when he saw that it pleased the Jews" (Acts 12:3). Acts thus presents, straight down the line, the same positive and negative evaluations of Roman and Jewish leaders that would have likely been found in the work of an elite Roman historian.

WE AND OTHER IN ACTS

These motifs in Acts would not likely have been aimed at a non-Christian audience, but were part of a construction of a self-image within Christianity: Christians should be seen as respectable members of the Roman Empire.[24] The negative depiction of the Jews and a positive self-presentation before Romans would go together as opposite sides of the same coin. They are not to be pursued as separate themes in the composition of Luke-Acts, but express a coordinated impulse, to define the construction of one relationship and the deconstruction of another: (1) Christians are the rightful heirs of pristine Judaism and Israelite tradition, and model citizens who should be protected under the wing of Rome; (2) Jews, as encountered in the Roman world in the later progress of the mission (and also as encountered in the time period of the audience), are prone to violence and sedition. The first defines the We and the second defines the Other. Still, it is possible that the real, contemporary opponents of Luke and Luke's audience are not Jews but observant Jesus-believers who would reject Paul's abrogation of the law. If that was the case, then Acts, like many of the texts we have analyzed, is constructing an external Other—opposing Jews—in order to counter an internal Other—observant Jesus-believers (Theorem 6: Internal Other linked).

Further, the pattern isolated here should not be considered in isolation. Mitzi Smith-Spralls has recently explored a number of literary patterns in Acts that, although seemingly unrelated, work together to communicate a single "meta-narrative."[25] The narrative themes she analyzes are:

1) The apostles are depicted as *passive* while the providential action of God makes their progress unstoppable.

2) In contrast to this, Jews are almost always depicted as *active* opponents to the mission of the apostles.
3) The charismatic opponents of the apostles are also parallel but contrasting, creating mirror images.
4) The named women characters among the followers of Jesus are contrasted with Peter and other named male apostles and are treated as lesser authorities.

These narrative themes are related in this respect: they depict the providential mission of God. The principal protagonists in this constructed world are the male apostles.[26] At the same time, various contrasting groups are constructed, either as internal or external Others: Jews and charismatic opponents are equal but external to the male apostles, while women within the movement are unequal but internal. The interwoven threads of the construction of the We and Other, or of We and several different kinds of Other, both internal and external, are thus traced (Theorem 6: Internal Others linked).

We can also be more specific about the We. Since Acts follows in the tradition of Paul, we might assume that, like that apostle, the author here treats gentiles as the Other that becomes We through conversion. But as Gary Gilbert observes, although we are prepared in almost every scene for the conversion of gentiles, this event, surprisingly, is never described.[27] After Acts 18, the story turns to Paul's increasing legal problems and does not mention any further converts. Throughout, and especially at the conclusion of the book, we are pointed ahead to a great influx of gentile converts, but it lies in the story's future, the audience's past. Although they are presumed, they are not described. Gilbert then draws our attention to another group, the "God-fearers." Luke introduces them as gentiles who revere God but have not converted to Judaism. They are quite central to the narrative, as some of the main events in the mission of the church involve gentiles who "fear God" (10:2, 35; 13:16; 16:14; 17:4; 18:7). There may have been a place in Jewish worship for those who were attracted to the theology of the one God but were not ready to convert to Judaism. Luke describes them as a group open to Paul's message, and it is often suggested that Paul preached among Jews, but found little reception there except among the God-fearers. They were thus a bridge between Jews and those gentiles who were unfamiliar with Judaism. Although some scholars argue that the God-fearers are Luke's literary creation, and others that they did in fact exist, both groups agree that their function in the narrative is as a bridge between the Jews who reject the message about Jesus and the gentiles who become the recipients. And since the gentile converts are not actually described, says Gilbert, the focus is on the God-fearers, who become the most important converts:

> From a literary viewpoint, God-fearers are not minor characters who stand between the two great pillars of Jew and Gentile. Rather, they exist as *the* alternative to the Jewish community, as the foil for Jews. . . . [T]he response by the God-fearers provides the model for how Jews should have acted, but did not."[28]

God-fearers are the ideal type for the gentile Christians of the author's day: they are an ambiguous group adopted as We (Theorem 7). Like Jews they are knowledgeable about Scripture, but unlike Jews they accept Jesus and are strongly positioned *against* Jewish observance.

CONCLUSION

Despite the fact that Paul and the earliest generation of apostles are depicted in Acts as pious and unobjectionable Jews, in Luke's mind the followers of Jesus had by the time of writing become a group separated from the body of Jews. They were "Christians." Luke-Acts has gone beyond Matthew and Paul in seeing the split between Christianity and Judaism as complete and in the past, and has even gone beyond John, who saw this split as irrevocable, but occurring contemporaneously. The narrative method of Luke is not so much to *state* a theological case as it is to *show* that after this separation Jews became every bit as disorderly and rebellious as one would expect from the fact that they were involved in three bloody rebellions in seventy years (66–135 CE). More to the point, the author demonstrates that Christians should be viewed *by the Roman authorities* as separate from Jews. Luke's depiction of a contrasting response of Jews on one hand and God-fearers on the other becomes what Meeks refers to as the constant message in the static of the narrative, the myth of earliest Christianity. One may say that the Christian tradition has inherited its view of Israel from Acts, its view of Paul and Peter from Acts, its view of the earliest Christians from Acts, and its view of Jews from Acts.

NOTES

1. But cf. the varying perspectives in Daniel Boyarin, *Border Lines: The Partition of Judaeo-Christianity* (Philadelphia: University of Pennsylvania Press, 2004); Daniel Boyarin, *Dying for God: Martyrdom and the Making of Christianity and Judaism* (Stanford, CA: Stanford University Press, 1999), 127–30; Adam H. Becker and Annette Yoshiko Reed, eds., *The Ways That Never Parted: Jews and Christians in Late Antiquity and the Early Middle Ages* (Tübingen, Germany: Mohr [Paul Siebeck], 2003);

Judith Lieu, *Neither Jew nor Greek? Constructing Early Christianity* (London and New York: Clark, 2002), esp. 15, 19–20; Judith Lieu, *Image and Reality: The Jews in the World of the Christians in the Second Century* (Edinburgh, UK: Clark, 1996); and Miriam Taylor, *Anti-Judaism and Early Christian Identity: A Critique of the Scholarly Consensus* (Leiden, Netherlands, and New York: Brill, 1995). On the first uses of *Christianos*, see David G. Horrell, "The Label *Christianos*: 1 Peter 4:16 and the Formation of Christian Identity," *Journal of Biblical Literature* 126 (2007): 361–81.

2. Jerome Neyrey, *The Passion according to Luke* (New York and Mahwah, NJ: Paulist, 1985), 69–84. On the Pauline Passion see Charles H. Talbert, *Literary Patterns, Theological Themes, and the Genre of Luke-Acts* (Missoula, MT: Scholars Press, 1975), 17–23.

3. Jack Sanders, "The Jewish People in Luke-Acts," 71, and Marilyn Salmon, "Insider or Outsider? Luke's Relationship with Judaism," 81, both in *Luke-Acts and the Jewish People*, ed. Joseph B. Tyson (Minneapolis, MN: Augsburg, 1988). I have been much influenced by Sanders' major work on this topic, *The Jews in Luke-Acts* (Philadelphia: Fortress, 1987), as well as by many stimulating conversations with him.

4. Ernst Haenchen, "Judentum und Christentum in der Apostelgeschichte," *Zeitschrift für die neutestamentliche Wissenschaft* 54 (1963): 155–89; Ernst Haenchen, *The Acts of the Apostles* (Philadelphia: Westminster, 1971), 721–32; Stephen Wilson, *The Gentiles and the Gentile Mission in Luke-Acts* (Cambridge, UK: Cambridge University Press, 1973), 219–38; Lloyd Gaston, "Anti-Judaism and the Passion Narrative in Luke and Acts," in *Anti-Judaism in Early Christianity*, ed. P. Richardson, 2 vols. (Waterloo, ON: Wilfred Laurier University Press, 1986), 1:127–53; and Robert Maddox, *The Purpose of Luke-Acts* (Edinburgh, UK: Clark, 1982).

5. Hans Conzelmann, *The Theology of St. Luke* (London: SCM, 1982), 145–48.

6. Jacob Jervell, *Luke and the People of God* (Minneapolis, MN: Augsburg, 1972).

7. Gerhard Lohfink, *Die Sammlung Israels* (Munich: Kösel, 1975), 55.

8. Sanders, *Jews in Luke-Acts*, 81. The thoughtful rejoinder to Sanders by James D. G. Dunn ("The Question of Anti-Semitism in the New Testament," in *Jews and Christians: The Parting of the Ways A.D. 70 to 135,* ed. D. G. Dunn [Tübingen, Germany: Mohr (Siebeck), 1992], 187–95) fails in my mind because he does not consider sufficiently the retrospective view of Luke, who could see a range of Jewish responses in the earlier period which over the course of the narrative become more clearly defined as negative. The apostles, and any other Jews who early on joined the church, were the bearers of the good that was in Israel, but—in the author's day—Jews who failed to join disrupt God's mission and are bad Roman citizens into the bargain. See also Shelly Matthews, "Perfect Martyr: The Stoning of Stephen and the Construction of Christianity in Acts" (forthcoming). She points out that the prayers of Jesus and Stephen for God to have mercy on their tormentors function as a rhetorical contrast with the murderous Jews. It is ironic that the superior and peace-loving ethic of Jesus and Stephen here becomes a means of casting the Jews as permanent Other, while Jesus and Stephen appear in the line of the persecuted prophets.

9. Erich Auerbach, *Mimesis: The Representation of Reality in Western Literature* (Princeton, NJ: Princeton University Press, 1953), 33–40. See also J. S. McClelland, *The Crowd and the Mob* (London: Unwin Hyman, 1989); and Ramsay MacMullen, *Enemies of the Roman Order* (Cambridge, MA: Harvard University Press, 1966), 170–72.

10. Robert F. Stoops, Jr., "Riot and Assembly: The Social Context of Acts 19:23–41," *Journal of Biblical Literature* 108 (1989): 73–91. Crowd scenes in Greek romances are treated by Richard Pervo, *Profit with Delight: The Literary Genre of the Acts of the Apostles* (Philadelphia: Fortress, 1987), 34–42; and Ronald F. Hock, "The Greek Novel," in *Greco-Roman Literature and the New Testament*, ed. David Aune (Atlanta, GA: Scholars Press, 1988), 139. However, in the romances riots are just another threat to the safety of the protagonists; Acts is closer in this regard to the histories in that riots also have political significance. The word *stasis* does not occur often in Luke-Acts, but when it does, its use is pointed: Luke 23:25, more than the other gospels, emphasizes that Barabbas is guilty of *stasis*, and Paul is *ironically* accused of *stasis* by a Jewish representative in Acts 24:5. Even more fascinating in regard to internal Others, at Acts 15:2 *stasis* is said to arise between Paul and Barnabas *when the latter sides with the observant Christians*. (Teorem 6)

11. Gregory E. Sterling, *Historiography and Self-Definition: Josephos* [sic], *Luke-Acts and Apologetic Historiography* (Leiden, Netherlands: Brill, 1992); Benjamin J. Hubbard, "Luke, Josephus and Rome: A Comparative Approach to the Lucan *Sitz-im-Leben*," in *Society of Biblical Literature 1979 Seminar Papers*, ed. P. J. Achtemeier, 2 vols. (Chico, CA: Scholars Press, 1979), 1:59–68; see also Eckhard Plümacher, *Lukas als hellenistischer Schriftsteller* (Göttingen, Germany: Vandenhoeck & Ruprecht, 1972).

12. Wayne Meeks, "The Man from Heaven in Johannine Sectarianism," *Journal of Biblical Literature* 91 (1972): 48.

13. See Haenchen, *Acts*, 537–41, on Luke's stylistic use of tension and release.

14. Loveday Alexander, "The Acts of the Apostles as an Apologetic Text," in *Apologetics in the Roman Empire: Pagans, Jews and Christians*, ed. Mark Edwards, Martin Goodman, and Simon Price (Oxford: Oxford University Press, 1999), 43–44.

15. David Balch, "*Metabolē Politeiōn*: Jesus as Founder of the Church in Luke-Acts: Form and Function," in *Contextualizing Acts: Lukan Narrative and Greco-Roman Discourse*, ed. Todd Penner and Caroline Vander Stichele (Atlanta, GA: Society of Biblical Literature, 2003), 139–88. On citizenship as a powerful metaphor in the Roman period, see Adela Yarbro Collins, "Insiders and Outsiders in the Book of Revelation and Its Social Context," in *"To See Ourselves as Others See Us": Christians, Jews, "Others" in Late Antiquity*, ed. Jacob Neusner and Ernst S. Frerichs (Chico, CA: Scholars Press, 1985), 188.

16. Jonathan Z. Smith, *Map Is Not Territory: Studies in the History of Religions* (Leiden, Netherlands: Brill, 1978), xiii–xiv, 98–102; "Here, There, and Anywhere," *Relating Religion: Essays in the Study of Religion* (Chicago and London: University of Chicago Press, 2004), 323–39.

17. Conzelmann, *Theology*, 145–48; Haenchen, "Judentum und Christentum."

18. Lohfink, *Sammlung*, 55; and Joseph B. Tyson, "The Problem of Jewish Rejection in Acts," in Tyson, *Luke-Acts*, 126–27.

19. Dixon Slingerland, "The Composition of Acts: Some Redaction-Critical Observations," *Journal of the American Academy of Religion* 56 (1988): 99–113.

20. David Tiede, "'Glory to Thy People Israel': Luke-Acts and the Jews," in Tyson, *Luke-Acts*, 21–34; Robert Tannehill, "Israel in Luke-Acts: A Tragic Story," *Journal of Biblical Literature* 104 (1985): 69–85; David P. Moessner, "The Ironic Fulfillment of Israel's Glory," in Tyson, *Luke-Acts*, 35–50; and Robert L. Brawley, *Luke-Acts and the Jews* (Atlanta, GA: Scholars Press, 1987), 151–59. Some of the "conciliatory" acts of Paul that they see, however, such as the circumcision of Timothy

(16:1–3) or the participation in a temple vow (21:17–26), must be seen as lying *in the past* from the point of view of the audience. They demonstrate Paul's irreproachability in terms of Jewish practice, so that any enmity between the camps must have arisen from the Jewish side. Even the reference in Acts 21:20 to the conversion of "myriads" is likely looking back from the audience's time frame to the early conversions, the "Jerusalem springtime," and establishing the historical view that the mission had begun by enjoying success among Jews. Thus all fault for the divorce between Jews and Christians—already in the past for Luke's community—must be ascribed to the growing rejection of Christianity by Jews. This process was for Luke prophesied in scripture but it remained for the Book of Acts to depict it historically.

21. Conzelmann, *Theology*, 138–44; Plümacher, *Lukas*, 16–27. Cf. in a similar but not identical vein the views of Sterling, *Historiography and Self-Definition*, 381–89; Paul W. Walaskay, *'And So We Came to Rome': The Political Perspective of St. Luke* (Cambridge, UK: Cambridge University Press, 1983), 1–14, 64–67; and Philip Esler, *Community and Gospel in Luke-Acts: The Social and Political Motivations of Lucan Theology* (Cambridge, UK: Cambridge University Press, 1987), 16, 210–19. A modified view of the pro-Roman apology in Acts is offered in a subtle analysis by François Bovon, "L'importance des médiations dans le projet théologique de Luc," *New Testament Studies* 21 (1974): 36–37, who sees in this text the reconciliation of Jewish particularism and Roman universalism.

22. Maddox, *Purpose*, 91–99, esp. 95. Richard J. Cassidy, *Society and Politics in the Acts of the Apostles* (Maryknoll, NY: Orbis, 1987), unconvincingly goes much further and argues that Luke is strongly anti-imperial, and describes the tensions between the nascent movement and Roman authorities. A better but still unconvincing case is made by Gary Gilbert, "Roman Propaganda and Christian Identity in the Worldview of Luke-Acts," in Penner and Vander Stichele, *Contextualizing Acts*, 233–56. A symbol system parallel to that of the Roman Empire is not necessarily challenging it; cf. the discussion in chapter seven.

23. Of those depicted negatively in Acts, Felix was condemned by Tacitus for his ignoble birth and his tyrannical abuse of office (*Histories* 5.9; *Annals* 12.54). Festus' brother Pallas was dismissed by Claudius and was not viewed positively by the class-conscious historians (Suetonius, *Claudius* 28; compare also Josephus, *Antiquities* 20.182). Of those depicted positively in Acts, Gallio was an older brother of Seneca, and Sergius Paulus was quoted as an authority by Pliny the Elder (*Natural History* book 1). Claudius Lysias was unknown outside of Acts, but his name indicates that he was adopted into the Claudian imperial family.

24. See Maddox, *Purpose*, 93–97; Esler, *Community and Gospel*, 217–19; and Stoops, "Riot," 90.

25. Mitzi Smith-Spralls, "The Function of the Jews, Charismatic Others, and Women in Narrative Instabilities in the Acts of the Apostles," Ph.D. dissertation, Harvard University, 2005.

26. See also Bovon, "L'importance des médiations."

27. Gary Gilbert, "The Disappearance of the Gentiles: God-Fearers and the Image of the Jews in Luke-Acts," in *Putting Body and Soul Together: Essays in Honor of Robin Scroggs*, ed. Virginia Wiles, Alexandra Brown, and Graydon F. Snyder (Valley Forge, PA: Trinity Press International, 1997), 172–84.

28. Gilbert, "Disappearance of the Gentiles," 179, 182.

9

⚜

Conclusion

In John Ford's American epic film *Drums along the Mohawk*, a young husband and wife played by Henry Fonda and Claudette Colbert have settled on the frontier in upstate New York on the eve of the American Revolution. The menacing, one-eyed Tory played by John Carradine has enlisted the Mohawk Indians to fight the homesteaders. But Fonda's problems are not just the Native Americans. When Colbert becomes hysterical over her unsettled conditions, the Christian Indian Blue Back places a stick in Fonda's hands and says "Beat her good!" Fonda tests the heft of the stick thoughtfully, but turns and places it over the mantle, where a rifle would normally hang, as if to say, "I won't be using that. But if I ever need it, it's there." Thus in the course of the film Fonda, the frontier hero, while being aided by an adopted Other (the Christian Blue Back) defeats the external Others (Native Americans) who are linked with an internal Other (man with a disability), and reestablishes control over another internal Other (his wife). In American social memory, this is epic time, a period of primeval anarchy, of primal people, when the constitution of the We is first created in a savage land by a conquest over the Other.

The social memory of the birth of the United States is not very different from that of Israel or Christianity. The We and the Other are mutually constructed, and internal and external Other are linked. But at the same time that we can perceive analogous processes between American epic film and biblical constructions of the Other, we have to reckon with the fact that there are important differences as well, not just those between twentieth-century American film and the biblical texts, but also between the various depictions of the Other within the Bible itself. Despite their own internal claims, the texts exhibit almost no stability in terms of passing on the same view of the Other that they inherited from a religious forebear. In other words, there is no orthodoxy in terms of who is Other, yet this should hardly surprise us. This apparent contradiction of similarity and yet difference may perhaps be explained. The biblical texts reveal differences in *essences*—what constitutes the Other—yet they are similar—and so are John Ford's films—in terms of *processes*. We may express this in the same terms used in the introduction. Each culture or period may understand the essences of A and B differently, but the *relation between* A and B may be quite analogous cross-culturally or trans-historically. The various ways of constructing the relation of We and Other—the theorems of the introduction—are common to many human cultures. The essence of the Other, what the Other is really like, is always different and perhaps unknown, but the *construction* of the Other will always sound familiar.

But we may also reflect on the particularities of these texts, how their Others are different. This reflection on the Other in the Bible has encompassed texts written over about a thousand years under very different conditions. Each text inhabits a different world. The early texts of the Hebrew Bible differentiate between a bygone Other (Canaanites), the great empires (Egypt, Assyria, Babylon), and real neighbors who are sometimes treated as descendants of the Canaanites (Ammonites, Moabites, and so on). Ezra-Nehemiah redraws the boundaries of Israel for a new day. True Israel is not the same as "Greater Israel," but is composed of those Judeans who were tested by God by being sent into exile to Babylon and brought back, and the Other is not the descendants of Canaan, but the "mixed" population of the land of Judah which is now like the foreign nations. First and Second Maccabees, reacting to yet another change of empire, constitute the We in a way similar to other Hellenistic indigenous kingdoms, but not in precisely the same way. In 1 Maccabees the Other is only the gentiles who threaten Israel, but in 2 Maccabees it is Hellenistic culture in general. Matthew takes over the gospel narrative of Mark, but only one group in Israel is singled out as the conspicuous opposite of true faith in God, the Pharisees. John imbues the gospel narrative with an unreal cast, and the Other becomes "the Jews" or even "the world." Next we considered the subtleties of Paul's discussion of "Jew and Greek." Contrary to the later claims of Christian tradition, Paul did not define the Jew as Other but rather the gentile, but this Other could become We by being baptized at the end of time and adopted as a child of God and of Abraham. Jews are not removed from God's plan, but gentiles are added. My analysis concluded with one of the later texts of the New Testament, the Book of Acts, which asserts a clearer program of the transfer of God's dispensation from Jews to gentile Christians, the view that became normative for the later church's Other. My discussion might well have been continued into the second- and third-century Christian texts and Jewish texts, but here I have chosen to limit discussion to texts that have been, in one canon or another, part of the Bible of the West.

Not only are the constructions of the Other all different, but they also only address a very particular context, a short moment in history. Although most westerners think of the biblical stories as universal, from our global and historical perspective we also see that each text arises in a small pond. How many worshipers of Yahweh were there in 1000 BCE? Perhaps twenty thousand? How many followers of Jesus were there in 100 CE? Perhaps ten thousand? The biblical We is actually a tiny group, and so is the Other. Ancient Assyria was not the Other for Israel, but rather, the supposed descendants of the Canaanites, nations also numbering in the mere thousands. Assyria was a great empire which could be either good or bad, and ultimately was seen as a bad empire before it perished, but it was not the Other. Neither was Rome the Other in Matthew, but the Pharisees, a group limited to a few thousand.[1] The closer, more similar Other is the obsessive Other. What the various Others in the Bible have in common are these qualities: varied, constructed, small. Yet an eternal significance is attributed to the Other (Theorem 9). The external Other is always assimilated to an eternal Other, the platonic form of Other. But the platonic form of Other always bears a striking resemblance to the We (Theorem 3).

There is clearly a relation between constructions of the Other, prejudice, and violence. The three are not identical, but understanding any one of these three requires an understanding of the other two. They form a triangular relationship. Prejudices either arise from constructions of the Other or are assimilated to them; that is, they either start there or they go there, in search of a cognitive cause for conflict. In regard to violence, it is becoming increasingly common to search out the prior conditions that give rise to violence and genocide. The peace activist Johan Galtung set himself the task of analyzing the role of violence in society, and in the process turned to the category of "cultural violence," the collection of cultural codes that precondition people to commit violent acts against certain people.[2] Cultural violence is the construction of the Other. As Regina Schwartz has said: "Violence is not only what we do to the other. It is prior to that. Violence is the very construction of the other."[3] The biblical texts reflect a very human process.

Texts here are considered in their historical context, but there is no reason to think that violence and negative constructions of the Other were any better or worse before the Bible, were any better or worse at a later stage than at an earlier one, nor that they are better or worse in enlightened western democracies. Indeed, some of the most extreme examples of constructing the ethnic Other in world history have occurred in the last few centuries: the European colonization of nonwhite peoples and western slavery, the holocaust of European Jews, the Armenian genocide, and more recently the slaughter of over a million people in southern Africa. But what is striking is that, no matter how the blanks of We and Other are filled in, the *processes* of constructing the Other—and the tragic consequences—are so similar. Those of us who survived the twentieth century can confirm that in regard to the Other the only thing that improved in that period was the technical means of mass murder, and a change in media that allowed a huge number of people to construct the same Other at the same time.

The focus of this study might be seen as negative—and it is. But it is not just because it focuses on the deep prejudices that the Bible formalizes. This study also, in Jonathan Z. Smith's words, defamiliarizes the Bible, "making the familiar seem strange *in order to enhance our perception of the familiar*."[4] Perceiving the negative theme forces us to view the familiar biblical texts in an unfamiliar and unsettling light, as texts that are not protected by an assumption of safety. Other scholars have written books that concentrate on the formation of community in the Bible, the construction of the We. A short list might include Paul Hanson, Howard Clark Kee, Ilana Pardes, and Sharon H. Ringe.[5] There certainly are passages in which the We is constructed peacefully or the Other is at least treated more fairly, such as the books of Ruth and Jonah, Isaiah 19:19–25, or Mark 12:28–34. Another area of hope lies surprisingly in the "alternative teaching" of the interpenetration of good and evil. Certain texts of the Bible, such as Judges, Job, Ruth, and Jonah, explore the interpenetration of good and evil and coexist with our constitutional texts as biblical misfits. Yet these texts are often rendered marginal to the constitutional texts of the Hebrew Bible and New Testament. To be honest to the biblical texts usually considered more central, one cannot hold up the ideal of community found there without also recognizing the way they simultaneously construct those who are *not* God's people. Perhaps the two most destructive passages in western history are Deuteronomy 7:2, "When the Lord your God gives them over to you and you defeat them, then you must utterly destroy them," and John 14:6, "I am the Way, the Truth, and the Life. No one comes to the Father except through me."

Modern pluralists may be tempted to see biblical pluralism as good and biblical exclusion as bad, but that is not the main point to be taken, and if readers simplistically assume that, they will be ill-equipped for the complexities of the twenty-first century. The larger lesson is that all cultures, monotheistic and polytheistic, those more exclusive and those more inclusive, construct their opponents and some of their own members as the Other, and we must try to understand the process in which we all engage.

This analysis focuses on texts that are part of the very constitution of our culture. Other cultures, polytheistic and more inclusive, have found other means to construct the Other—for example, civilized/barbarian in China or pure/impure in India—in order to subjugate peoples, to impose control, and to treat others as less than fully human. Further, in the twentieth century some of the worst violations of Others were conducted by regimes that were either irreligious or only nominally religious. The construction of the Other is not an exclusively religious process, and the new turn in studies of *religious* violence is to make broader comparisons to other root causes of conflict as well.[6]

Perhaps it is not even possible to forgo constructing the Other. It does not simply result from a failure of goodness or innocence. That is a dangerous romantic fallacy, perhaps the most dangerous there is. Constructing the Other is a fundamental part of what it means to be human, somewhat like anger: there are clear negative consequences, but it is not possible for human societies to transcend it. Ultimately, the problem is not so much that the ancient authors did something wrong, but that, first, human beings refuse to grant that their views of the Other are constructions, and second, these constructions form the basis of the ordering of society. The first step in undoing the damage inherent in these processes is to perceive the construction of the Other in all cultures and to recognize its relationship to power.

Thus the problem is not that we construct the Other, but that we deny it.

NOTES

1. It can be plausibly argued that for some New Testament texts, especially Revelation, Rome is the Other, but it is my view that this is not true for Matthew, John, Paul, or Acts. The two exceptions of those treated here—that is, texts with a great Other—are 2 Maccabees, for whom Hellenistic culture was in some sense the Other, and Paul, for whom gentile religion is the Other.

2. Johan Galtung, "Cultural Violence," *Journal of Peace Research* 27 (1990): 291–305.

3. Regina Schwartz, *The Curse of Cain: The Violent Legacy of Monotheism* (Chicago and London: University of Chicago Press, 1997), 5.

4. Jonathan Z. Smith, *Imagining Religion: From Babylon to Jonestown* (Chicago: University of Chicago Press, 1982), xiii.

5. Paul Hanson, *The People Called: The Growth of Community in the Bible; With a New Introduction* (Louisville, KY: Westminster John Knox, 2001); Howard Clark Kee, *Who Are the People of God? Early Christian Models of Community* (New Haven, CT: Yale University Press, 1995); Ilana Pardes, *The Biography of Ancient Israel: National Narratives in the Bible* (Berkeley: University of California Press, 2000); Sharon H. Ringe, *Wisdom's Friends: Community and Christology in the Fourth Gospel* (Louisville, KY: Westminster John Knox, 1999). Some books which address the negative side

also include the positive passages as well: Jonathan Sacks, *The Dignity of Difference: How to Avoid the Clash of Civilizations*, 2nd ed. (London and New York: Continuum, 2003), 52–59. His work is admirable, but not quite honest about the role of the negative passages of the Hebrew Bible. One consideration of negative passages as such is Patrick D. Miller, "God's Other Stories: On the Margins of Deuteronomic Theology," in *Realia Dei: Essays in Archaeology and Biblical Interpretation in Honor of Edward F. Campbell, Jr. at His Retirement*, ed. Prescott H. Williams, Jr., and Theodore Hiebert (Atlanta, GA: Scholars, 1999), 185–94.

6. Donald L. Horowitz, *Ethnic Groups in Conflict* (Berkeley: University of California Press, 1985), xv; William T. Cavanaugh, "Does Religion Cause Violence?" *Harvard Divinity Bulletin*, Spring/Summer 2007: 24–35.

Appendix: Theorems for the Analysis of the Other

Theorem 1: From Other to We. The construction of the Other serves to construct the We.

Theorem 2: From We to Other. Just as the construction of the Other serves to construct the We, so also the construction of the We serves to construct the Other.

Theorem 3: Other similar to We. The Other is often in reality very similar to the We.

Theorem 4: Seductive power of Other. The Other has the ability to corrupt or infect the We, and the We is vulnerable.

Theorem 5: Other distorted. The depiction of the Other is often unreal, distorted, monstrous, mythical, and taboo.

Theorem 6: Internal Others. There are internal as well as external Others, and they are often seen as linked.

Theorem 7: Ambiguous groups reassigned. Ambiguous groups are often reassigned either as an Other or as a special case of an adopted We or internal Other.

Theorem 8: Origins of practices reassigned. Ancient, native, or traditional practices may be redefined as new or foreign and associated with the

Other, while an originally foreign practice may be redefined as ancient, native, and traditional, now associated with the We.

Theorem 9: Eternal Other. The Other is viewed as having existed from time immemorial and continues to exist, and cannot be permanently extirpated.

Select Bibliography

Allport, Gordon W. *The Nature of Prejudice*. Cambridge, MA: Addison-Wesley, 1954.

Anderson, Benedict R. *Imagined Communities: Reflections on the Origin and Spread of Nationalism*. 2nd ed. London and New York: Verso, 1991.

Barth, Fredrik. "Introduction." Pages 1–26 in *Ethnic Groups and Boundaries: The Social Organization of Cultural Differences*. Boston: Little, Brown, 1969.

Baumann, Gerd. *Contesting Culture: Discourses of Identity in Multi-Ethnic London*. Cambridge and New York: Cambridge University Press, 1996.

———. *The Multicultural Riddle: Rethinking National, Ethnic, and Religious Identities*. New York: Routledge, 1999.

Baumann, Gerd, and Andre Gingrich, eds. *Grammars of Identity/Alterity: A Structural Approach*. New York and Oxford: Berghahn, 2004.

Baumgarten, Albert I. *The Flourishing of Jewish Sects in the Maccabean Era: An Interpretation*. Leiden: Brill, 1997.

Becker, Adam H., and Annette Yoshiko Reed, eds. *The Ways That Never Parted: Jews and Christians in Late Antiquity and the Early Middle Ages*. Tübingen: Mohr (Siebeck), 2003.

Benbassa, Esther, and Jean-Christophe Attias. *The Jew and the Other*. Ithaca, NY, and London: Cornell University Press, 2004.

Bhabha, Homi. *The Location of Culture*. London and New York: Routledge, 1994.

Biale, David. *Power and Powerlessness in Jewish History*. New York: Schocken, 1986.

Blenkinsopp, Joseph. "A Jewish Sect of the Persian Period." *Catholic Biblical Quarterly* 52 (1990): 5–20.

———. "The 'Servants of the Lord' in Third Isaiah: Profile of a Pietistic Group in the Persian Period." *Proceedings of the Irish Biblical Association* 7 (1983): 1–23.

———. "The Nehemiah Autobiography." Pages 199–212 in *Language, Theology and the Bible: Essays in Honor of James Barr*. Edited by Samuel Balentine and John Barton. Oxford: Clarendon/New York: Oxford University Press, 1994.

Bloch-Smith, Elizabeth. "Israelite Ethnicity in Iron I: Archaeology Preserves What Is Remembered and What Is Forgotten in Israel's History." *Journal of Biblical Literature* 122 (2003): 401–25.

Bovon, François. "L'importance des médiations dans le projet théologique de Luc." *New Testament Studies* 21 (1974): 23–39.

Boyarin, Daniel. *Border Lines: The Partition of Judaeo-Christianity*. Philadelphia: University of Pennsylvania Press, 2004.

———. *Dying for God: Martyrdom and the Making of Christianity and Judaism*. Palo Alto, CA: Stanford University Press, 1999.

———. "The *Ioudaioi* in John and the Prehistory of 'Judaism.'" Pages 216–39 in *Pauline Conversations in Context: Essays in Honor of Calvin J. Roetzel*. Edited by Janice Capel Anderson, Philip Sellew, and Claudia Setzer. London: Sheffield Academic Press, 2002.

———. *A Radical Jew: Paul and the Politics of Identity*. Berkeley: University of California Press, 1994.

Brett, Mark G., ed. *Ethnicity and the Bible*. Leiden: Brill, 1996.

Buell, Denise Kimber. *Why This New Race? Ethnic Reasoning in Early Christianity*. New York: Columbia University Press, 2005.

Cavanaugh, William T. "Does Religion Cause Violence?" *Harvard Divinity Bulletin* Spring/Summer (2007): 24–35.

Certeau, Michel de. *Heterologies: Discourse on the Other*. Minneapolis and London: University of Minnesota Press, 1986.

Cohen, Shaye J. D. *The Beginnings of Jewishness: Boundaries, Varieties, Uncertainties*. Berkeley: University of California Press, 1999.

Cohn, Robert L. "Negotiating (with) the Nations: Ancestors and Identity in Genesis." *Harvard Theological Review* 96 (2003): 147–66.

———. "The Second Coming of Moses: Deuteronomy and the Construction of Israelite Identity." Pages 59–71 in *Proceedings of the Twelfth World Congress of Jewish Studies* (Division A: The Bible and Its World). Jerusalem: World Union of Jewish Studies, 1999.

———. *The Shape of Sacred Space*. Chico, CA: Scholars Press, 1981.

Cohn, Robert L., and Laurence J. Silberstein, eds. *The Other in Jewish Thought and History: Constructions of Jewish Culture and Identity*. New York/London: New York University Press, 1994.

Collins, Adela Yarbro. "Insiders and Outsiders in the Book of Revelation and Its Social Context." Pages 187–218 in *To See Ourselves as Others See Us: Christians, Jews, 'Others' in Late Antiquity*. Edited by Jacob Neusner and Ernst S. Frerichs. Chico, CA: Scholars Press, 1985.

Collins, John J. *The Bible after Babel: Historical Criticism in a Postmodern Age*. Grand Rapids, MI: Eerdmans, 2005.

———. "The Zeal of Phinehas: The Bible and the Legitimization of Violence." *Journal of Biblical Literature* 122 (2003): 3–21.

Coser, Lewis. *The Functions of Social Conflict*. Glencoe, IL: Free Press, 1956.

Delaney, Carol. *Abraham on Trial: The Social Legacy of Biblical Myth*. Princeton, NJ: Princeton University Press, 1998.

Derrida, Jacques. "Deconstruction and the Other." Pages 107–26 in *Dialogues with Contemporary Thinkers*. Edited by Richard Kearney. Manchester: Manchester University Press, 1984.

Doran, Robert. "Independence or Coexistence: The Responses of 1 and 2 Maccabees to Seleucid Hegemony." Pages 1.102–3 in *Society of Biblical Literature Seminar Papers Vol. 38.* 2 vols. Atlanta: Society of Biblical Literature, 1999.

Douglas, Mary. "Holy Joy: Rereading Leviticus: The Anthropologist and the Believer." *Conservative Judaism* 46 (1994): 3–14.

———. "Justice as the Cornerstone: An Interpretation of Leviticus 18–20." *Interpretation* 53 (1999): 341–50.

———. *Natural Symbols: Explorations in Cosmology.* New York: Pantheon, 1970.

———. *Purity and Danger.* 2nd ed. Harmondsworth: Penguin, 1970.

———. "Who Was the Stranger?" *Archives européennes de sociologie* 35 (1994): 283–98.

Eilberg-Schwartz, Howard. *The Savage in Judaism: An Anthropology of Israelite Religion and Ancient Judaism.* Bloomington: Indiana University Press, 1990.

Eisenbaum, Pamela. "Paul as the New Abraham." Pages 130–45 in *Paul and Empire: Religion and Power in Roman Imperial Society.* Edited by Richard A. Horsley. Harrisburg, PA: Trinity Press International, 1997.

———. "A Remedy for Having Been Born of Woman: Jesus, the Gentiles, and Genealogy in Romans." *Journal of Biblical Literature* 123 (2004): 671–702.

Eskenazi, Tamara Cohn. "Ezra-Nehemiah." Pages 123–30 in *Women's Bible Commentary.* Edited by Carol A. Newsom and Sharon H. Ringe. Louisville, KY: Westminster/John Knox, 1992.

———. *In an Age of Prose: A Literary Approach to Ezra-Nehemiah.* Atlanta: Scholars, 1988.

Forkman, Gören. *The Limits of the Religious Community: Expulsion from the Religious Community within the Qumran Sect, within Rabbinic Judaism, and within Primitive Christianity.* Lund: Gleerup, 1972.

Frankfurter, David. *Evil Incarnate: Rumors of Demonic Conspiracy and Ritual Abuse in History.* Princeton, NJ: Princeton University Press, 2006.

———. "The Legacy of Sectarian Rage: Vengeance Fantasies in the New Testament." Pages 114–28 in *Religion and Violence: The Biblical Heritage.* Edited by Jonathan Klawans and David Bernat. Sheffield: Sheffield Phoenix, 2008.

Fredriksen, Paula, and Adele Reinhartz, eds. *Jesus, Judaism, and Christian Anti-Judaism: Reading the New Testament after the Holocaust.* Louisville and London: Westminster/John Knox, 2002.

Freyne, Seán. "Vilifying the Other and Defining the Self: Matthew's and John's Anti-Jewish Polemic in Focus." Pages 117–43 in *To See Ourselves as Others See Us: Christians, Jews, 'Others' in Late Antiquity.* Edited by Jacob Neusner and Ernst S. Frerichs. Chico, CA: Scholars Press, 1985.

Gager, John G. *Kingdom and Community: The Social World of Early Christianity.* Englewood Cliffs, NJ: Prentice-Hall, 1975.

———. *Reinventing Paul.* Oxford: Oxford University Press, 2000.

Galtung, Johan. "Cultural Violence." *Journal of Peace Research* 27 (1990): 291–305.

Gaston, Lloyd. *Paul and the Torah.* Vancouver: University of British Columbia Press, 1987.

Gibson, E. Leigh, and Shelly Matthews. *Violence in the New Testament.* Edinburgh: T & T Clark, 2005.

Gilman, Sander. *Difference and Pathology: Stereotypes of Sexuality, Race, and Madness.* Ithaca, NY: Cornell University Press, 1985.

Goodblatt, David M. *Elements of Ancient Jewish Nationalism*. New York: Cambridge University Press, 2006.

Grabbe, Lester. *Ezra-Nehemiah*. London/New York: Routledge, 1998.

Greifenhagen, F. V. *Egypt on the Pentateuch's Ideological Map: Constructing Biblical Israel's Identity*. Sheffield: Sheffield Academic Press, 2002.

Grosby, Steven. *Biblical Ideas of Nationality Ancient and Modern*. Winona Lake, IN: Eisenbrauns, 2002.

Gruen, Erich. *Diaspora: Jews amidst Greeks and Romans*. Cambridge, MA, and London: Harvard University Press, 2002.

——. *Heritage and Hellenism: The Reinvention of Jewish Tradition*. Berkeley: University of California Press, 1998.

Halbwachs, Maurice. *On Collective Memory*. Chicago: University of Chicago Press, 1992.

Hall, Jonathan M. *Ethnic Identity in Greek Antiquity*. Cambridge: Cambridge University Press, 1997.

Hanson, Paul D. *The People Called: The Growth of Community in the Bible*. San Francisco: Harper & Row, 1986.

Hayes, Christine. *Gentile Impurities and Jewish Identities: Intermarriage and Conversion from the Bible to the Talmud*. Oxford: Oxford University Press, 2002.

Heard, R. Christopher. *Dynamics of Diselection: Ambiguity in Genesis 12–36 and Ethnic Boundaries in Post-Exilic Judah*. Atlanta: Society of Biblical Literature, 2001.

Heschel, Susannah. "Anti-Judaism in Christian Feminist Theology." *Tikkun* 5 (1990): 25–28, 95–97.

Himmelfarb, Martha. "Judaism and Hellenism in 2 Maccabees." *Poetics Today* 19 (1998): 19–20.

——. "'A Kingdom of Priests': The Democratization of the Priesthood in the Literature of Second Temple Judaism." *Journal of Jewish Thought and Philosophy* 6 (1997): 89–102.

Horowitz, Donald. *Ethnic Groups in Conflict*. Berkeley: University of California Press, 1985.

Hostetter, Edwin C. *Nations Mightier and More Numerous: The Biblical View of Palestine's Pre-Israelite Peoples*. N. Richmond Hills, TX: BIBAL Press, 1995.

Janzen, David. *Witch-hunts, Purity and Social Boundaries: The Expulsion of the Foreign Women in Ezra 9–10*. Sheffield: Sheffield Academic Press, 2002.

Japhet, Sara. "People and Land in the Restoration Period." Pages 103–25 in *Das Land Israel in biblischer Zeit*. Edited by Georg Strecker. Göttingen: Vandenhoeck & Ruprecht, 1983.

——. "Sheshbazzar and Zerubbabel—Against the Background of the Historical and Religious Tendencies of Ezra-Nehemiah." Parts I and II. *Zeitschrift für die alttestamentliche Wissenschaft* 94 (1982): 66–98; 95 (1983): 218–30.

Johnson, Luke T. "The New Testament's Anti-Jewish Slander and the Conventions of Ancient Polemic." *Journal of Biblical Literature* 108 (1989): 419–41.

Johnson Hodge, Caroline. *"If Sons, Then Heirs:" A Study of Kinship and Ethnicity in Paul's Letters*. Oxford: Oxford University Press, 2007.

Kaminsky, Joel S. "Did Election Imply the Mistreatment of Non-Israelites?" *Harvard Theological Review* 96 (2003): 398–99.

Kee, Howard Clark. *Who Are the People of God?: Early Christian Models of Community*. New Haven, CT: Yale University Press, 1995.

Kelber, Werner H. "Metaphysics and Marginality in John." Pages 129–54 in *What Is John? Readers and Readings of the Fourth Gospel*. Edited by Fernando F. Segovia. Atlanta: Scholars, 1996.

Killebrew, Ann E. *Biblical Peoples and Ethnicity: An Archaeological Study of Egyptians, Canaanites, Philistines, and Early Israel 1300–1100 BCE*. Atlanta: Society of Biblical Literature, 2005.

Kimelman, Reuven. "*Birkat Ha-Minim* and the Lack of Evidence for an Anti-Christian Jewish Prayer in Late Antiquity." Pages 2.226–44 in *Jewish and Christian Self-Definition*. Edited by E. P. Sanders. (3 vols. Philadelphia: Fortress, 1981.

Kirk, Alan, and Tom Thatcher, eds. *Memory, Tradition, and Text: Uses of the Past in Early Christianity*. Atlanta: Society of Biblical Literature, 2005.

Klawans, Jonathan. *Impurity and Sin in Ancient Judaism*. Oxford: Oxford University Press, 2000.

Knust, Jennifer Wright. *Abandoned to Lust: Sexual Slander and Ancient Christianity*. New York: Columbia University Press, 2006.

Kriesberg, Lewis. *The Sociology of Social Conflicts*. Englewood Cliffs, NJ: Prentice-Hall, 1973.

Kristeva, Julia. *Powers of Horror: An Essay on Abjection*. New York: Columbia University Press, 1982.

———. *Strangers to Ourselves*. New York: Columbia University Press, 1991.

Kugel, James. "The Holiness of Israel and the Land in Second Temple Times." Pages 21–32 in *Texts, Temples, and Traditions: A Tribute to Menachem Haran*. Edited by Michael V. Fox, Victor Hurowitz, and Avi Hurvitz. Winona Lake, IN: Eisenbrauns, 1996.

Lakoff, George. *Women, Fire, and Dangerous Things: What Categories Reveal about the Mind*. Chicago: University of Chicago Press, 1987.

Leach, Edmund. "Anthropological Aspects of Language: Animal Categories and Verbal Abuse." Pages 153–65 in *Reader in Comparative Religion: An Anthropological Approach*. Edited by William Lessa and Evon Vogt. New York: Harper & Row, 1979.

Lévinas, Emmanuel. *Ethics and Infinity: Conversations with Philippe Nemo*. Pittsburgh: Duquesne University Press, 1985.

———. *Time and the Other [and Additional Essays]*. Pittsburgh: Duquesne University Press, 1987.

Lieu, Judith. *Image and Reality: The Jews in the World of the Christians in the Second Century*. Edinburgh: Clark, 1996.

———. *Neither Jew nor Greek? Constructing Early Christianity*. London and New York: Clark, 2002.

Longxi, Zhang. *Mighty Opposites: From Dichotomies to Differences in the Comparative Study of China*. Palo Alto, CA: Stanford University Press, 1998.

Lüdemann, Gerd. *The Unholy in Holy Scripture: The Dark Side of the Bible*. Louisville, KY: Westminster John Knox, 1997.

Machinist, Peter. "Biblical Traditions: The Philistines and Israelite History." Pages 53–83 in *The Sea Peoples and Their World: A Reassessment*. Edited by Eliezer D. Oren. Philadelphia: University Museum of University of Pennsylvania, 2000.

———. "On Self-Consciousness in Mesopotamia." Pages 183–202 in *The Origins and Diversity of Axial Age Civilizations*. Edited by S. N. Eisenstadt. Albany: State University of New York, 1986.

———. "The Question of Distinctiveness in Ancient Israel: An Essay." Pages 198–212 in *Ah, Assyria . . . : Studies in Assyrian History and Ancient Near Eastern Historiography Presented to Hayim Tadmor.* Edited by Mordechai Cogan and Israel Eph`al. Jerusalem: Magnes, 1991.

———. "The *Rab Šāqēh* at the Wall of Jerusalem: Israelite Identity in the Face of the Assyrian 'Other.'" *Hebrew Studies* 41 (2000): 151–68.

Magonet, Jonathan. "The Attitude towards Egypt in the Book of Exodus." Pages 11–20 in *Truth and its Victims.* Edited by Wim Beuken, Seán Freyne, and Anton Weiler. Edinburgh: Clark, 1988.

Martyn, J. Louis. *History and Theology in the Fourth Gospel.* 2nd ed. Nashville, TN: Abingdon, 1979.

McKenzie, Steven L. *All God's Children: A Biblical Critique of Racism.* Louisville, KY: Westminster/John Knox, 1997.

Meeks, Wayne A. "The Man from Heaven in Johannine Sectarianism." *Journal of Biblical Literature* 91 (1972): 44–72.

Mendels, Doron. *Memory in Jewish, Pagan and Christian Societies of the Graeco-Roman World.* London and New York: T & T Clark International, 2004.

———. *The Rise and Fall of Jewish Nationalism: Jewish and Christian Ethnicity in Ancient Palestine.* Grand Rapids, MI: Eerdmans, 1992.

Miller, Patrick D. "God's Other Stories: On the Margins of Deuteronomic Theology." Pages 185–94 in *Realia Dei: Essays in Archaeology and Biblical Interpretation in Honor of Edward F. Campbell, Jr. at His Retirement.* Edited by Prescott H. Williams, Jr., and Theodore Hiebert. Atlanta: Scholars, 1999.

Moore, R. I. *The Formation of a Persecuting Society.* 2nd ed. Oxford: Blackwell, 2007.

Mullen, E. Theodore. *Ethnic Myths and Pentateuchal Foundations: A New Approach to the Formation of the Pentateuch.* Atlanta: Scholars, 1997.

———. *Narrative History and Ethnic Boundaries: The Deuteronomistic Historian and the Creation of Israelite National Identity.* Atlanta: Scholars Press, 1993.

Nickelsburg, George W. E. "Revealed Wisdom as a Criterion for Inclusion and Exclusion: From Jewish Sectarianism to Early Christianity." Pages 73–91 in *To See Ourselves as Others See Us: Christians, Jews, 'Others' in Late Antiquity.* Edited by Jacob Neusner and Ernst S. Frerichs. Chico, CA: Scholars Press, 1985.

Niditch, Susan. *Chaos to Cosmos: Studies in the Biblical Patterns of Creation.* Chico, CA: Scholars Press, 1985.

Olyan, Saul. "'And with a Male You Shall Not Lie the Lying Down of a Woman:' On the Meaning and Significance of Leviticus 18:22 and 20:13." *Journal of the History of Sexuality* 5 (1994): 179–206.

———. "'Anyone Blind or Lame Shall Not Enter the House:' On the Interpretation of Second Samuel 5:8b." *Catholic Biblical Quarterly* 60 (1998): 218–27.

———. *Asherah and the Cult of Yahweh in Ancient Israel.* Atlanta: Scholars Press, 1988.

———. "Purity Ideology in Ezra-Nehemiah as a Tool to Reconstruct the Community." *Journal for the Study of Judaism* 35 (2004): 1–16.

———. *Rites and Rank: Hierarchy in Biblical Representations of Cult.* Princeton, NJ: Princeton University Press, 2000.

Pardes, Ilana. *The Biography of Ancient Israel.* Berkeley: University of California Press, 2000.

Petersen, Norman R. *The Gospel of John and the Sociology of Light: Language and Characterization in the Fourth Gospel.* Valley Forge, PA: Trinity Press International, 1993.

Poo, Mu-chou. *Enemies of Civilization: Attitudes toward Foreigners in Ancient Meso-potamia, Egypt, and China*. Albany: State University of New York Press, 2005.

Reinhartz, Adele. *Befriending the Beloved Disciple: A Jewish Reading of the Gospel of John*. New York and London: Continuum, 2001.

———. "The Johannine Community and Its Jewish Neighbors: A Reappraisal." Pages 111–38 in *What Is John? Volume 2: Literary and Sociological Readings of the Fourth Gospel*. Edited by Fernando F. Segovia. Atlanta: Scholars Press, 1998.

———. "Love, Hate, and Violence in the Gospel of John." Pages 109–23 in *Violence in the New Testament*. Edited by E. Leigh Gibson and Shelly Matthews. Edinburgh: T & T Clark, 2005.

———. *The Word in the World: The Cosmological Tale in the Fourth Gospel*. Atlanta: Scholars Press, 1992.

Rensberger, David. "Anti-Judaism and the Gospel of John." Pages 120–57 in *Anti-Judaism and the Gospels*. Edited by William R. Farmer. Harrisburg, PA: Trinity Press International, 1999.

———. *Johannine Faith and Liberating Community*. Philadelphia: Westminster, 1988.

Ringe, Sharon H. *Wisdom's Friends: Community and Christology in the Fourth Gospel*. Louisville, KY: Westminster John Knox, 1999.

Rowlette, Lori L. *Joshua and the Rhetoric of Violence: A New Historicist Analysis*. Sheffield: Sheffield Academic Press, 1996.

Sacks, Jonathan. *The Dignity of Difference: How to Avoid the Clash of Civilizations*. 2nd ed. London and New York: Continuum, 2003.

Said, Edward. *Orientalism*. London: Routlege & Kegan Paul, 1978.

Saldarini, Anthony J. "The Gospel of Matthew and Jewish-Christian Conflict." Pages 38–61 in *Social History of the Matthean Community: Cross-Disciplinary Approaches*. Edited by David L. Balch. Minneapolis, MN: Fortress, 1991.

———. "The Delegitimation of Leaders in Matthew 23." *Catholic Biblical Quarterly* 54 (1992): 659–80.

Sanders, E. P. *Paul and Palestinian Judaism: A Comparison of Patterns in Religion*. Philadelphia: Fortress, 1977.

———. *Paul, the Law, and the Jewish People*. Philadelphia: Fortress, 1983.

Sanders, Jack T. *The Jews in Luke-Acts*. Philadelphia: Fortress, 1987.

———. *Schismatics, Sectarians, Dissidents, Deviants: The First One Hundred Years of Jewish-Christian Relations*. Valley Forge, PA: Trinity Press International, 1993.

Satlow, Michael L. *Jewish Marriage in Antiquity*. Princeton, NJ, and Oxford: Princeton University Press, 2001.

———. *Tasting the Dish: Rabbinic Rhetorics of Sexuality*. Atlanta: Scholars Press, 1995.

Schüssler Fiorenza, Elisabeth. *Jesus and the Politics of Interpretation*. New York: Crossroad, 2000.

Schwartz, Daniel R. "The Other in 1 and 2 Maccabees." Pages 30–37 in *Tolerance and Intolerance in Early Judaism and Christianity*. Edited by Graham N. Stanton and Guy G. Stroumsa. Cambridge: Cambridge University Press, 1998.

Schwartz, Regina. *The Curse of Cain: The Violent Legacy of Monotheism*. Chicago: University of Chicago Press, 1997.

Schwartz, Seth. "The Hellenization of Jerusalem and Shechem." Pages 37–46 in *Jews in a Graeco-Roman World*. Edited by Martin Goodman. Oxford: Clarendon, 1998.

———. "Israel and the Nations Roundabout: 1 Maccabees and the Hasmonean Expansion." *Journal of Jewish Studies* 42 (1991): 16–38.

Segovia, Fernando F. *The Farewell of the Word: The Johannine Call to Abide*. Minneapolis, MN: Fortress, 1991

——. "Inclusion and Exclusion in John 17: An Intercultural Reading," Pages 183–210 in *What Is John? Vol. 2: Literary and Social Readings of the Fourth* Gospel. Edited by Fernando F. Segovia. Atlanta: Scholars, 1998.

——. "The Love and Hatred of Jesus and Johannine Sectarianism." *Catholic Biblical Quarterly* 43 (1981): 258–72.

Sen, Amartya. *Identity and Violence: The Illusion of Destiny*. New York: Norton, 2006.

Shankman, Steven, and Massimo Lollini, eds. *Who, Exactly, Is the Other? Western and Transcultural Perspectives*. Eugene: University of Oregon Books, 2002.

Siker, Jeffrey S. *Disinheriting the Jews: Abraham in Early Christian Controversy*. Louisville, KY: Westminster/John Knox, 1991.

Simmel, Georg. *Conflict*. Glencoe, IL: Free Press, 1955.

Smith, Anthony D. *The Ethnic Origins of Nations*. Oxford: Blackwell, 1986.

——. *Chosen* Peoples. Oxford and New York: Oxford University Press, 2003.

Smith, Jonathan Z. "*Dayyeinu*." Pages 483–87 in *Redescribing Christian Origins*. Edited by Ron Cameron and Merrill P. Miller. Atlanta: SBL, 2004.

——. "Differential Equations: On Constructing the Other." Pages 231–37 in *Relating Religion: Essays in the Study of* Religion. Chicago: University of Chicago Press, 2004.

——. *Imagining Religion: From Babylon to Jonestown*. Chicago: University of Chicago Press, 1982.

——. *Map Is Not Territory: Studies in the History of Religions*. Leiden: Brill, 1978.

——. "What a Difference a Difference Makes." Pages 3–48 in *"To See Ourselves as Others See Us:" Christians, Jews, "Others" in Late Antiquity*. Edited by Jacob Neusner and Ernst S. Frerichs. Chico, CA: Scholars Press, 1985.

Smith, Mark. *The Early History of God: Yahweh and the Other Deities in Ancient Israel*. San Francisco: Harper & Row, 1987.

Smith, Morton. *Palestinian Parties and Politics That Shaped the Old Testament*. New York: Columbia University Press, 1971.

Smith-Spralls, Mitzi. "The Function of the Jews, Charismatic Others, and Women in Narrative Instabilities in the Acts of the Apostles." Ph.D. dissertation, Harvard University, 2005.

Sparks, Kenton L. *Ethnicity and Identity in Ancient Israel: Prolegomena to the Study of Ethnic Sentiments and Their Expression in the Hebrew Bible*. Winona Lake, IN: Eisenbrauns, 1998.

Stendahl, Krister. *Paul Among Jews and Gentiles, and Other Essays*. Philadelphia: Fortress, 1976.

Sternberg, Meir. *Hebrews Between Cultures: Group Portraits and National Literature*. Bloomington: Indiana University Press, 1998.

Stowers, Stanley K. *A Rereading of Romans: Justice, Jews, and Gentiles*. New Haven, CT: Yale University Press, 1994.

Stroumsa, Gedaliahu Guy. *Barbarian Philosophy: The Religious Revolution of Early Christianity*. Tübingen: Mohr Siebeck, 1999.

Sugirtharajah, R. G. ed. *Postcolonial Bible*. Sheffield: Sheffield Academic Press, 1998.

——, ed. *Voices from the Margins*. Maryknoll, NY: Orbis, 1995.

Tajfel, Henri, and John C. Turner, "The Social Identity Theory of Intergroup Behavior." Pages 7–24 in *Psychology of Intergroup Relations*. Edited by W. G. Austin and S. Worchel. Chicago: Nelson Hall, 1986.

Talmon, Shemaryahu. "The Emergence of Jewish Sectarianism in the Early Second Temple Period." Pages 165–201 in *King, Cult and Calendar in Ancient Israel: Collected Studies*. Jerusalem: Magnes, 1986.

Taylor, Miriam. *Anti-Judaism and Early Christian Identity: A Critique of the Scholarly Consensus*. Leiden and New York: Brill, 1995.

Todorov, Tzvetan. *The Morals of History*. Minneapolis/London: University of Minnesota Press, 1995.

Weinfeld, Moshe. *The Promise of the Land: The Inheritance of the Land of Canaan by the Israelites*. Berkeley: University of California Press, 1993.

Weitzman, Steven. *Surviving Sacrilege: Cultural Persistence in Jewish Antiquity*. Cambridge, MA: Harvard University Press, 2005.

White, L. Michael. "Crisis Management and Boundary Maintenance: The Social Location of the Matthean Community." Pages 211–47 in *Social History of the Matthean Community: Cross-Disciplinary Approaches*. Edited by David L. Balch. Minneapolis, MN: Fortress, 1991.

Wills, Lawrence M. "The Aesop Tradition." Pages 222–37 in *The Historical Jesus in Context*. Edited by John Dominic Crossan, Dale Allison, and Amy-Jill Levine. Princeton, NJ: Princeton University Press, 2006.

———. "Ascetic Theology before Asceticism? Jewish Narratives and the Decentering of the Self." *Journal of the American Academy of Religion* 74 (2006): 902–25.

———. "The Death of the Hero and the Violent Death of Jesus." Pages 79–99 in *Religion and Violence: The Biblical Heritage*. Edited by Jonathan Klawans and David Bernat. Sheffield: Sheffield Phoenix, 2008.

———. *The Jew in the Court of the Foreign King: Ancient Jewish Court Legends*. Minneapolis, MN: Fortress, 1990.

———. "Methodological Reflections on the Tax Collectors in the Gospels." Pages 251–66 in *When Judaism and Christianity Began: Essays in Memory of Anthony J. Saldarini*. Edited by Alan J. Avery-Peck, Daniel Harrington, and Jacob Neusner. Leiden and Boston: Brill, 2004.

———. *The Quest of the Historical Gospel: Mark, John and the Origins of the Gospel Genre*. London and New York: Routledge, 1997.

Yee, Gale A. *Class Acts: Marginalization in Ancient Israel*. Louisville: Westminster John Knox, forthcoming.

Yerushalmi, Yosef. *Zakhor: Jewish History and Jewish Memory*. Seattle: University of Washington Press, 1996.

Young, Robert J. C. *Colonial Desire: Hybridity in Theory, Culture and Race*. London and New York: Routledge, 1995.

Young-Bruehl, Elisabeth. *The Anatomy of Prejudices*. Cambridge, MA: Harvard University Press, 1996.

Younger, K. Lawson Jr. *Ancient Conquest Accounts: A Study in Ancient Near Eastern and Biblical History Writing*. Sheffield: Sheffield Academic Press, 1990.

Zerubavel, Yael. *Recovered Roots: Collective Memory and the Making of Israeli National Tradition*. Chicago: University of Chicago Press, 1995.

Index of Modern Authors

Ahlström, G., 48n19
Akenson, Donald, 16n10
Albertz, Rainer, 25, 46n4
Alexander, Loveday, 201, 208n14
Allison, Dale, 126, 128n2, 131n23, 132n36, 132n37
Allport, Gordon W., 10, 17nn17–18
Alt, Albrecht, 25, 46n4
Anderson, Benedict R., 8, 16n8
Armstrong, John, 16n10
Attias, Jean-Christophe, 18n27, 76, 85n35, 86n41
Attridge, Harold, 162n30
Auerbach, Erich, 198, 207n9

Balch, David, 201–2, 208n15
Banks, Robert, 130n20, 131n31
Barrett, C. K., 160n11
Barstad, Hans M., 81n1
Barth, Fredrik, 6–7, 15n2, 98, 100n18
Bassler, Jouette, 140–41, 161n17, 191n20
Baumann, Gerd, 7, 12, 15n2, 16n6, 18n25, 86n41
Baumgarten, Albert I., 82n7, 129n5
Becker, Adam H., 206n1
Beckford, James A., 82n8

Benbassa, Esther, 18n27, 76, 85n35, 86n41
Berger, Peter, 130n12
Berko, Alexis, 84n31
Berquist, Jon L., 82n4, 82n10, 85n34
Bhabha, Homi, 14, 16n8, 18n24, 19n30, 100n17, 191n26
Biale, David, 49n33, 51n43
Bickerman, Elias, 99n2
Bigger, Stephen F., 51n44
Black, Matthew, 168, 180, 189n3
Blenkinsopp, Joseph, 56, 60, 69, 81n3, 82n7, 82nn10–11, 83nn17–18, 83n20, 84n28
Bloch-Smith, Elizabeth, 37, 49n29
Bovon, François, 209n21
Bowe, Barbara, 165n52
Boyarin, Daniel, 84n24, 86n45, 99n10, 138, 141, 160n12, 161n14, 162n20, 180, 186–87, 190n18, 191n25, 192n25, 192n34, 193n38, 206n1
Boyd, W., 164n47
Branham, Joan, 15–16n5
Brawley, Robert L., 208n20
Brett, Mark G., 16n61
Brettler, Marc Z., 47n10, 48n23, 49n28, 83n14, 84n27

Index of Ancient Literature

DEUTERO-CANONICAL JEWISH LITERATURE

NEW TESTAMENT

POST–BIBLICAL JEWISH LITERATURE

Subject Index

About the Author

Lawrence M. Wills is the Talbot Professor of Biblical Studies at Episcopal Divinity School in Cambridge, Massachusetts, and has also taught at Harvard Divinity School and Wesleyan University. Among his previous books is *The Jewish Novel in the Ancient World*, which was named an Outstanding Academic Book of 1995 by *Choice* magazine for academic librarians.